New Subaltern Politics

New Subaltern Politics

Reconceptualizing Hegemony and Resistance in Contemporary India

Edited by

ALF GUNVALD NILSEN

and

SRILA ROY

OXFORD
UNIVERSITY PRESS

OXFORD
UNIVERSITY PRESS

Oxford University Press is a department of the University of Oxford.
It furthers the University's objective of excellence in research, scholarship,
and education by publishing worldwide. Oxford is a registered trademark of
Oxford University Press in the UK and in certain other countries

Published in India by
Oxford University Press
YMCA Library Building, 1 Jai Singh Road, New Delhi 110 001, India

ISBN-13: 978-0-19-945755-7
ISBN-10: 0-19-945755-7

Typeset in Trump Mediaeval LT Std 9.5/13
by The Graphics Solution, New Delhi 110 092

Contents

II IMAGINATION, FAITH, AFFECT

III   CASTE AND COMMUNITY IN CIVIL/POLITICAL SOCIETY

POSTSCRIPT

Acknowledgements

This volume builds upon a series of conference panels and workshops that we organized between 2011 and 2013, in such diverse places as Honolulu, Nottingham, and Bergen. We would like to thank the University of Nottingham's Integrating Global Societies Research Priority Group, and UiB Global for the grants that made the workshops in Nottingham and Bergen possible. Obviously, this volume would not have been possible without its contributors, and we extend a heartfelt thanks to Kenneth, Aparna, Manali, Rashmi, Subir, Ajantha, and Luisa. We would especially like to thank David Arnold for agreeing to participate in the workshop in Bergen and for providing us with a very incisive postscript to this volume. Along the way, we are also fortunate to have benefited from the participation of Alpa Shah, Sumi Madhok, Dag Erik Berg, and Neera Chandhoke. The anonymous referees of the manuscript provided encouragement and critical inputs. We are grateful to them for a thorough engagement with all contributions and useful suggestions to structure the manuscript through the use of subsections. It has been a pleasure to work with Oxford University Press. We would like to thank Mishta Roy for the fitting cover design and Laurence Cox for churning out the index with such efficiency. Finally, Srila would like to thank Alf for persuading her to take up this project and sticking with it through maternity leave and transcontinental moves—he has proved, time and again, to be an intellectual interlocutor, collaborator, and friend, par excellence.

Alf Gunvald Nilsen and Srila Roy
Johannesburg 2015

Acknowledgements

Abbreviations

BCC	Basic Christian Community
BJP	Bharatiya Janata Party
CEB	Communidades Eclesiales de Base
CMC	Christian Medical College (Vellore)
CMM	Chhattisgarh Mukti Morcha
CSR	corporate social responsibility
DDWU	Delhi Domestic Workers' Union
FORRAD	Foundation for Rural Recovery and Development
GM	genetically modified (crops)
ICDS	Integrated Child Development Service
IIT	Indian Institute of Technology
IIT-JEE	IIT Joint Entrance Exam
IRDS	Integrated Rural Development Society
KSSS	Kottar Social Service Society
LGBT	lesbian, gay, bisexual, and transgender
MCD	Municipal Corporation of Delhi
MFC	Medico Friends Circle
MKP	Majur Kranti Parishad
MS	Mahila Samakhya
NCP	National Contact Point
NGO	non-governmental organization
OBC	Other Backward Class

OECD	Organisation for Economic Co-operation and Development
PUCL	People's Union for Civil Liberties
RSS	Rashtriya Swayamsevak Sangh
RWA	Residents' Welfare Association
SABKMS	Singur Akranta Bargadar Khet Majur Samiti
SIPCOT	State Industries Promotion Corporation of Tamil Nadu
SKJRC	Singur Krishi Jomi Raksha Committee
TMC	Trinamul Congress

Introduction

Reconceptualizing Subaltern Politics in Contemporary India

Alf Gunvald Nilsen and Srila Roy

What Is Subaltern Politics?

The term 'subaltern politics' refers in a broad sense to the political activity of social groups who are adversely incorporated into determinate power relations (see Green 2011a). Subaltern politics finds a number of manifestations, ranging from everyday forms of resistance, via rights-based campaigns on the terrain of civil society and participation in electoral democracy, to armed struggles for revolutionary transformation. However, cutting across these manifestations is the articulation of oppositional agency—that is, challenges to the extant structuring of power relations and the multiple forms of marginalization that are produced by this structuring. In this book, we are concerned with the conceptualization of the dynamics of these processes as they crystallize in the context of contemporary India.

In recent decades, India has emerged at the helm of the process that the United Nations Development Programme has dubbed 'the rise of the South'—that is, the 'dramatic rebalancing of global economic power' that has been propelled by impressive growth rates in the BRICS countries, namely, Brazil, Russia, India, China, and South Africa (UNDP 2013: 13). Indeed, the combination of economic dynamism with the remarkable stability and continuity of India's parliamentary democracy has led some observers to hail the country as one that holds valuable lessons for other developing countries in the global South (see, for example, Bhagwati and Panagariya 2013; Desai 2011; D. Gupta 2010, 2013). However, the story of India in the twenty-first century is not simply one of economic progress and democratic inclusion (Corbridge et al. 2013; Kohli 2012; Nayyar 2006; Sen and Drèze 2013). As Stuart Corbridge and Alpa Shah (2013) have recently pointed out, the much-lauded 'Indian boom' is blighted by the persistence of entrenched poverty and widening inequalities, a deepening agrarian crisis across large swathes of the countryside, and rampant exploitation of casual labour in the country's vast informal sector (see also Breman 2003; Walker 2008). Socio-economic marginalization in turn intersects with structures of power based on caste, gender, and sexuality to create the patterns of exclusion, vulnerability, stigma, and disenfranchisement that define subalternity in contemporary India (see, for example, Dave 2012; A. Sharma 2008; Waghmore 2013).

However, subalternity and the relations of power through which it is produced are also vigorously contested from below. In a process that Corbridge and Harriss (2000) refer to as 'the reinvention of India', dominant and subaltern groups engage in complex processes of negotiation, contestation, and struggle over the future form, direction, and meaning of democracy and development, redistribution and recognition, and—ultimately—the very edifice upon which the Indian state rests. And this scenario is arguably best understood as a manifestation of the protracted unravelling of the Nehruvian nation-building project from the late 1960s until the present (Ray and Katzenstein 2005).

The making of India's postcolonial state was predicated on the demobilization of mass-based movements that had played a key role in the struggle for independence (Ray and Katzenstein 2005). Simultaneously, the Congress Party constructed its hegemonic position in the electoral arena by incorporating the leading

representatives of large land-owning castes in a way that reinforced their power relative to lower castes and labouring classes
(Frankel 2005). The effect of these alignments was to reproduce
entrenched forms of power in Indian society at the same time as
the political agency of subaltern groups was contained and circumscribed by 'the strong hand of the Nehruvian state' (Ray and
Katzenstein 2005: 14).

During the second half of the 1960s, the worsening stagnation of
the Indian economy combined with the erosion of the 'dominant
party system' of the Congress to produce spaces for the articulation of new oppositional projects from below. The outbreak of
the Naxalite revolt in 1967 signalled the onset of two decades
that would witness the emergence of new social movements
moored in and mobilized around subaltern groups—for example,
women, Adivasis, informal-sector workers, Dalits—who had not
only been marginalized in relation to the postcolonial state, but
had also occupied a relatively peripheral position in left politics
since independence in 1947 (Omvedt 1993; Vanaik 1990). Adding
momentum to this upsurge was the process that Christophe
Jaffrelot (2003) has referred to as a 'silent revolution'—that is, the
rise of political parties that represented and mobilized Dalits and
lower-caste groups in electoral politics (see also Michelutti 2008).
This process, Jaffrelot (2003: 494) argues, is one in which power is
transferred 'on the whole peacefully, from the upper caste elites to
various subaltern groups'.

Whereas the onset of neoliberal reform in the early 1990s was
very much a manifestation of the political clout of India's globalizing elites,[1] the past two and a half decades have also witnessed
the further development of new forms of subaltern politics.
One prominent development is, of course, the re-emergence of
Maoism as a significant political force in India's 'Red Corridor'
(see Harriss 2011a; Mukherji 2012; A. Shah 2010; N. Sundar 2012)
and the intensification of struggles against land acquisition and
displacement (Levien 2012). Moreover, the combined impact of
development strategies that are increasingly centred on neoliberal forms of empowerment and the introduction of rights-based
legislation to protect civil liberties and social entitlements has
arguably 'reconfigured not only the material interactions between

the state and India's marginalized, but also the imagined spaces within which marginal groups renegotiate their relationships with the state' (Williams et al. 2011: 12; see also Corbridge et al. 2005; Madhok 2013; A. Sharma 2008).

The current conjuncture, then, is one in which multiple forms of subaltern politics are locked in a confrontation with what Corbridge and Harriss (2000, Chapter 6) refer to as 'elite revolts': hegemonic projects that seek to mould India's economy, polity, and society in ways that consolidate the power of the country's dominant social groups. The significance of this confrontation and its outcomes for India's future development is considerable, and it is ultimately this that compels us as researchers to think through the conceptual optics that we deploy in our engagement with the oppositional agency and political projects of subaltern groups.

Why Engage the Subaltern Studies Project?

This book and the project through which it has emerged undertake this rethinking through a critical engagement with the Subaltern Studies project. This might seem like an odd point of departure for a venture that is concerned with understanding the contemporary forms and dynamics of subaltern politics. After all, when the Subaltern Studies project was launched in the early 1980s, its primary purpose was to unearth the history of what Ranajit Guha (1982b: 4) called 'the politics of the people' in the wider context of the Indian struggle for independence from colonial rule.[2] And in its further evolution, the project turned increasingly towards an interrogation of metatheoretical questions related to the historiography of colonialism and modernity.[3] Indeed, in a recent article, Partha Chatterjee (2012: 49) has argued that the conceptual and methodological approaches that were originally developed in and through the Subaltern Studies project are not adequate to the task of understanding politics from below in contemporary India: 'Subaltern Studies was a project of its time; another time calls for other projects' (see also Chakrabarty 2013).

However, the Subaltern Studies project cannot simply be brushed aside as irrelevant to the study of subaltern politics in contemporary India. Despite being rooted in historiographical concerns, the project has been of singular importance in orienting scholarly attention towards the significance of popular politics and mobilization from below in postcolonial India (see Arnold, this volume). And as we as scholars focus our inquiries on the oppositional agency of subaltern groups, we tend to find ourselves drawing on and engaging in debates with the analytical templates that were central to the Subaltern Studies project—in particular, perhaps, the foundational argument that the politics of subaltern social groups should be conceived of as constituting an 'autonomous domain' that is different and distanced from the realm of 'elite politics' (see Ranajit Guha 1982b: 4). Interestingly, in Chatterjee's (2012: 45–7) engagement with the challenges facing the study of contemporary subaltern politics in India, it is precisely this conception that is singled out for critical discussion. A conceptual lens centred on the notion of subaltern communities that exist beyond the reach of hegemonic projects and apparatuses of governmentality, he argues, has become increasingly untenable due to significant changes in the Indian political landscape: 'The deepening and widening of the apparatuses of governmentality has, I believe, transformed the quality of mass politics in India in the last two decades' (Chatterjee 2012: 45–7). And for Chatterjee, this throws up the crucial imperative of redefining subalternity in order to be able to grasp the dynamics of subaltern politics in India today (Chatterjee 2012: 46).[4]

This volume can be read as an attempt to address this imperative. Crucially, our attempt does not revolve around devising a new singular template for understanding subalternity and subaltern politics in contemporary India. Rather, we seek to initiate a critical but constructive dialogue with the conceptual legacies of the Subaltern Studies project by bringing together a set of essays that draw on research into fields as diverse as the lifeworlds of urban subalterns in globalizing Gujarat, the activism of sexual subalterns in eastern India, discourses of merit in higher education institutions in Tamil Nadu, and struggles over land acquisition in rural West Bengal—to name but a few—to suggest possible ways in which to move towards new understandings of the agency that subaltern groups develop to negotiate and resist the workings of power from above in contemporary India. To highlight this guiding thread that runs throughout the volume, we turn in the remainder of this introduction to a more detailed discussion of the theorization of subalternity and hegemony.

Trajectories towards a Definition of the Subaltern

To put it simply, Gidwani (2009) says, subalternity is the state of being subaltern. What it means to be subaltern is, however, scarcely so simple, especially given the analytic extension and even over-use of the term since its popularity under the Subaltern Studies project. Gidwani (2009: 66) provides a descriptor of the term which is, as he puts it, working albeit elastic; that is, subalternity refers to 'persons and groups hierarchically positioned as subordinate or inferiors within nation states, capitalist production relations, or relations of patriarchy, race, caste, and so forth'. His usage of the term in this instance remains confined to an empirical grouping as it was for the early subaltern historians. For others within the group, the term 'subaltern', drawn from Antonio Gramsci, signalled relations of dominance and subordination—'in terms of class, caste, gender, race, language and culture' (G. Prakash 1994: 1477)—in Indian society as opposed to subordinate groups alone. Indeed, the meaning of the term subaltern is characterized by this tension between empirical designations of identity positions, on the one hand, and a critical understanding of how power, subordination, and agency are constituted within a specific set of social relations, on the other. As we show in what follows, the trajectory of the term within the Subaltern Studies project, especially the move from subaltern to subalternity, exhibits a shift of perspective from identity to power.

Ranajit Guha (1982a, 1982b) defined the subaltern rather loosely as that part of the population—the working classes, peasantry, and subordinate classes—who were not part of the elite. Subalternity was furthermore associated with subordination, subaltern being used 'as a name for the general attribute of subordination in South Asian society whether this is expressed in terms of class, caste, age, gender and office or in any other way' (Ranajit Guha 1982a: vii). It was also placed in a dichotomous relationship with the elite given that subordination is 'one of the constitutive terms in a binary relationship of which the other is dominance' (Guha 1982a: vii).

The category of the elite was divided, in a Weberian-like taxonomy, into a dominant (colonial) elite, an indigenous elite, and dominant indigenous groups at the local and regional levels. The last category of the indigenous elite at regional and local levels was not only a heterogeneous one, but one that differed from area to area owing to regional disparities with respect to socio-economic development. Consequently, 'the same class or element which was dominant in one area ... could be among the dominated in another' (Ranajit Guha 1982b: 8). While Guha here seems to recognize that the boundaries of his taxonomy might be blurred in some cases, its foundational assumption remains a 'structuralist populism' (Roosa 2006) that pits elites against people. It forms, moreover, the basis of Guha's (1982b: 4) argument that subaltern politics constitutes 'an autonomous domain'. As David Arnold (1984: 170–3) has pointed out, this autonomy was understood as resulting from the confluence of the village collectivities that emerged from the exigencies of agricultural production, the limited reach of precolonial polities and the relative insularity of agrarian economies, and finally the failure of the nationalist movement to incorporate the peasantry into the ambit of modern anticolonial nationalism. In an attempt to 'recover' the agency of the subaltern that had been denied by elite historiography, Guha (1982b: 4) argued that subalterns acted independently of elites and that their politics constituted an autonomous sphere, 'for it neither originated from elite politics nor did its existence depend on the latter'. The historical recovery of subaltern agency was in aid of constituting subalterns as autonomous subject-agents in their own right.

The idea of an autonomous subaltern is perhaps the aspect of the Subaltern Studies template that has received the most critical attention (O'Hanlon 1988; Sarkar 1997: chapter 3; Sivaramakrishnan 2002). The most well-known critique is associated with Gayatri Chakravorty Spivak, whose intervention into Subaltern Studies marks the turn away from using 'subaltern' as an empirical designation of identity positions and towards a critical perspective on power relations. In her most provocative intervention, 'Can the Subaltern Speak?', Spivak (1988a: 284–5) describes Guha's ideas of the elite and the people/subaltern, and his project of measuring the deviation of these from ideal types, as being 'essentialist and taxonomic'. As with the European philosophers Foucault and Deleuze, on the one hand, and Marxists on the other, Spivak (1988b: 5) finds a hidden essentialism in the attempt by subaltern historians like Guha to retrieve and represent subaltern consciousness 'in a positive and pure state'. Such an attempt is essentialist insofar as it negates the heterogeneity of subaltern groups and transforms them 'into an undifferentiated, humanist, and implicitly male subject agent' (Gidwani 2009: 68). The project of recovering subaltern agency is also positivist in as much as it presumes a 'firm ground' (Spivak 1988b: 10) or even an 'idealistic bedrock' (Spivak 1988a: 286), namely, subaltern consciousness that one can access unmediated by discourse, representation, or experience. This positing of some pure subaltern consciousness or essence bypasses entirely the problem and politics of representation, which, Spivak is at pains to show, is impossible to do.

In contrast, Spivak argues that the subaltern can only be retrieved and represented—be spoken for—in the terms set by dominant or elite ideology, discourse, and politics. There is no pure space from which she can speak and, insofar as she can speak through dominant discourse alone, the subaltern cannot speak. The ethics and politics of representation mean that even well-meaning attempts—like those of the subaltern historian or progressive Western intellectuals—to give voice to the subaltern or to restore her agency end by othering or objectifying her and reinforcing her subordinate status. This is in large measure because of the failure of these scholars to recognize their own complicity in practices of representation that render, in an act of further epistemic violence, their own subject positions transparent.

Spivak uses as an example the debate around sati or widow-sacrifice in colonial India to show the disappearance of the subaltern precisely in the act of representing her and her interests: 'Between patriarchy and imperialism, subject-constitution and object-formation, the figure of the woman disappears... . There is no space from which the sexed subaltern can speak' (1988a: 306–7). In not being given a subject position from which to speak (G. Prakash 1994), the colonized or Third World woman is, unlike the politically organized proletariat, paradigmatic of subalternity borne out of silencing, epistemic violence, and erasure. Her silencing marks the limits of what can be historically retrieved (subaltern voice) and epistemologically known (experience). It is well known that the early Subaltern Studies project absented women as subjects and did not employ gender as a category of analysis. For Spivak, in contrast, the subaltern is an inherently sexed and racialized subject. The Third World woman is doubly effaced—'more deeply in shadow' (1988a: 287)—than her male counterpart by virtue of gender and race and the twin pillars of patriarchy and imperialism.

The upshot of Spivak's critique is threefold: there is no escape from the politics and ethics of representation (Gidwani 2009). There is consequently no pure space from which intellectuals or social movements can hope to speak on behalf of, or represent, subaltern interests (Kapoor 2008). Relatedly, there is no outside of power structures. The subjectivity of the subaltern does not lie in some pure, autonomous space outside of power relations, but is constituted through these. This poststructuralist shift from conceptualizing the subject as autonomous of (elite) discourse to seeing it as an 'effect of discursive systems' (G. Prakash 1994: 1480) was a major outcome of Spivak's intervention. Finally, an understanding of gendered subalternity goes to the heart of Spivak's reading of subalternity, as being removed from all lines of social mobility (Sharpe and Spivak 2002; Spivak 2005; Spivak et al. 1996). She says in a later interview of 'Can the Subaltern Speak?':

> In the essay I made it clear that I was talking about the space as defined by Ranajit Guha, the space that is cut off from the lines of mobility in a colonized country. You have the foreign elite and the indigenous elite. Below that you will have the vectors of upward, downward, sideward, backward mobility. But then there is a space which is for all practical purposes outside those lines. (Spivak et al. 1996: 288–9)

Subalterns are not just the non-elite but those who are 'so displaced they lack political organization and representation' (Green 2002: 18). So they are not simply cut off from elite politics but from politics per se: 'subalternity is where social lines of mobility, being elsewhere, do not permit the formation of a recognisable basis of action' (Spivak 2005: 476). It is in this sense that Spivak contends that the proletariat is not a subaltern group because it is organized in most instances (Green 2002).

More recently, however, Spivak (2000a, 2000b) writes of Third World women as 'new subalterns' who are not outside of circuits of power but integrated into them in problematic ways, especially by a feminist-inspired neoliberal developmentalism. Subaltern consciousness is once again key, not for the purposes of resistance (as it was in the analytics of early Subaltern Studies) but for the sake of justifying global developmental projects premised on the 'agency' of Third World women. The complicity of international feminism in such a project also makes evident Spivak's non-iden-titarian use of the category of subaltern: that it does not refer to women per se or to anyone in the formerly 'Third World' or to ethnic minorities in the West who are all, by virtue of their class position and culture, complicit in 'a corporate globalization that maintains subaltern women in a position of subalternity' (Sharpe and Spivak 2002: 610). In more recent work, she defines subalter-nity as a position without identity or, as Morris (2010) puts it, a predicament that is shaped by being structurally obstructed from accessing power and voice. At least since Spivak's intervention and *Subaltern Studies III*, the term 'subaltern' has been employed less as an empirical or identity category than as 'a position of critique' (G. Prakash 1994: 1481) or a 'perspective' (Das 1989) on dominant discourse or a set of hierarchical relations.

But does the unspeakability of the subaltern leave any room for agency? Prominent critics of Spivak have noted that her posi-tion might constrain subaltern agency so as to effectively efface any possibility of resistance. It is true that Spivak has been more interested in exposing the structures and imbrications of power-knowledge than in 'the possibility of resistance on the part of the objects of the power-knowledge nexus' (Varadharajan 1995: xii). Her critique has been involved, in other words, with 'the unremit-ting exposure of complicity rather than the charting of opposition' (Varadharajan 1995: xii). Some, like Benita Parry (1987), have gone so far as to charge Spivak with never letting the subaltern speak, and of recentring the master discourse (of imperialism) even in the act of opposing it. Even if one must reject an 'essentialist, utopian politics' (Spivak 1988a: 276; Varadharajan 1995: 93), is the assertion that the subaltern cannot speak the only alternative? And is it the case that all resistance ultimately feeds back into power?

In fact, for Spivak, one stops being subaltern as soon as one acts politically to achieve representation within a hegemonic formation. She says in an interview:

> I don't think that I declare myself to be allied to the subaltern. The subaltern is all that is not elite, but the trouble with those kinds of names is that if you have any kind of political interest you name it in the hope that the name will disappear. That's what class consciousness is in the interest of: the class disappearing. What politically we want to see is that the name would not be possible. So what I'm interested in is seeing ourselves as namers of the subaltern. If the subaltern can speak then, thank God, the subaltern is not a subaltern any more. (Spivak 1990: 158)

In what has been called a problem of the 'disappearing subaltern' (Hershatter 1993), certain groups like the organized working class cease to be 'subaltern' in Spivak's formulation, even as it is clear, as we argue later, that subalternity cannot be reduced to the politics of representation alone. Not only does such a formulation posit subalternity in dramatically opposite terms to agency, but also to agency that is available and manifest, above all, in subaltern politics. Even as 'new subalterns' are theorized as not being victimized in the same way as historical subalterns, they are positioned as entirely subjected to hegemonic power in ways that negate, once again, subaltern agency and the possibility of political resistance (see S. Roy 2014).

Thus, as much as Spivak's intervention advances our understanding of subalternity by unmooring the concept from its structuralist focus on identity, her alternative conceptualization is nevertheless problematic in that it suggests a position of absolute exteriority in relation to hegemonic formations—the condition of being cut off from lines of social mobility—and in that it deprives subaltern groups of agential capacities. Given what we know about the ability of subaltern groups to develop oppositional agency even in extremely repressive contexts—slave revolts being a case in point in this respect (see, for example, Blackburn 1988; da Costa 1994; Shuler 2009; Sidbury 1997)—this proposition is less than convincing.

Rethinking Subalternity

So how can we think about subalternity in an alternative way? We suggest an understanding that is: (a) relational—that is, subalternity is above all a positionality of adverse incorporation in a certain set of socio-historical power relations; (b) intersectional—that is, subalternity is constituted along several axes of power, whose specific empirical form must be deciphered in concrete empirical settings; and (c) dynamic—subalternity does not preclude agency, but agency arises and develops within and in relation to dominant discourses and political forms. Taken together, the volume presumes and purports an expansive, relational, and intersectional account of subalternity that locates it in a wide social field of power relations to address a plurality of context-specific manifestations of power. Such an approach underscores the limitations of understanding marginalization in relation to class alone, or indeed along any single axis. It is also able to account for subaltern agency as not being entirely subsumed, as in Spivak, under the power of dominant discourse, or being, as in Guha, entirely voluntarist.

One way to develop such a conceptualization of subalternity is to go back to Gramsci, from whom the historians of the Subaltern Studies project originally took the term 'subaltern'. Marcus Green's (2002, 2011a) reading of Gramsci's work is highly instructive. Crucially, Green (2011a: 388) argues that, by subscribing to the thesis that Gramsci used the term 'subaltern' as code for 'proletariat' in his *Prison Notebooks*, the Subaltern Studies scholars 'limit Gramsci's expansive conception of subalternity'. Consequently, they elide the ways in which Gramsci located subordination in a dense social field in specific historical contexts, and conceived of subalternity as being constituted by 'exclusion, domination, and marginality in their various forms' (Green 2011a: 388). As we will detail later in this Introduction, Green also proposes, *contra*

Spivak, an understanding of subalternity in which political agency is recognized.

Against the equation of the subaltern with the proletariat and subalternity with class domination alone, Green shows that Gramsci's original conception of subalternity was not limited to understanding marginalization in relation to class or class domination, even as class was a major element in his understanding of power and subordination: 'subalternity [in Gramsci] was not merely defined by class relations but rather an intersection of class, race, culture, and religion that functioned in different modalities in specific historical contexts' (Green 2011a: 395). Thus, Gramsci treated the question of the subordination of women separately (albeit briefly) without subsuming it under class domination. To the extent that gender subordination functions differently from that of class, he recognized the suppression of women as a phenomenon that occurs across classes (see Moe 2010).

Subalternity was thus conceptualized in relation to multiple social groups and the power relations between them. It was not reducible to any singular social axis—class or gender—as it was in the early subaltern historians' privileging of economic relations over other social relations, especially as these manifested themselves in conflicts between peasant communities and the political economy of colonial capitalism. The pure subaltern subject was invariably measured in class terms, given the original conceptualization of the category in terms of the non-elite. Earlier in this discussion, we noted the blurring of the categories of elite and subaltern even in Guha's rigid taxonomy in which he allows—as deviations from ideal types—the possibility of one social group being hegemonic in one context and subordinate or subaltern in another. What the (inadvertent) inclusion of such ambiguity in his classification allows is the recognition of the production of exclusion, oppression, and otherness in distinctive and interlocking terms, whether based on class, caste, gender, sexuality, or religion, as has become typical of intersectional understandings of (primarily gender-based) forms of social inequality and exclusion. One can thus read an intersectional deployment of subalternity even in early works (Chatterjee 1993; Spivak 1988a). This is especially evident in the manner in which the concept was employed to address the 'shadowy figure' of the female subaltern in Spivak, including middle-class women whose political exclusion constituted the realm of democratic citizenship. Such a focus complicates any quest for a 'pure' subaltern, circumventing problems of empirical classification of the 'real' subaltern besides opening up a wider discursive field to rethink subalternity from the perspective of the intersectionality of race, class, gender, sexuality, and religion (Green 2011a).

Finally, Green (2002) rereads Gramsci in a manner that offers a way out of the impasse of the 'disappearing subaltern' in at least two ways. Against Spivak's aporetic position that the subaltern ceases to be so the moment she is politically intelligible, Gramsci does not equate such political agency with the end/termination of subalternity. This is because Gramsci recognizes, according to Green (2002: 18), that a subaltern group can exercise political organization and agency 'without any level of hegemony and therefore still be subject to the activity of dominant groups'. Political mobilization does not mean the transformation of subaltern groups into dominant groups, and neither does it necessarily transform the root causes of subalternity. Subaltern groups can only cease to be subaltern once their subalternity is addressed, 'once they have transformed the relations of subordination that cause their marginalization' (Green 2002: 20).

Second, and *contra* Spivak's polarization of political agency and subalternity, Gramsci sees political organizing as being an integral aspect of the condition of being subaltern: 'Subaltern groups have to become conscious of their social position, organize, and struggle to transform their social positions, since organization and representation alone will not transform the relations of subordination' (Green 2002: 19). Green points out that Gramsci thought of subalternity as existing 'in degrees or levels of development' (Green 2002: 16), and that 'subaltern groups develop in various degrees or phases that correspond to levels of political organization' (Green 2002: 15). Some are more organized and exhibit higher levels of political consciousness than others. Subalternity is thus not pitted against politics; political struggle is understood, instead, as being intrinsic to subalternity.

The political struggles and mobilizations of subaltern groups do not, however, take place in some autonomous domain, but in and through the institutions and relations through which hegemony is constituted. 'Subaltern groups', Gramsci (1971: 182) argued, 'are always subject to the activity of ruling groups, even when they rebel and rise up'. What he meant by this is that subaltern agency—ranging from everyday negotiations of the workings of power from above to collective action challenging adverse incorporation into a social formation—will tend to proceed by engaging institutional ensembles, framing claims through discourses, and mobilizing through political forms that are commensurable with and geared towards the reproduction of unequal structures of power. This is, in turn, a result of the fact that the compromises that have been struck in and through hegemonic processes remain ones 'in which the interests of the dominant social groups prevail' (Gramsci 1971: 182): subaltern groups are positioned in relation to socio-economic relations, political institutions, and cultural forms that, despite concessions and compromises, buttress the reproduction of hegemony. Consequently, subaltern resistance is conditioned by and mediated through 'the social condensations of hegemony' (Morton 2007: 92).

Taken together, Gramsci enables an understanding of subalternity that embraces a notion of political agency as: (a) always being mediated; and (b) as not necessarily guaranteed to be successful or transformative of the conditions of subalternity. This takes us somewhat beyond the impasse identified earlier, between positing a subaltern subject that is entirely autonomous and one that is entirely subject to structures of dominance and silenced. In challenging this idea of 'subaltern consciousness [as] either a completely independent product or ... a mere reflection of a totalising hegemony from above', Haynes and Prakash (1992: 19) emphasize the entanglement of power and resistance in everyday life in South Asia.

While such a formulation has become fairly commonsensical since these debates took place in the wake of Subaltern Studies (and its critique by Spivak), the expectation of autonomy and purity has not abated in current ruminations on subaltern resistance and politics. Contemporary movements of subalterns are invariably located—by those reading them—in domains outside of the state and market and as uninformed by understandings of state, law, and citizenship or as unmediated by trans/national actors including scholars, activists, NGOs, and representatives of the state. The expectation of purity has also inevitably led to proclamations of such movements as being inadequately representative of subaltern interests or voices when mediated by discourses of rights and practices of solidarity (see Sinha 2012). One hears, for instance, repeated condemnations of the Indian women's movement as having become 'NGO-ized', not without a touch of nostalgia amongst 'older' feminists committed to the ideals if not practices of autonomy (see S. Roy 2011). Such anachronistic ways of reading current subaltern movements—amongst academics and activists alike—are partly a legacy of Subaltern Studies that, in associating subalterns with autonomy on the one hand, or alterity on the other, mitigated its own analytical purchase in addressing a more messy, impure field of subaltern mobilization that traverses elite and subaltern domains, civil and political society, and the bounds of the 'global' and 'local'. And as an extension of conceiving of subalternity in this way, it also becomes necessary to rethink our conceptualization of hegemony.

Rethinking Hegemony

Compared to the rich debates on subalternity, relatively little attention has been devoted to the conceptualization of hegemony in relation to the Subaltern Studies project. Indeed, writing in 1984, David Arnold commented that the project's participants had 'not, as yet, given sufficient attention to the forms that domination and hegemony took in colonial India' (Arnold 1984: 175). This would remain the case until Ranajit Guha penned two long essays, 'Dominance without Hegemony and Its Historiography' and 'Discipline and Mobilize', for the sixth and seventh volumes of the series, respectively, which subsequently came to form the core of the important book *Dominance without Hegemony: History and Power in Colonial India* (Guha 1998).

Essentially a development of the proposition that he had formulated in the introductory statement that launched the Subaltern Studies project in 1982, Guha's essay on dominance without hegemony put forward an analysis of the organization of political power under British colonial rule. This analysis was anchored in a theoretical model in which power is understood as being constituted by the interaction between domination and subordination. According to Guha, domination and subordination are animated by the intersecting dynamics of coercion/persuasion and collaboration/resistance. And on this reading, hegemony is to be understood as 'a condition of dominance (D), such that in the organic composition of D, Persuasion (P) outweighs Coercion (C)' (Guha 1998: 23).

Hegemony, for Guha, is the hallmark of the political in Western capitalist democracies. In this context, he argues, the bourgeoisie had gained the consent of subaltern groups as it emerged at the helm of the struggle against feudalism. Following the paradigmatic bourgeois revolutions in England and France, a hegemonic liberal political culture was crafted that incorporated subaltern groups within the ambit of democratic nation-states. In contrast, the colonial state established by the British in India rested fundamentally on coercion: 'As an absolute externality, the colonial state was structured like a despotism, with no mediating depths, no space provided for transactions between the will of the rulers and that of the ruled' (Guha 1998: 65). Furthermore, the political culture that the colonial overlords sought to craft was one in which the central idioms of rule—order, improvement, obedience, and rightful dissent—were mediated through 'the precolonial political traditions of the colonized' (Guha 1998: 24). Consequently, colonial rule failed to generate a hegemonic ruling culture: 'One of the consequences of that failure has been to inhibit the homogenization of the domain of politics. For, under conditions of dominance without hegemony, the life of civil society can never be fully absorbed into the activity of the state' (Guha 1998: 72).

Dominance without hegemony, Guha argues, was reproduced under the postcolonial state. This was, above all, the result of the ways in which the leadership of the Indian bourgeoisie shaped the form and trajectory of the Indian freedom struggle: 'Pliant and prone to compromise from their inception, they lived in a state of happy accommodation with imperialism for the greater part of their career as a constituted political force from 1885 to 1947.... Compromise and accommodation were equally characteristic of their attitude to the semi-feudal values and institutions entrenched in Indian society' (Guha 1998: 5). The willingness to compromise and accommodate with landlordism and the colonial state, Guha argues, combined with 'the failure of nationalism to assimilate the class interests of peasants and workers effectively into a bourgeois hegemony' (Guha 1998: 133). Ultimately, the upshot of this failure was the reproduction of 'dominance without hegemony' under the postcolonial state (Guha 1998: xiii, 97).

Vivek Chibber (2013) has recently articulated a strong critique of Guha's perspective. At the heart of his argument is the contention that Guha's contrast between hegemonic and non-hegemonic forms of bourgeois rule is flawed. Revisiting the scholarship on the English and French Revolutions, Chibber argues that their trajectories differ substantially from how they are portrayed by Guha. In particular, he argues, the link between bourgeois revolutions and political liberalism is very tenuous: 'What they bequeathed was an oligarchic state with an expanded scope for political participation—but only for members of the ruling order that had hitherto been excluded' (Chibber 2013: 77). Crucially, Chibber notes that whereas subaltern agency was imperative in energizing these transformations in particular phases, this did not mean that the political projects of dominant groups accommodated the claims and demands articulated from below: 'the leaders' intention, far from incorporating mass demands, was to marginalize them as much as possible, and to keep the political agenda confined to the preferences of the elite groupings... . The goal was to force through an elite pact, not to transform the condition of the lower orders' (Chibber 2013: 85). Ultimately, the inclusion of subaltern groups in these new political orders was an achievement of mobilization from below, rather than an intrinsic feature of bourgeois hegemony: 'For more than a century after the new states were installed, laboring classes had to wage unceasing struggle to gain any substantial political rights—the very rights that Guha seems to associate with a hegemonic order' (Chibber 2013: 87).

Chibber's critique is instructive in the sense that it clears the ground for a necessary rethinking of hegemony. In Guha's work, hegemony is arguably conceived of in a way that, on the one hand, elides the significance of subaltern agency in the construction of hegemonic formations, and, on the other hand, exaggerates the element of consent over coercion. As Florencia Mallon (1995: 6) has argued, it is necessary to move beyond an understanding of hegemony as 'a belief in, or incorporation of, the dominant ideology' towards a conception of hegemony as 'a set of nested, continuous processes through which power and meaning are contested, legitimated, and redefined at all levels of society' (Mallon 1995: 6). Indeed, thinking of hegemony in processual terms brings us closer to Gramsci's original formulation of the concept, which focused on how hegemony emerged through 'a continuous process of formation and superseding of "unstable equilibria" ... between the interests of the fundamental group and those of the subordinate groups' (Mallon 1995: 182). Hegemony, then, 'does not just passively exist as a form of dominance', but is actively produced through contentious negotiations between dominant and subaltern groups (R. Williams 1977: 112). To the extent that dominant groups are capable of gaining consent through such processes, the oppositional projects of subaltern groups 'will be reorganized and redefined, obfuscated and partially buried' (Mallon 1995: 7). Moreover, Gramsci (1971: 263) was very clear that hegemony was always 'protected by the armour of coercion'—in other words, whereas dominant groups will accommodate the claims and demands of some subaltern groups in their bid for hegemony, the oppositional projects of other subaltern groups will be violently repressed by the coercive apparatus of the state (Mallon 1995: 7). Ultimately, then, the 'compromise equilibrium' (Gramsci 1971: 168) that results from such processes—what Mallon (1995: 7) dubs a 'hegemonic outcome'—is a constellation that will always be vulnerable to new rounds of assertion and contestation, which in turn means that hegemony 'has continually to be renewed, recreated, defended, and modified' in active relation to the renewal and recreation of subaltern politics (R. Williams 1977: 112).

Viewing hegemony in this way—as a contested process in which consent and coercion are closely intertwined—is particularly apt for understanding the character of India's neoliberal turn. The character, impact, and outcomes of the neoliberal project clearly reflect the salience of elite interests. Witness, for example, the coeval increase in economic growth and income disparities between 1991 and the present (see Jayadev et al. 2011), and the state has certainly shown its willingness to mobilize coercive power in the face of popular resistance, especially in relation to the ongoing Maoist insurgency in the country's Red Corridor (see, for example, N. Sundar 2007: chapter 10, 2012).[5] However, the trajectory of neo-liberalization in India is simultaneously criss-crossed by political processes that seek to garner consent from below. Chief among these is arguably the emergence of what Sanjay Ruparelia (2013: 569) refers to as 'the new rights agenda'—that is, the enactment of several national laws that entrench both civil liberties and socio-economic entitlements 'through legally enforceable rights' (see also Chopra et al. 2011).[6] Subaltern politics—in particular, the pro-liferation of socio-legal activism and the expansion of the popular foundations of parliamentary democracy—has been a key driving force in this process. Of course, it remains to be seen whether this new agenda will serve as an effective resource for mobilization or as a modality for co-optation and depoliticization, but, regardless of this, the fact that liberties and entitlements have increasingly been enshrined in law in recent years does testify to the negotiated character of neoliberalism as a hegemonic project in contemporary India.

What Follows...

The essays in this volume eschew expectations of purity in reading both subalternity and subaltern politics as being firmly embedded in particular historical and social conjunctures and as being potentially transformative of the same through the use of available political technologies. Ajantha Subramanian (2011) underscores the dual character of subalternity as both embedded and transformative, as offering a 'productive dialectic between the historical embeddedness of subaltern life—its emergence from within formations of state and capital—and how through art and politics, subaltern actors attempt to reach beyond and transform their conditions of existence'. Such an approach takes us away from what she calls 'definitional exercises to assess whether par-ticular groups are authentically subaltern' (or not), to analyse not merely contemporary forms of subalternity but also 'processes of subalternization and challenges to it from within spaces of power' (Subramanian 2011).

The contributions to the volume provide hard-hitting critiques of the underlying assumptions of Subaltern Studies-inspired approaches to subaltern politics: the presumption of purity and autonomy, the bifurcation of civil and political spaces and elite and subaltern domains, the absence of (elite) mediation, and the unrepresentability of the subaltern, to name but a few. Several call for a reconsideration of Gramscian/Marxian analytical approaches to subaltern politics, especially in the face of a more recent, Foucauldian turn to governmentality, in proposing ways forward in South Asian studies as well as postcolonial studies more broadly.

The three chapters that constitute the first part of the book, 'Engaging Gramsci', take up this project explicitly and contribute to the bigger argument about hegemony that the collection forwards within and against poststructuralist deployments of the Gramscian concept (see especially Nilsen and Desai's contributions, this volume). Alf Gunvald Nilsen's contribution opens up the discussion with a dense historical and theoretical discussion of state–subaltern relations, which are presented in a bifurcated view not just in Subaltern Studies but also in more recent Foucauldian readings of the same. Both fail, he shows, to fully appreciate the production of subaltern political agency and its containment in and through the state, and how subalterns use the full resources of 'democracy' and 'modernity' available to them, traversing Chatterjee's spatial divide of 'civil' and 'political' society. Nilsen turns to Gramsci to provide a conceptual armoury capable, on the one hand, 'of grasping how subaltern politics is always-already imbricated in state–society relations, and how, on the other hand, state–society relations simultaneously enable and constrain subaltern politics'.

Manali Desai and Ajantha Subramanian equally address the question of hegemony. Desai does so through a perceptive analysis of emergent political subjectivities of informal-sector workers in Ahmedabad, Gujarat. Arguing for a conceptual approach that recognizes the negotiated and fractured nature of hegemony, she explores how the hegemonic project of the Bharatiya Janata Party

(BJP), which has been centred on the fusion of majoritarian Hindu communalism and neoliberal developmentalism, is appropriated by Dalit and Other Backward Class workers in the informal economy. Desai's analysis reveals ambivalence as the defining feature of the political subjectivities of subaltern groups, which, in turn, destabilizes the BJP's hegemonic project and renders it potentially vulnerable to assertion from below. The ambivalent nature of these subjectivities opens up ways of remobilizing the concept of hegemony in critical dialogue with studies conducted through conceptual optics centred on Foucault's concept of governmentality, thereby opening up ways of rethinking the character and form of subaltern resistance.

While several chapters of the book critique the presumption of autonomy in early Subaltern Studies, Subramanian shows how autonomy does exist as a belief and a fought-for privilege amongst upper-caste elites. Lower-caste mobilization has had a considerable impact in terms of challenging upper-caste hegemony in contemporary India. However, the study of caste in Indian politics, she contends, remains incomplete if we do not take cognizance of upper-caste responses to such assertion. In the context of her case study of Indian technical education, this response has materialized in the form of a discourse in which 'merit' and 'meritocracy' are systematically related to being upper caste and to the reproduction of hegemony. Subramanian underscores the ways in which the politics of the powerful is shaped by the politics of the powerless, emphasizing the need to think of hegemony in processual and dynamic terms rather than as a monolithic ideological edifice.

The next part of the book, 'Imagination, Faith, Affect', enhances given definitions of subalternity and subaltern politics through foregrounding the imaginative, affective, secular, and religious dimensions of subaltern as well as elite identity, practices, and life. Rashmi Varma's chapter takes on Spivak's conceptualization of the subaltern not just as a position of 'social, economic, and political subordination', but as one of 'radical, and indeed an irretrievable alterity … that has profound implications for the politics of representation'. The problem of representation, posed in this manner in postcolonial theory, not only silences the subaltern subject but disallows political voice and subjectivity that can partly be developed through projects of solidarity. Varma recovers the figure of the Adivasi—'the unrepresentable par excellence'—as a political subject-agent in a number of literary texts, against the preoccupation of postcolonial theory with the limits and (im)possibilities of representation. She also incorporates, in this manner, a perspective on and critique of postcolonial theory that offers 'ironic analogies' with the materialist approaches to subalternity offered elsewhere in the volume.

Aparna Sundar similarly challenges the presumption of subaltern religiosity as being autonomous not only of religious institutions but also of 'the secular democratic politics of the elite'. Subaltern religiosity has, moreover, been pitted against elite secularism in recent (albeit limited) attempts to understand the role of religion in politics in ways that flatten out the complex imbrications of both religious and secular domains, especially when it comes to religious minorities. Sundar's case study of the Catholic fishing communities of Kanyakumari district, Tamil Nadu, ethnographically and analytically illustrates her contention that, 'far from being an autonomous and self-enclosed sphere, subaltern religiosity must be read within the context of changing political economies, caste, national, subnational, and even geopolitical shifts'.

The conception of the political is further extended—beyond its association with autonomy or elitism—in Srila Roy's discussion of the affective dimensions of sexual rights activism in contemporary India. Not only does sexuality provide new analytical and empirical purchase on the concept of the subaltern, but the ethnographic instance of lesbian activism that Roy turns to displaces some of the central presumptions of the original Subaltern Studies project that had to do with the normative rational male subject. Sexual subalternity also provides a stronger case for mobilizing a more expansive, relational, and intersectional conceptualization of the subaltern even as it implicitly underscores, as David Arnold notes in his postscript to this volume, the potential of this concept to encompass a diverse range of marginalized subjects beyond what was originally imagined. Indeed, the essays of this volume incorporate under the sign of 'subaltern' a diverse range of subjects, including sexual minorities, Dalits, and Adivasis, whose subalternity is understood in terms of locally specific configurations of power and powerlessness and vis-à-vis dominant groups such as local activists, privileged upper-caste educators, religious majorities, and sexually normative identities and practices.

The final chapters, in the third part titled 'Caste and Community in Civil/Political Society', engage with Partha Chatterjee's new conceptual framework for addressing contemporary as opposed to historical forms of subaltern politics. They join a host of critical voices that show how this framework fails to capture the actual, on-the-ground dynamics of the politics of contemporary subaltern groups in India (see, for example, Baviskar and Sundar 2008; M. Shah 2008; Sundar and Sundar 2012; and also Nilsen, this volume). In drawing on rich case studies to make their critiques, the contributions in this section provide a more fully fleshed out version of contemporary subaltern politics and how such politics is embedded in regional particularities and the on-the-ground dynamics of class, caste, and gender.

Luisa Steur develops a critique of Chatterjee's argument that Marxian perspectives of agrarian transition have been rendered irrelevant by the introduction of social policy regimes that ameliorate the ramifications of contemporary forms of primitive accumulation. Drawing on the work of Eric Wolf, she argues that Chatterjee's contention that social policy has to be understood as a purely political phenomenon, detached from the economic dynamics of neoliberalization in India, fails to capture the dialectical interrelations between dispossession as a form of 'structural power' that operates on the macro-level of global capitalism, and social policy as a form of 'tactical power' that seeks to ensure the popular legitimacy of neoliberal projects in determinate locales. Through an analysis of Dalit activism around land acquisition in Tamil Nadu, Steur investigates how corporate social responsibility works to deflect the collective action of subaltern groups as it obfuscates the workings of structural forms of power at play in contemporary processes of primitive accumulation.

A critique of Chatterjee's now infamous civil–political society dichotomy and what it does for the conceptualization of 'community' in Subaltern Studies is what is at stake in Kenneth Bo Nielsen's contribution to this volume. While the early subalternists presumed pre-existing community formations and solidarities, later works by Partha Chatterjee argue that communities are strategically created in the course of political action. Notwithstanding this theoretical advancement over the earlier conception of community, Chatterjee's 'community' appears 'curiously bereft' of an appreciation of internal power dynamics and social hierarchies, thus reinforcing romanticized notions of unified subaltern collectives and consciousness. Nielsen uses his case study of the movement against land acquisition and industrialization in rural West Bengal to show how hierarchies pertaining to caste and class complicate straightforward assumptions of community formation and solidarity.

The idea that state interventions in contemporary India reverse the social consequences of primitive accumulation is also the subject of critique of the final chapter by Subir Sinha. Discussing the mobilization of transnational solidarity for the wrongfully jailed Binayak Sen and the politics of a Delhi-based Residents' Welfare Association, Sinha problematizes Chatterjee's trifurcated conceptualization of the political domain into civil society, political society, and 'an outside beyond the boundaries of political society' (Chatterjee 2008: 61). It is a perspective, he claims, that fails to capture the actual political fault lines generated by contemporary processes of primitive accumulation. Particularly, Sinha argues that the claim that welfare programmes constitute a significant region of 'political society'—separate from the domain of civil society—is rendered problematic by the multi-level solidarity networks that mediate and translate between dispossessed subaltern groups and the liberal democratic discourses of universal rights and entitlements.

The discussions and arguments that are presented in this volume relate most immediately to the contemporary Indian context. However, the processes that we are concerned with—namely, the ways in which subaltern groups mobilize collectively to contest and resist the dispossession, disenfranchisement, oppression, and stigma that are wrought by hegemonic formations—should resonate beyond this specific empirical reference point. In his postscript to this volume, David Arnold notes that Subaltern Studies was always meant to be relevant beyond 'the massed ranks of the academy'. That ambition remains as important and as valid as ever today, when, across the global South, the advent and unfolding of the neoliberal project have redefined the fault lines of political mobilization over the past three decades, thus giving rise to what Prashad (2012: 9) refers to as 'a world of protest; a whirlwind of creative activity'. We hope, therefore, that this book might serve as a constructive contribution to an informed and engaged debate about the prospects for politics from below across the regions of the global South.

Notes

1. See Corbridge and Harriss (2000, chapter 7), Kohli (2006a, 2006b), and Vanaik (2001) for accounts of the elite-driven nature of economic reform in India.

2. See Chakrabarty (2002, chapter 1), Chaturvedi (2000b), and Ludden (2002a) for accounts of the evolution of the Subaltern Studies project. The key contributions to the critical debates that were spawned by the Subaltern Studies project are collected in Chaturvedi (2000a) and Ludden (2002b).

3. The most significant contribution to this turn is arguably Dipesh Chakrabarty's (2000) *Provincializing Europe: Postcolonial Thought and Historical Difference*, which sets out to destabilize and transcend Eurocentric narratives of transitions towards the modern. Other significant contributions include Gyan Prakash (1990, 1994) and Ranajit Guha (2002). The debate between O'Hanlon and Washbrook (1992) and Gyan Prakash (1992) is also important in this respect, as is Sumit Sarkar's (1994) critical intervention on Saidian frameworks in the writing of modern Indian history.

4. Chatterjee (2004, 2008) has attempted to carry out such a redefinition by suggesting that subaltern politics in contemporary India operates on the terrain that he refers to as 'political society'—that is, the terrain constituted by the apparatuses of governmentality that attach to the state. Political society is contrasted to civil society where the principles of liberal democracy prevail. In Chatterjee's account, civil society remains a domain of elite politics. Sinha, Nielsen, and Steur discuss the adequacy of Chatterjee's formulation in detail in this volume. See also Gudavarthy (2012) for a collection of essays on Chatterjee's recent work.

5. Violence and coercion are, of course, also central features of the Indian state's presence in Kashmir and the North-East states (see Baruah 1999; Duschinski 2009).

6. These include, for example, the Right to Information Act, the Right to Food Act, the Right of Children to Free and Compulsory Education Act, the National Rural Employment Guarantee Act, the Forest Rights Act, and the recent Right to Fair Compensation and Transparency in Land Acquisition, Rehabilitation and Resettlement Act.

I

Engaging Gramsci

1

For a Historical Sociology of State–Society Relations in the Study of Subaltern Politics

ALF GUNVALD NILSEN[*]

This chapter presents a critical discussion of the theoretical frameworks through which state–society relations have been conceptualized in the study of subaltern resistance in colonial and postcolonial India. In developing this discussion, I will argue for the necessity of developing a historical sociology of state formation moored in Marxian theory in order to be adequately equipped to analyse the ways in which subaltern resistance articulates with state power and the institutions, discourses, and technologies of rule through which this power is effectuated.

The first part of the chapter presents a critical assessment of the way in which the Subaltern Studies project has conceptualized

[*] I would like to thank the participants at the workshop 'Reconceptualizing Subaltern Politics in Contemporary India' (University of Bergen, 4–5 October 2013) for their instructive comments on an initial draft of this chapter. I have also benefited greatly from Srila Roy's critical reading and generous discussion of the chapter.

the relationship between the state and subaltern groups in colonial and postcolonial India. Engaging with the work of Ranajit Guha, Partha Chatterjee, and Sudipta Kaviraj, I call attention to the problems that attach to a persistently bifurcated view of state power and subaltern resistance. This perspective, I argue, fails to appreciate how subaltern groups appropriate the institutions, discourses, and governmental technologies of the state as and when they engage in collective resistance.

I then consider an alternative to this perspective that has recently come to the fore, namely, ethnographic studies of everyday forms of state–society relations that draw on Foucault's notion of governmentality. Focusing on the work of Akhil Gupta and Aradhana Sharma, I argue that these perspectives have been of great importance in terms of crafting a more relational conception of the multifarious ways in which subaltern groups in India conceive of and engage with the state. However, due to their commitment to a decentred and dispersed understanding of power, these perspectives fail to engage sufficiently with how historically determinate relations of class power tend to both enable *and* constrain the pursuit of subaltern politics in and through the state.

In the third and final section, I outline an alternative approach to the study of state–society relations that is grounded in Gramsci's conceptions of subalternity, hegemony, and state formation. The objective of this exercise is to craft a foundation for a historical-sociological approach to the study of subaltern politics that enables us to decipher the dialectics of enablement and constraint that emerge at the point of convergence between the contemporary micro-dynamics of everyday state–society relations and the macro-structural *longue durée* of state formation.

State–Society Relations in the Subaltern Studies Project

As is well known, the Subaltern Studies project took its point of departure in Ranajit Guha's founding statement in the essay 'On Some Aspects of the Historiography of Colonial India', in which he argued for a conceptualization of the politics of subaltern groups as an 'autonomous domain' that 'neither originated from elite politics, nor did its existence depend on the latter' (Guha 1982b: 4).

This conception of subaltern politics as an autonomous domain had significant ramifications for how state–society relations were conceived of by key participants in the Subaltern Studies project. Indeed, a close reading of the relevant texts reveals the contours of a conceptual narrative that runs as follows: the precolonial state was a very distant entity for most subaltern groups, who seem to have inhabited something akin to James Scott's (2010) 'non-state spaces'. Despite intentions and attempts to the contrary, the marginality of the state in relation to the lifeworlds of India's subaltern minorities was reproduced under colonialism. And the postcolonial state has at best been only partially successful in overcoming this schism, which in effect means that it remains alien and irrelevant to the articulation and pursuit of subaltern politics.

Precolonial and Colonial State–Society Relations in the Subaltern Studies Project

In his early contributions to the Subaltern Studies project, Partha Chatterjee (1982, 1983) focuses on how different 'modes of power' structure and animate particular social formations. Chatterjee argues that precolonial peasant societies have their base in a 'communal mode of power', which binds together the peasantry in a community where 'the collective is always prior to the individual parts and its authority larger than the mere sum of its parts' (Chatterjee 1982: 12). Peasant consciousness, in turn, is one in which 'the state is always distant'—it remains 'an entity which is not organic or integral to the familiar sphere of everyday social activity' (Chatterjee 1982: 31–32). Thus, when 'peasant-communal politics' engages with the state—and the state and its functionaries are perennial targets of peasant discontent—'it is always the concept of the community as a whole, a form of authority incapable of being brought down into consistent parts, which shapes and directs peasant politics *vis-à-vis* the state' (Chatterjee 1982: 34–5; see also Chatterjee 1983). Sudipta Kaviraj has developed a similar perspective in which he argues that the precolonial state was 'a distant, formally all-encompassing empire' that commanded ceremonial deference from its subjects, but had little actual capacity for inter-vention in their communities, lifeworlds, and livelihoods (Kaviraj 2010a: 12). In this sense, the precolonial state was situated at the centre of 'a circle of circles of caste and regional communities' in which monarchical rulers were afforded 'deep obeisance at the cost of a certain marginality' (Kaviraj 2010b: 53).

Now, the advent of colonial rule brought in its tow a serious commitment to overcoming this marginality. In the political realm, this revolved around a partial introduction of modernist political discourse, centred on 'the idea of the state as an imper-sonal regime of relations, the idea of an individual subject ... the equality of rights or rightlessness ... and, finally, a state which ... pretended to represent the collective interest of society, and whose legitimate interference in society was morally immune' (Kaviraj 2010a: 12).[1] Education served as a means to induct a small Indian elite into the running of the new politico-administrative apparatus, and more generally into the incipient public sphere that—despite its exclusions and inequalities—was constituted by and through the colonial project. In other words, the imperial polity 'provided a discursive space on which nationalist ideas could eventually be framed' (Kaviraj 2010b: 50) by turning 'the political point of this discourse against colonial authority itself' (Kaviraj 2010b: 20).

For Chatterjee, of course, the formation of the Indian national state was a paradigmatic case of 'passive revolution' in which a structurally weak but aspiring bourgeoisie sought to build 'the larg-est possible nationalist alliance ... against the political rule of the colonial power' (Chatterjee 1986: 48). But this also entailed con-fronting the 'fundamental cultural problem' (Chatterjee 1986) of overcoming the parochial traditionalism of the peasant's worldview.

In *Nationalist Thought and the Colonial World*, Chatterjee (1986) traces the career of this problem through the sequential development of Indian nationalist ideology across three phases—the moments of departure, manoeuvre, and arrival, respectively—as these are embodied in the thought of three leading nationalists: Bankimchandra Chattopadhyay, Mahatma Gandhi, and Jawaharlal Nehru. The key point for Chatterjee is that throughout these three moments, the peasantry and its politics remained marginalized. This marginalization was ultimately institutionalized when

Indian nationalism became 'a *state ideology*' (Chatterjee 1986: 132) in and through the Nehruvian nation-building project, in which 'the life of the nation' was subsumed under 'the life of the state' (Chatterjee 1986: 161).

Similarly to Chatterjee, Kaviraj sees anticolonial nationalism as a project that germinated among the narrow Indian elite that was incorporated into the colonial state machinery, and who then turned the precepts of liberal political discourse against the colonial rulers: 'Indian nationalism, at least the form in which it came to be enshrined in the Congress, was primarily a product of this discourse, a complex of dissatisfactions worked out by the modernist-rationalistic elite' (Kaviraj 2010a: 20). The postcolonial state that eventually emerged as a result of anticolonial mobilization consequently also reproduced many of the exclusions that had been constitutive of the colonial state. Indeed, according to Kaviraj (2010a: 23), the mobilizing strategies of the Indian freedom movement established an elite–subaltern relation that after 1947 'would be written as the state–society relation'.

Finally, it is worth taking note of Ranajit Guha's own formulation of this argument in the long essay 'Dominance without Hegemony' (Guha 1989). Guha takes his point of departure in the argument that in colonial India, 'power simply stood for a series of inequalities between the rulers and the ruled as well as between classes, strata and individuals among the latter' (Guha 1989: 229).[2] Guha attributes these unequal relationships and power differentials to a specific structuring of dominance and subordination under the Raj. Hegemony, Guha argues, is a form of dominance in which persuasion outweighs coercion. However, the colonial state 'failed to generate a hegemonic ruling culture' (Guha 1998: 64). Ultimately, the reason for this failure is located in the essentially alien and imposed character of the colonial state: 'The colonial state in India did not originate from the activity of Indian society itself... . As an *absolute externality*, it was *structured like a despotism* with no mediating depths, no space provided for a transaction between the will of the rulers and that of the ruled' (Guha 1989: 274–5). Under these conditions, British rule over Asian subjects came to rely 'more on force than consent' (Guha 1989: 281)—that is, 'dominance without hegemony' (Guha 1989: 282).

The fundamental problem with the underlying narrative in these accounts lies in its postulation of a profound disjuncture between subaltern groups and precolonial and colonial forms of state. This is, quite simply, a claim that fails to measure up to the historical evidence. Precolonial peasant protest—such as the *dhandak* (bringing a complaint before the king) in the Tehri-Garhwal Himalayas—was clearly animated by a culture of resistance that operated through an oppositional appropriation of the ideology of kingship that undergirded precolonial states (Ramachandra Guha 1985, 1999). Now, obviously, the 'infrastructural power' (Mann 1984) of precolonial states was constricted by 'the political economy of appropriation' (Haldon 1993) that undergirded tributary modes of production (see also Banaji 2010; Berktay 1991). Nevertheless, the fact that cultures of resistance such as the dhandak existed suggests that it is highly problematic to construe the peasant community and the state as independent and opposing entities that only enter into an external relation with each other in and through conflictual clashes.

Similar problems attach to claims about the colonial state and subaltern resistance during the Raj. Contrary to the claim that peasant communities simply opposed the state as an externality, a recent study of Adivasi resistance in colonial Chota Nagpur has shown that the tribal peasantry in this region would petition the state all the way from the local level to London, deploying a rhetoric that 'admirably mimics the official discourse of colonial primitivism' (Chandra 2013a: 154). Even when they made politico-theological claims to sovereignty, the demand was for 'quasi-national autonomy under British colonial overlordship' (Chandra 2013a: 157). Moreover, as Kaushik Ghosh (2006: 525) points out, these struggles left an imprint on the state, which was compelled to introduce protective legislation that cannot be understood as anything other than 'a cumulative effect of massive and persistent tribal revolts against the colonial system of 18th and 19th-century India and Jharkhand'.

In other words, actual historical dynamics seem to compel us to develop a far more fine-grained analytic of relations between the precolonial and colonial states and subaltern groups than a formulation like 'dominance without hegemony' allows for.

Postcolonial State–Society Relations in and Beyond the Subaltern Studies Project

Dominance without hegemony during the Raj was, according to Ranajit Guha (1989: 307), reproduced by its 'successor regime'—the postcolonial Indian state. Whereas this claim is not developed in any depth in Guha's own work, it has been a central theme in the critiques of the Indian nation-state that have been issued by Kaviraj and Chatterjee.

According to Sudipta Kaviraj, the Nehruvian nation-building project was by no means grounded in the political vocabulary of the popular classes. Rather, it was anchored in ideals that were intelligible and relevant only to the modernizing elite that had taken over the reins of power from the British. Therefore, the commanding heights of the state came to be dominated by an elite that 'did not try to create or re-constitute popular common sense around the political world, taking the new conceptual vocabulary of rights, institutions, and impersonal power into the vernacular discourse of rural or small-town Indian society' (Kaviraj 2010a: 29).

As the Indian state expanded, this created a bifurcation between the 'upper' and 'lower' discourses of the state: 'The new elite could not create its own hegemony, or create a dialogic relation with the subaltern classes' (Kaviraj 2010b: 81). The postcolonial state came to rely on 'a vast lower-order population'—those that did not 'inhabit the modernist discourse'—in recruiting its personnel and implementing its policies (Kaviraj 2010b: 26, 30). This means that, at the point of implementation, major government policies infused with elite conceptions of governance and development have been 'reinterpreted beyond recognition' (Kaviraj 2010b: 30). Thus, despite the fact that the state 'in its sordid everyday structures' has become more familiar to India's subaltern groups, there remains a deep-seated 'problem of intelligibility of the political institutions of the state ... at the heart of the Indian democratic system' (Kaviraj 2010b: 246).

The central arguments presented in Chatterjee's second treatise on Indian nationalism—*The Nation and Its Fragments*—tap a similar vein. The postcolonial nation-state, Chatterjee argues, has constructed its self-definition 'from the ideology of the modern, liberal-democratic state' and, as a result of this, 'autonomous forms of imagination of the community were, and continue to be, overwhelmed and swamped by the history of the postcolonial state' (Chatterjee 1993: 10–11).

It is nevertheless possible to detect a slight change in the tenor of Chatterjee's argument—a change that in many ways mirrors the claims put forward by Kaviraj—in that he stresses a certain tenuous rapprochement between elite and subaltern politics in relation to the postcolonial state. The fact that both communalism and populism have become increasingly salient phenomena within the context of India's liberal constitutional order is interpreted as an indication of a two-pronged change: on the one hand, Indian elites have come to recognize that their political fortunes depend to a large extent on electoral support from subaltern groups, and that this can only be achieved through the construction of demotic idioms and imaginaries; on the other hand, the subaltern domain of politics 'has increasingly become familiar with, and even adapted itself to, the institutional realms of the elite domain' (Chatterjee 1993: 13). Still, it is all too clear that Chatterjee's analytical optic continues to rest upon the assumption that there exist two separate political domains—one defined by 'the hegemonic project of nationalist modernity', and the other by 'the numerous fragmented resistances to that project' (Chatterjee 1993: 13, see also 218–19). In his more recent work, Chatterjee has suggested that—'as a result of the deepening reach of the developmental state under electoral democracy' (Chatterjee 2008: 54)—subaltern groups have become more familiar with the governmental technologies of the state. However, as many critics have noted—for example, Nandini Sundar (2011) and Sinha (2012)—Chatterjee's distinction between 'civil society' as a sphere of elite politics and 'political society' as a sphere of subaltern politics fails to capture how actually existing subaltern politics is often crafted around oppositional claims for citizenship (see also Agarwala 2013; Baviskar and Sundar 2008; Chandra 2013b; Chopra et al. 2011; Nilsen 2015; Subramanian 2009).

It is clearly necessary to develop a fine-grained understanding of the mutual imbrication of subaltern politics and the institutions, discourses, and technologies of rule of the state. In the next part of this chapter, I therefore move on to discuss a body of scholarship that seeks to do this by employing Foucauldian concepts in the ethnographic study of state–society relations.

Foucauldian Studies of State–Society Relations in India

Foucauldian ethnographies of state–society relations in India have mushroomed in recent years through the work of scholars as diverse as Akhil Gupta (1995, 1998, 2001, 2012), Aradhana Sharma (2006, 2008; see also Gupta and Sharma 2006a, 2006b), Corbridge et al. (2005), Fuller and Harriss (2001), and Williams et al. (2011). In the following, I will focus predominantly on the work of Akhil Gupta and Aradhana Sharma, as they are arguably the ones who have developed this perspective in the richest and most stimulating manner since the middle of the 1990s.[3]

Akhil Gupta on Governmentality and Subaltern Politics in Rural India

In a landmark article on the discursive construction of the state, Akhil Gupta (1995: 375) argues that 'the state has become implicated in the minute texture of everyday life' in contemporary India. However, in contrast to Kaviraj's notion of upper-order and lower-order discourses about the state, Gupta insists on the importance of not conceiving of the local state as a coherent spatial unit that encapsulates its own reality. Whereas the *tehsil* (sub-district) is obviously the arena where the vast majority of Indians come into contact with the state and where their imaginaries of the state are forged, Gupta argues for the necessity of acknowledging that the local state is itself criss-crossed by translocal processes, discourses, and practices that in turn inflect subaltern imaginaries of the state (Gupta 1995: 377).

Using the example of corruption, Gupta (1995: 389) argues that 'the imagined state' crystallizes at the confluence of the experience of encounters with corruption in the practices of the local bureaucracy, on the one hand, and the discourse of corruption as it is articulated in public culture, on the other. Local experiences with corruption are endemic, but also variegated; in Gupta's account they range from cases where villagers fail to master the art of giving a bribe, thereby finding themselves under the thumb of local revenue officials, via the recalcitrant low-caste farmer who is at least partially successful in challenging corruption in a government housing programme, to the militant farmers of the Bharatiya Kisan Union, who regularly cajole local officials into delivering state development schemes.

What cuts across these experiences and encounters, however, is that the state is perceived as being embedded in and entwined with local relations of power (Gupta 1995: 384). Practical experiences of corruption, and the awareness that this generates about how the state is implicated in local power relations, in turn mesh with the discourse of corruption that circulates in public culture—in particular, through the vernacular press. This discourse, Gupta argues, constructs an opposition between an exploitative state and an exploited people, and in doing so it appeals to the notion of citizenship that was so central to the establishment of the post-colonial state. The state is therefore constructed discursively as an entity that is accountable to the people: 'The discourse of corruption, by marking those actions that constitute an infringement of such rights, thus acts to represent the rights of citizens to themselves…. The discourse of corruption…plays this dual role of enabling people to construct the state symbolically and to define themselves as citizens' (Gupta 1995: 389).

Gupta draws out a series of implications for the study of the state and state–society relations from this argument. Most importantly, perhaps, the state must be conceptualized in a more disaggregated and less bounded way than has been the case hitherto—that is, it is necessary to conceive of the state as a space constituted at the intersection of local, regional, national, and global political flows. In political terms, it also means that making absolute distinctions between collaboration and resistance is unsatisfactory. Strategically, Gupta argues, it is important to exploit the contradictions in the workings of state institutions, discourses, and governmental technologies. These 'fissures and ruptures' enable subaltern groups 'to create possibilities for political action and activism' (Gupta 1995: 394; see also Gupta 2012: chapter 3).

This perspective is developed further and takes on a more explicitly Foucauldian character in Gupta's (2001) analysis of the Integrated Child Development Services (ICDS) programme in Uttar Pradesh. According to Gupta, the ICDS is best conceptualized via Foucault's notion of governmentality—that is, a form of power that is exercised through the workings of dispersed techniques of government that seek to improve the welfare of a population in various ways.[4] Given its preoccupation with 'the size and quality of the population' and its reliance on 'techniques of *regulation, enumeration, and accountability*', the ICDS has propelled a vast expansion of the scope and reach of the state into the lives of poor people in the Indian countryside, and, in particular, into the lives of lower-caste women and their children (Gupta 2001: 74).

However, Gupta (2001: 66) is keen to emphasize that the implementation of the ICDS did not merely create new subjects—it also created 'new kinds of resistances'. Each node in the ICDS chain of command was also a site where these resistances played themselves out: in the face of *anganwadi* (daycare centre for children) workers who tried to collect a variety of statistics and data from and about them, poor rural women would refuse anganwadi workers access to their homes and to provide certain kinds of information; in the face of bureaucrats who defined them as 'volunteers', women anganwadi workers challenged this lowly status and defined themselves as 'teachers' (Gupta 2001: 74–92). Thus, whereas the contemporary Indian state is clearly involved in a concerted effort to 'alter, regulate, monitor, measure, record, and reward the conduct of politically disempowered groups of lower-caste women and children' so as to 'manage the size and quality of the population', it is also and conversely a fact that 'the conduct of government itself' changes as a result of the interaction that goes on in and through state–society relations, as subaltern groups imbue 'the state with their own agendas, interpretations, and actions' (Gupta 2001: 92; see also Gupta 2012: chapter 7).

Aradhana Sharma on Neoliberal Empowerment and Subaltern Assertion

Aradhana Sharma (2006, 2008) develops the Foucauldian approach to the understanding of state–society relations in contemporary

India with reference to the intersection between NGO activism and official policy strategies for women's empowerment.

Sharma investigates the workings of the Mahila Samakhya (MS)—the Indian government's flagship programme for women's empowerment in Uttar Pradesh. Now, on the part of the state, MS represents a turn away from a developmentalist form of governmentality centred on welfare, towards a neoliberal form of governmentality centred on efforts 'to empower marginalized subjects to care for themselves' (Sharma 2006: 69). A common criticism of NGO and activist participation in programmes such as these is that it ultimately leads to their co-optation and depoliticization. However, according to Sharma, this view is too one-sided: despite their neoliberal tinge, she maintains, programmes like MS 'do not depoliticize struggle as much as they open up new vistas and forms of political action' (Sharma 2008: 64).[5]

In Sharma's study, this is brought out most clearly when she hones in on how MS workers mobilized around issues that involved the state in some way, and that necessitated confrontation and claims-making. Formally speaking, MS workers were government employees, and state officials would use this fact actively as a way of preventing the MS programme from becoming too activist in its orientations. Therefore, MS workers had to find ways to circumvent strictures imposed on them as a result of being government staff. Sharma (2008: 77) details how MS staff 'worked around the state's disciplinary strategies' to achieve empowerment. Crucially, this entailed the use of bureaucratic proceduralism—both to shield themselves from punitive responses from the state and to be able to pursue claims and struggles on behalf of subaltern women (Sharma 2008: 76–9).

Sharma argues that whereas empowerment programmes such as MS clearly governmentalize women's everyday lives and subject them to the disciplinary reach of the state, they also generate knowledge, skills, and aptitudes that enable assertion: 'encountering officials, gaining information about how bureaucracies work, and learning statist methods can also be seen as enabling subaltern women to mobilize and demand accountability and entitlements from state agencies' (2006: 75). These reflections echo Akhil Gupta's concern with the necessity of using the contradictions, cracks, and fissures in the workings of policies and programmes to advance the concerns of subaltern groups, and focus attention on what might be called the 'unintended consequences' of neoliberal governmentality.

Neoliberal policies, then, may well be geared towards redirecting poor people's gaze from the state and towards 'themselves, their communities and other civil society bodies', but an unintended consequence of their workings is to generate assertive and oppositional practices that target the agencies of the state: 'this is a politics of citizenship centred on demanding resources as rights from government bodies' (Sharma 2008: xxii). What ultimately emerged from these processes was a discourse of 'justice, rights and citizenship, albeit not one limited to the bourgeois precepts of the individual rights-bearing citizen' (Sharma 2008: 143). Rather, the subaltern communities that Sharma focuses on developed a 'culturally coded, collectively informed' conception of citizenship that effectively denaturalized 'the legalistic discourse on citizenship that writes out questions of class, caste and gender inequality and appears to treat all citizens as formally equal' (Sharma 2008: 144).

Foucauldian Ethnographies: Towards a Critique

Foucauldian ethnographies have situated subaltern politics in contemporary India in 'relational spaces of connection and articulation' (Moore 1998: 347), and in doing so they have been of singular importance in terms of moving beyond the impasses that I discussed in my interrogation of the Subaltern Studies project earlier in this chapter. Moreover, by highlighting how the state—rather than being a behemoth defined by 'verticality' and 'encompassment' (Ferguson and Gupta 2002)—is 'a multi-layered and conflictual ensemble' (Gupta and Sharma 2006a: 291), these ethnographies are politically enabling as they make it possible to pursue a debate about how activism can best exploit the schisms that might exist between different scales and regions of the state.

However, despite these significant virtues, I nevertheless believe that this approach to the study of state–society relations and subaltern politics suffers from a theoretical elision that ultimately also limits its political fecundity. This elision flows from its theoretical mooring in the analytics of state power that Foucault developed in his lectures on biopolitics and governmentality at the Collège de France (see especially Foucault 2007, 2008). The key problem with this shift is that it leaves us ill equipped to address the crucial dialectic between what Bob Jessop (1982: 224) has referred to as 'conjunctural possibilities' and 'structural constraints' in subaltern encounters with state power.

The basic problem is this: the argument that 'the state' is not an entity endowed with a clearly demarcated and bounded unity, positioned over and above society, also entails that 'the political power that is pre-eminently ascribed to the state' (Poulantzas 1978: 147) comes to function as a modality in and through which the ability of dominant social groups to control social relations is institutionalized and consolidated. This is perhaps most clearly evidenced in those historical conjunctures when the exercise of state power achieves a certain unity across dispersed sites as and when hegemonic groups are faced with concerted challenges from below. However, it is equally visible in the fact that the state is structured in such a way that dominant groups are better able to pursue collective projects in and through the state (Jessop 1990: 250).

If we return to the empirical terrain in question—the postcolonial Indian polity—we find examples of the former in state-orchestrated mobilizations of organized violence in various forms in response to the collective action of subaltern groups,[6] as well as in Indira Gandhi's declaration of a state of emergency in 1975. In a less dramatic but no less significant manner, extensive networks of middlemen, advisers, contractors, and criminals are capable of hollowing out the actual state apparatus, depleting it of funds, and running it according to their own interests (Harriss-White 2003). Similarly, dominant farming communities often combine their extensive networks of contact and influence with their substantial purchasing power in the informal market for government jobs to colonize the state apparatus, and put this to use as a modality in the systematic reproduction of class advantage (Jeffrey 2001; see also Jeffrey and Lerche 2001). These are aspects of the workings of state power that Foucauldian ethnographies of the state cannot adequately grasp. Indeed, in the work of Gupta and Sharma, there is no systematic discussion of how class power moulds the institutional modalities of the state, and how this structuring in turn reproduces the hegemony of dominant groups.[7]

These elisions arguably echo lacunae in Foucault's theorization of power relations and the state that persisted throughout the different phases of his work. As much as Foucault's early work examined 'sites of new power relations' that were integral to 'the capitalist-liberal state' (Kalyvas 2002: 117), it was still marked by a refusal to interpret 'this materiality of power (and thus of the state) as rooted in the relations of production and social division of labour' (Poulantzas 1978: 67). However, Foucault did eventually start to grapple with some of these questions in his later work, where the focus was on how some technologies of power were selected over others, and then brought together in stable ensembles and strategies of government (Poulantzas 1978: 151; see also Jessop 2008: chapter 6). As part of this shift, Foucault also increasingly engaged with the existence of 'a general line of force that traverses the local oppositions and links them together' (Foucault 1990: 94; cf. Jessop 2008: 153).

Nevertheless, Foucault remained profoundly vague about what the general line that traverses the 'micro-diversity of power relations' is actually grounded in and congealed from (Jessop 2008: 140, 148, 152–3). And it is precisely this silence that resurfaces in the inability of Foucauldian ethnographies of state–society relations to sufficiently grasp how a determinate form of state will be constituted in such a way as to structurally constrain the advance of subaltern political projects through its institutional ensemble. Thus, my contention is this: in order to adequately grasp the dialectic of conjunctural opportunities and structural constraints in subalterns' encounters with state power, it will be necessary to fuse our ethnographic attentiveness to the situated and quotidian aspects of state–society relations with a historical awareness of the macro-structural dynamics of capitalist development and state formation as 'master change processes' (Tilly 1984: 44). This, in turn, takes us towards the domain of historical sociology and a concern with how '[the] shaping of action by structure and transforming of structure by action both occur as processes in time' (Abrams 1982: 6).

Towards a Historical Sociology of State–Society Relations in the Study of Subaltern Politics

In this part of the chapter, I move on to address the challenge of constructing a conceptual approach that, on the one hand, is capable of grasping how subaltern politics is always-already imbricated in state–society relations, and how, on the other hand, state–society relations simultaneously enable and constrain subaltern politics. I do so by proposing a dialectical rethinking of subalternity and hegemony that focuses on the nature of contestation in and through the lattice-work of 'connective tissues' (Gramsci, cited in Morton 2007: 70) between subaltern and dominant groups that is mediated by 'the integral state' (Gramsci 1971: 239).

Subalternity, Fields of Force, and Hegemony

If we want to restore a dialectical sensibility to our understanding of subaltern politics, we need to start by rethinking subalternity itself as a determinate positionality within a set of historically constituted relations between social groups that are differentially situated and endowed in terms of 'the extent of their control of social relations and ... the scope of their transformative powers' (Sewell 1992: 20). Subalternity, then, must be related to the moulding, over time, of 'a societal "field-of-force"' (Thompson 1978: 151) through the contentious unfolding of 'hegemonic processes' (Mallon 1994a: 70).[8]

In trying to understand subalternity and hegemony in these terms, it is imperative to recall that Gramsci (1971: 182) thought of the construction of 'the hegemony of a fundamental social group over a series of subordinate groups' as a gradual process. Through such processes, dominant or ascendant social groups develop political projects that enable them to gain the consent of subaltern groups 'to the general direction' (Gramsci 1971: 12) that they seek to impose on social life. Subaltern consent, however, can only be gained through 'a continuous process of formation and superseding of unstable equilibria ... between the interests of the fundamental group and those of the subordinate groups' (Gramsci 1971: 182). Thus, hegemony will bear the imprint of this: as a result of the making of concessions, what emerges from a hegemonic process is necessarily 'an always dynamic or precarious balance ... among contesting forces' (Mallon 1994a: 70).

How do we then understand the positionality and agency of subaltern groups within such fields of force?[9] 'Subaltern groups', Gramsci (1971: 182) argued, 'are always subject to the activity of ruling groups, even when they rebel and rise up.' Thus, subaltern agency of various kinds—ranging from everyday negotiations of the workings of power from above, to collective action challenging adverse incorporation into a social formation[10]—develops through engagements with institutional ensembles, framing claims through discourses, and mobilizing through political forms that are commensurable with and geared towards the reproduction of unequal structures of power. This dynamic follows from the fact that the compromises that have been reached in and through hegemonic processes are ostensibly ones 'in which the interests of the dominant social groups prevail' (Gramsci 1971: 182): subaltern groups are positioned in relation to socio-economic relations, political institutions, and cultural forms that ultimately undergrid reproduction of hegemony. Consequently, subaltern collective agency is conditioned by and mediated through 'the social condensations of hegemony' (Morton 2007: 92).

Gramsci conceived of the development of oppositional projects from below as a trajectory in which subaltern groups strive to develop political strategies and forms that will better enable them 'to transform their subordinate social positions' (Green 2002: 15). The starting point of this trajectory is always the 'objective formation' of a given subaltern group as the result of the reorganization of a determinate social formation—in other words, capitalist development and state formation as master change processes. From this point, Gramsci conceives of the articulation of subaltern politics in terms of attempts to move from active or passive affiliation to 'dominant political formations' that have been developed 'to secure the assent of the subaltern groups and to maintain control over them' (Gramsci 1971: 52). Initially, these attempts will take the form of limited claims and demands, but the experience of impasses in the pursuit of these claims may prompt the development of political organizations that press for more comprehensive, autonomous claims—albeit within the parameters of the extant social and political order. Finally, subaltern groups may move towards the development of genuinely counterhegemonic projects that assert their 'integral autonomy' (ibid.) against the dominant social groups and aim for thoroughgoing systemic transformation. Crucially, Gramsci does not posit the unfolding of this trajectory as a teleological necessity. Rather, the tendency towards unification that exists in the collective agency of subaltern groups 'is continually interrupted by the activity of the ruling groups' (Gramsci 1971: 55) and therefore cannot be taken for granted. With these foundations in place, the next step is to consider the role of state formation in hegemonic processes and subaltern politics.

Subalterns and State Formation in Hegemonic Processes

The construction of hegemony, in Gramsci's view, is intrinsically linked to state formation and the workings of state power: it is in and through the state that dominant groups ultimately articulate and gain consent for hegemonic projects, which in turn enable them to give form and direction to trajectories of social change (Gramsci 1971: 52).

In opposition to liberal conceptions that compartmentalize the different regions of social formations, Gramsci (1971: 263) argued that 'State = political society + civil society, in other words hegemony protected by the armour of coercion'. Political society is constituted by 'the apparatus of state coercive power which "legally" enforces discipline on those groups who do not "consent" either actively or passively' (Gramsci 1971: 12)—or, as Peter Thomas (2009: 137) has put it, 'the machinery of government and legal institutions'. Civil society, on the other hand, is the sphere in which 'the spontaneous consent' of subaltern groups is organized and reproduced through 'the ensemble of organisms commonly called "private"' (Gramsci 1971: 12)—such as schools, religious institutions, and trade unions (see Buttigieg 1995). And Gramsci (1971: 239) coined the term 'the integral state' to denote 'the unity of the moments of civil society and political society' (Thomas 2009: 157).

The notion of the 'integral state' is significant for our understanding of the construction of hegemony because it denotes a distinctive feature of modern processes of state formation, namely, 'an increasingly more sophisticated internal articulation and condensation of social relations within a given state form' (Thomas 2009: 140). A crucial part of this is the increasingly salient orientation of the state in capitalist modernity towards the construction of relations between dominant and subaltern groups (see Thomas 2009: 27–8). In contrast to previous ruling groups, dominant groups under capitalism seek 'to construct an organic passage from the other classes into their own' (Gramsci 1971: 260) through a state that operates through institutions, discourses, and technologies of rule that effect the 'capillary and permanent direction of an entire social fabric' (Burgio, cited in Thomas 2009: 144; see also Morton 2007: 92–3).

The converse side of the centrality of the integral state to the working out of hegemonic projects from above is, of course, its centrality as a modality through which oppositional politics is articulated and pursued by subaltern social groups. There are two points that are vital in this respect: one relates to the contradictions of 'moral regulation' (Corrigan and Sayer 1985) in processes of state formation; the other relates to how the state as 'a *site* and a *centre* of the exercise of power' (Poulantzas 1978: 148) is constituted in ways that ultimately undergird the reproduction of hegemonic structures of power.

The Contradictions of Moral Regulation

It is precisely because of the construction of organic passages between dominant and subaltern social groups that state formation as a master change process comes to articulate with the 'local rationalities' (Nilsen 2009; Nilsen and Cox 2013) that animate subaltern politics. State formation is a profoundly cultural process, predicated on forms of 'moral regulation' that are geared towards encouraging some ways of organizing social life 'whilst suppressing, marginalizing, eroding, and undermining others' (Corrigan and Sayer 1985: 4). An integral aspect of this regulation is the emphasis put on unification: 'Centrally, state agencies attempt to give unitary and unifying expression to what are in reality multifaceted and differential historical experiences of groups within society, denying their particularity' (Corrigan and Sayer 1985: 4).

This is achieved partly through the totalizing idioms of loyalty and identity tied to nationalism, and partly through individualizing projects that register people within the state as citizens, taxpayers, and so on and so forth. Thus, one can think of the 'organic passage' that dominant social groups seek to construct between themselves and subaltern social groups through the integral state as being constructed by projects of moral regulation. In this way, 'subaltern classes are intertwined with processes of state formation' (Morton 2007: 62). Indeed, the emphasis on unification and erasure of particularity and systematic inequality in processes of modern state formation is precisely the definitive feature of civil society as a moment of the integral state (Thomas 2009: 144).

The crucial point, however, is that the moral regulation of the state does not proceed untrammelled and without contestation. There will, unavoidably, be scope for dissonance to arise between the 'unifying representations' that are at the heart of bourgeois state formation and actual lived experiences of 'inequality, domination and subordination' (Corrigan and Sayer 1985: 6). As a result of this dissonance, the 'universalizing vocabularies' of the modern state do not merely serve as pillars of hegemony, but also become 'sites of protracted struggle as to what they mean and for whom' as subaltern groups mobilize to contest their adverse incorporation in a given social formation (Corrigan and Sayer 1985: 7, 6; see also Nugent and Alonso 1994: 211).

In this sense, then, popular struggles 'do not take up a position absolutely external to power: they are always an integral part of the power edifice and make their own mark on the state by reason of its complex articulation with the totality of power mechanisms' (Poulantzas 1978: 151; see also Joseph and Nugent 1994: 20).

The Structuring of the State

The state in its 'integral form' has to be understood not as 'a sovereign instance above civil society' but as 'a network of social relations for the production of consent, for the integration of the

subaltern classes into the expansive project of historical development of the leading social group' (Thomas 2009: 143, 343). This
is highly significant in terms of understanding the equations of
conjunctural opportunities and structural constraints in subaltern
engagements with the state. As I argued earlier, the social relations that undergird hegemony are not shaped by the unilateral
exercise of power by dominant social groups, but through a trajectory of contentious negotiations that culminates in a 'compromise
equilibrium' in which 'account is taken of the interests and the
tendencies of the groups over which hegemony is to be exercised'
(Gramsci 1971: 161).

Now, given its ontological moorings in these relations, it also
follows that the state 'above all is the condensation of a relationship of forces defined precisely by struggle' (Poulantzas 1978: 151).
This means that in a given structuration and institutionalization
of state power, there will always be 'internal limits imposed by the
struggles of the dominated' (Poulantzas 1978: 151). And, crucially,
it is these limits that generate conjunctural opportunities for subaltern groups to pursue their political projects via the modalities of
state power. Yet, it remains the case that the compromise equilibrium that makes hegemony possible 'cannot touch the essential'
(Gramsci 1971: 161). The equilibrium, after all, sustains the hegemonic position of the dominant social group. The consequence of
this is the simple but important fact that 'the state is an ensemble of
power centres that offer unequal chances to different forces within
and outside the system to act for different political purposes' (Jessop
2008: 37). Bob Jessop (1990, 2008) has referred to this as the 'strategic selectivity' of the state—a selectivity that is manifest in the
greater ease with which dominant social groups are able to use the
state in their pursuit of hegemonic projects and, on the other hand,
the structural constraints faced by subaltern social movements as
they seek to harness the state to oppositional projects.

Thus, when we study the ways in which subaltern groups pursue oppositional projects in relation to the state, the key challenge
is to delineate *both* the enablements *and* the constraints that characterize such processes in specific contexts and particular scales.
For a historical-sociological approach to the study of subaltern
politics, this means that it will be necessary to trace the origins of

a particular structuring of a determinate form of state to previous cycles of contestation and struggle between dominant and subaltern groups. And to extend this analysis in a politically relevant direction, it will be necessary to developed grounded understandings of what subaltern groups can achieve by appropriating the institutions, discourses, and technologies of rule of the state while simultaneously raising questions about how oppositional projects from below can destabilize and rupture the structures of social power from which the state is ultimately congealed.

* * *

In the context of contemporary India, the need for such an approach is, arguably, particularly urgent. On the one hand, recent years have witnessed the deepening of Indian democracy through the emergence of what Ruparelia (2013) calls 'the new rights agenda'— that is, national rights-based legislation to secure civil liberties and socio-economic entitlements—and an increasing tendency of subaltern politics to be oriented towards socio-legal activism. On the other hand, Indian democracy is at the same time being hollowed out by an elite-led process of neoliberal restructuring that has thrown up new forms of uneven development and has failed to enhance the life chances of India's subaltern populations (see Nilsen and Roy, this volume). In this conjuncture, knowing 'what is to be done' will, by necessity, mean knowing something about what to do in relation to the state.

Notes

1. This should, of course, not be read as an argument that the colonial state was founded on liberal principles. As Kaviraj (2010b: 60) notes, the colonial state was profoundly authoritarian. The problem, however, in Kaviraj's account is that he overlooks how the modern western state was only democratized gradually, through popular mobilization that challenged the reactionary alliance of emergent bourgeoisies that emerged after the revolutionary convulsions of 1848 (Halperin 2004; Silver 2003).

2. Similarly to Kaviraj, Guha is arguably operating with a slightly caricatured view of the development of the bourgeois state in the metropolitan

context, in which the popular classes are seen as always-already incorporated into its ambit as citizens with democratic rights (see note 1; see also Chibber 2013).

3. See Nilsen (2011) for an engagement with Fuller and Harriss (2001) and Corbridge et al. (2005).

4. The literature on governmentality is too vast to summarize here. See Foucault (2007, 2008) for the original statements of the idea, and Rose (1999) and Dean (2009) for instructive discussions.

5. A similar argument can be found in the work of Sumi Madhok (2013), who has focused on the Women's Development Programme in Rajasthan—a forerunner to MS. Due to constraints of space, I do not engage with her work in this chapter.

6. See, for example, Baruah (1999) and Duschinski (2009) on the use of direct military force in the North-East and Kashmir, respectively; Nandini Sundar (2006, 2007, 2010) on the use of paramilitary outfits like the Salwa Judum in response to the Maoist insurgency in Bastar; Ashwani Kumar (2008) on the use of landlord armies against militant Dalits as 'surrogate arms of the state'; and Menon and Nigam (2007) and Pati (2006) on state violence against democratic resistance to displacement.

7. I owe this point to Alpa Shah's comments on Akhil Gupta's book in 'Thinking Allowed: Family Funerals; Red Tape', which aired on BBC Radio 4 on 3 December 2012, http://www.bbc.co.uk/programmes/b01p0hnv (accessed on 2 March 2015). See also Harriss and Jeffrey (2013).

8. See Roseberry (1994) for a set of instructive comments on Thompson's concept of 'field of force'.

9. See Green (2011b) for a profoundly instructive reading of the richness of Gramsci's notion of the 'subaltern'.

10. See Nilsen (2009) and Nilsen and Cox (2013) for a discussion of the different phases and forms of 'movement processes' from below.

2

Rethinking Hegemony

Caste, Class, and Political Subjectivities among Informal Workers in Ahmedabad

MANALI DESAI

This chapter explores the puzzle of why the concept of hegemony was relatively neglected in the Subaltern Studies project, and thereby raises some questions about the concept's Gramscian lineage itself. I argue that, to develop a useful notion of hegemony that can be employed in a reinvigorated Subaltern Studies project, we need to employ some conceptual and analytical tools drawn from the post-structuralist extensions of Gramsci's work. Although the works of Laclau and Mouffe (1985) and Stuart Hall (1996) are most closely associated with these extensions, some highly pertinent scholarship on political subjectivities under neoliberalism goes beyond the Gramscian preoccupation with hegemony, turning to Foucault's less top–down notion of governmentality instead (Ong 2006, 2007). While I employ some crucial insights from this literature, I argue that hegemony remains a vitally important concept and a potentially better analytical tool for understanding change, process, and resistance compared to the concept of governmentality. A more developed concept of hegemony can surpass the top–down implications of governmentality with its conceptual neglect of the subaltern, in part by accounting for the fissures, contradictions, and counter-hegemonic spaces that are an inherent part of hegemonic condensations. A distinct contribution of this chapter is therefore to push the conceptualization of hegemony in this direction, in part by pointing towards the desire and ambivalence that mark subaltern political subjectivities, rendering them more complex and open than the binary between acquiescence and resistance would suggest. In doing so, this chapter addresses a key concern raised in the Introduction to this volume, namely, the manner in which subaltern resistance is conditioned and mediated by hegemonic processes rather than being autonomous from them. Drawing on in-depth interviews with dalit and Other Backward Class (OBC) informal workers in Ahmedabad,[1] it shows how the category 'subaltern' is overridden by so many different political claims that any recovery of political authenticity and homogeneous subject formation as implied in the original Subaltern Studies project is rendered impossible. Even as neoliberal tenets have become central to global hegemonic projects, the erosion of security and rise in labour's precarity creates a field of fragmented heterogeneity, with complex subjectivities and identifications that are deeply ambivalent towards neoliberal hegemonies. Subalternity is thus, as Ananya Roy describes it, 'a heterogeneous, contradictory and performative realm of political struggle' (2011: 230).

This essay develops the concept of hegemony in a novel way by arguing that subalterns neither fully accept nor reject the rationale of hegemonic claims, but instead appropriate these claims in order to surpass the constraints and strictures of mundane life. This conceptualization allows us to avoid splitting hegemony into either ideational or material forms of imbrication/subjection, and instead weaves them together into a performative conceptualization that problematizes stable notions of agency, identity, and indeed, subalternity. Through emotions ranging from deep ambivalence to acceptance of these claims, our respondents discussed how they negotiated the views and values of dominant groups to individually and collectively transcend their position as 'subaltern'. The essentially dynamic analytical stance that is developed in the chapter helps to erode the inevitable structural binaries between elite and subaltern politics that emerged in the original Subaltern Studies project (a point discussed extensively in this volume). I argue that keeping both aspects—the position of subalternity and the desire to transcend it by working *through* hegemonic claims—within the same analytical frame is a necessary if difficult challenge. It cautions against the assumption that hegemony is ever complete, yet allows us to recognize its power in shaping how dreams and desires are felt and articulated. The ambivalence that emerged so prominently in the interviews at times represented a deep-seated rejection of the very frame of politics, yet equally cautioned against the romantic notions of nihilist rejection that are implicit in some discussions of subaltern politics. Instead, what emerged clearly was that subaltern appropriations of hegemonic projects can be creative even as such appropriations are made in conditions not of their own choosing. In turn, this suggests that the foundational notion of consent that underpins the concept of hegemony as it is widely used fails to do justice to the complex subjectivity of precarious labour under capitalism.

Hegemony: Subaltern Studies and Beyond

The Subaltern Studies project, despite its early and sometimes reiterated debt to Gramsci, was less concerned with the problem of hegemony than the question of force or dominance, given the long colonial experience from which India had emerged during the 1940s. In a sense, the theoretical question about India's post-colonial trajectory lay somewhere between the problem of the West and the East. Ranajit Guha's impressive *Dominance without Hegemony* (1998) sought to highlight the impossibility of hegemony in the colonial state, where a Western colonizing power ruled the East without assimilating civil society (as it did in its country of origin). Instead, coercion was the primary means by which it stabilized its rule over an alien country. For Guha and other Subaltern Studies historians, particularly as outlined in Partha Chatterjee's *Nationalist Thought and the Colonial*

World (1986) and *The Nation and Its Fragments* (1993), the elite–subaltern split that was maintained through non-hegemonic coercion under colonialism was, in the post colonial state, largely unresolved through nationalism. Instead, Indian nationalism perpetuated a new, yet equally potent split between the two domains, this time not through coercion, but an equally non-hegemonic ideology that papered over the split. It is the exclusion of the subaltern from hegemony itself, the marginalization of autonomous and authentic forms of subaltern self-activity and expression, and the attempted absorption and normalization of subaltern activity within the nationalist narrative, that became the key preoccupation of the group of insurgent historians. What was needed was a methodology of recovery, through unearthing new historical sources and reading existing ones 'against the grain'.

Ranajit Guha's early statements did much to promote the importance of subaltern conceptual and theoretical autonomy in the writing of history. It was precisely because elites had exercised *dominance* rather than hegemony that subaltern actors had in fact always acted independently of the elite. In his words, subaltern politics constituted 'an autonomous domain, for it neither originated from elite politics not did its existence depend on the latter' (Guha 1982b: 40). In part, this was a method for explaining peasant rebellions in colonial India, which had too often, Guha argued, been appropriated to colonial, nationalist, and Marxist narratives (G. Prakash 1994). The central theme was appropriation—tied in particular to the passive revolution that, Partha Chatterjee argued, had marginalized forms of subaltern agency and resistance that did not fit with the nationalist project of modernity, while at the same time attempting to normalize other forms of subaltern aspirations and desires (G. Prakash 1994: 1481). In all of these formulations, there is a distinct sense of a domain outside the elite that is at once autonomous and subject to appropriation. This often left, as Gyan Prakash has argued, the subaltern as 'position', as 'compass or stance' with no objective base. Indeed, the emphasis on the subaltern as a position of critique, or as a 'discursive effect', potentially left little room for the voice of the subaltern (G. Prakash 1994: 1488).

Perhaps the more important implication of Guha's conception of the subaltern, particularly for the discussion in this chapter, is that the problem of hegemony was largely glossed over. As Florencia Mallon (1994b: 1512) noted, Guha assumed the failure of the Indian bourgeoisie to truly mobilize (and thus hegemonize) the masses. But this notion of hegemony relies upon a somewhat orthodox interpretation of Gramsci's emphasis on the Jacobin party, and of France in 1789. As 'not-France', India is perpetually defined as the failure of capitalism or liberalism to fully material-ize, yet at this level of generality what is missed are the alternative routes to hegemony (and alternative hegemonic processes) that are discussed not only by authors such as Foucault (albeit indirectly), but in Gramsci's own work.

This particular critique of Guha can be linked to a wider prob-lem in the use of the term 'hegemony', which tends to be so unevenly deployed in the literature that it has lost some of the conceptual edge that it had acquired in Gramsci's theory. Perhaps the most consistent definition of the term is as an outcome in which the interests of the dominant (ruling) class have become coeval with those of the ruled (Arrighi 1994).[2] Some scholars are, however, concerned with hegemony not so much as an outcome, but rather as a process through which dominant groups attempt to shape reality and perceptions of reality in their own image. This recognizes the incomplete and fragile nature of hegemony, with 'resistance' or counter-hegemony being seen as its direct coun-terpart. Thus, for example, in a critical and landmark discussion, authors in the volume *Everyday Forms of State Formation* (Gilbert and Nugent 1994) pay close attention to the fragility of hegemonic projects. Florencia Mallon (1994a: 71) argues that 'hegemony can-not exist or be reproduced, without the constant, though partial, incorporation of counterhegemony'. In the same volume, William Roseberry proposes that 'we use hegemony not to understand con-sent, but to understand struggle' (1994: 360). In his words, 'to the extent that the dominant order establishes ... legitimate forms of procedure, to the extent that it establishes not consent but pre-scribed forms for expressing both acceptance and discontent, it has established a common discursive framework' (Roseberry 1994: 364). Of course, these frameworks, as he acknowledges, are frag-ile and problematic, giving rise to an effectively bilingual space where the dominant and subordinate speak different languages with different intentions. Nevertheless, one can argue that the conceptualization of hegemony rests exclusively upon a notion of practice, through emphasis on language, procedures, and rituals, rather than subjectivity. Thus, Derek Sayer argues that it is not ideology or belief, but the 'materiality of everyday forms of state formation' that both compels and constrains its subjects, while potentially liberating them at the same time (1994: 377).

The fractured and fragile character of hegemony has been amply contrasted to the assumption of hegemonic projects as grand, settled conjunctures. However, what is critically missing in this otherwise compelling discussion of hegemony is the question of subjectivity, which was arguably central to Gramsci's own concerns. Do the languages and procedures established by dominant groups work only as prescriptions, or do the subordinate effectively come to believe in them and inhabit them as their own, albeit in different ways from dominant groups? Bringing political subjectivity into the discussion allows us to examine these questions. The concept itself has multiple connotations; as Krause and Schramm (2011: 118) note, it simultaneously incorporates two older and often opposing notions of political belonging—primordial attachment and legal-instrumental membership of the state. They suggest that political subjectivities should be thought of as the *effects of practices* by which political subject positions come into being, that is, not simply as the result of practices of inclusion and exclusion, as one might attribute to practices of state formation, but equally as the result of practices that bring about longing and desire (belonging). Following Werbner (2002), Krause and Schramm (2011: 126) argue that subjectivity is best viewed as being simultaneously about 'subjection to power, experiencing new agency and gaining recognition'.

The question of subjectivity, I argue, is integral to understanding what Gramsci meant by hegemony. In other words, for Gramsci, the question of hegemony operated simultaneously at the level of the state, civil society, and the individual and his/her lived experience. As Thomas (2009) convincingly argues, in Gramsci's thought, hegemony is conceptually linked to other key concepts, and its particular status was always as a *provisional* and *practical* concept. It is linked in particular to two key concepts—

the 'integral state' and 'passive revolution'—which together create the significance of the concept of hegemony. The integral state is the unity of political society and civil society, a critical move by Gramsci to conceptually remove the distinction between state and society that is central to liberal political thought. Civil society, for Gramsci, is the terrain upon which social classes seek hegemony, although, in the last instance, capturing the legal monopoly of the means of violence in political society was paramount to achieving this hegemony (Thomas 2009).

The exceptional revolutionary contribution of the bourgeoisie, compared with all previous dominant classes, was its lack of conservatism, its promise of freedom for all social classes. This thoroughly revolutionized the political sphere by creating the basis for moving from state-led coercion as the primary means of securing a bourgeois order, towards consent as its primary cementing force. However, this idealized claim was thrown into crisis with the Europe-wide revolts of 1848, during which the universalist basis of bourgeois hegemony was revealed as, in fact, particularistic and exploitative. The revolutionary expansionary movement of the bourgeoisie was thus halted in favour of a passive revolution. This was a new type of bourgeois initiative aimed at restoring its leadership in civil society, but through the *'inverted spectral distortion'* (Thomas 2009: 148; my emphasis) of the former mode of hegemony, namely, of the 'real and substantive image of freedom' (Thomas 2009: 148). In other words, freedom became the dominant sign of its inverse, which was the passive revolution. As a revolutionary process, it proceeded by creating the image of freedom while absorbing and neutralizing emerging oppositional forces initially through a molecular and peaceful 'depoliticization' process, and then by securing a more fundamental passage of left revolutionaries into the moderate camp. But hegemony also has to work at the level of the self: to mould and remould conceptions of the world, and create a common sense through the inculcation of discipline, responsibility, consumption, and values and practices that were integral to capitalist subjects.

The concept of passive revolution has been applied to the Indian case by several authors who argue that the dominant agrarian and industrial classes created a ruling pact through the absorption of the Indian masses first under the banner of Indian nationalism, then the state form of parliamentary democracy (Chatterjee 1986, 2008; Kaviraj 1994). But there has been very little discussion of the subjective dimensions of this absorption. The Subaltern Studies school at its origins had effectively denied the possibility that subaltern groups would consent to their own subjection. Rather than passivity, it was *activity* that became the focus—various modes of rebellion that were written out of the archive of official accounts, all but lost to later generations of historians. But this may have been too partial a reading of Gramsci. Instead, for Gramsci, there were several aspects of subaltern life and consciousness that had to be integrated in order to construct an appropriate methodology for studying subaltern history. These included the 'objective formation' of subaltern classes, their *'passive or active adherence to dominant political formations'* (my emphasis), the formations of subaltern classes themselves, and various successive modes through which subaltern classes sought to create autonomous assertions of their class interests (Green 2002: 9). These aspects of subalternity implied some imbrication in dominant class institutions and formations, such that a proper analysis of subalternity would of necessity have to work with the complexities of this imbrication.

In rethinking Subaltern Studies for contemporary times, Chatterjee (2012) has discussed some of the ways that a new subaltern project could move forward. He argues that contemporary conditions of capitalist modernity have removed the 'archaic from the modern' and shaped the practices of subaltern actors increasingly through the technologically modern industry of mass production. We could see this new conjuncture, therefore, as an opportunity to rethink the structuralist bias of the Subaltern Studies school's conceptual edifice, and identify the elements of a less romanticized conceptualization of subjectivity.[3] Although there is much that can be said in favour of and against this attempt at rethinking the Subaltern Studies project, a crucial problem lies in the conceptualization of the term 'subaltern' in relation to elite domains. Indeed, Chatterjee's notion of 'subaltern' reproduces the idea of subaltern as *popular*, one that presumes an underlying agency and identity, replicating the problem with earlier conceptions of 'subaltern' in the original project. Rather, it might be useful to draw on Spivak's (2005: 476) contention that 'subalternity is a position without identity' (see also Ismail 2013). This theoretical move from thinking of the subaltern as the domain of 'demographic difference' towards one inflected with the flexibility and performativity of inhabitants of spaces 'in-between', at the periphery, and in 'zones of exception' (Ong 2006; A. Roy 2011) offers an important way forward. The consideration of subalterns as inhabitants of sites where sovereign power and global finance capitalism criss-cross situated social relations such as ethnicity and class allows us a much more contingent and flexible theorization of contemporary subaltern subjectivities. It thoroughly loosens up the structural dichotomy between elite and subaltern, offering us the opportunity to investigate the contradictory and messy political subjectivities and expressions that emerge from the zoning of space and territory as we see in the case of the eastern part of neoliberalizing Ahmedabad, where our interviewees lived and worked, and where our interviews were conducted.

Subalternity and Hegemony in Ahmedabad

The discussion in this chapter draws upon 30 in-depth interviews conducted between August and December 2012 in east Ahmedabad (Vatva, Shahpur, Naroda, Amraiwadi, Juhapura, Khadia, Dariapur) with dalit and OBC men and women employed in a range of occupations such as rickshaw drivers, bricklayers, casual labour, and the marginally self-employed, many of whom had moved in and out of employment. The purpose of the interviews was to gain insight into the political subjectivities of two generations of 'lower' castes who were engaged in Gujarat's neoliberalizing economy in mostly precarious work. Although the informal sector has always dominated the economy in Ahmedabad, there has been a notable casualization of work and increased precarity in the context of declining welfare since the mid-1980s. As Gujarat's developmental model has been consolidated during the same period, particularly taking a neoliberal turn since the late 1990s, the interviews were specifically intended to probe what meaning the hegemonic constructions of 'development' held for those who were engaged in such work.

Gujarat is one of the most dynamic regional economies in India, with the highest growth rate among Indian states (11.3 per cent, compared with the Indian average of 9 per cent in 2010–11) (Bagchi et al. 2005: 3039). Gujarat's urban labour force was substantially transformed during the 1980s, from its relatively stable base in the famous textile industry which dominated Ahmedabad, to rapid casualization and informalization. The first liberalization policy in 1985 created a loss of almost 100,000 jobs in Ahmedabad (Breman 2001: 4804). The new factories that arose on the outskirts of the city paid less than half the former wages and practically no benefits (Spodek 2011: 198). Our research showed that the remaining workers were forced to accept work as contract labourers with poor pay and extreme insecurity.

The brutality of the new 'social Darwinian order' has been poignantly described by Breman (2004). As I discuss subsequently, the intensification of a neoliberal model in Gujarat was based on dismantling Congress-era welfare pacts between the state and lower castes, in particular dalits. Caught between the precarity of work and a state increasingly facing away from the poor, dalits became 'unchained' from the previous order in which their subject positions had come into being. As older forms of caste patronage disappeared, OBCs and dalits (in different ways) became the subject of competing discourses and claims in an increasingly politicized environment. It is crucial to note at this point that the terms 'dalit' and 'OBC' do not refer to stable or homogeneous categories. Such 'analytical groupism' in scholarship risks deploying the language of the state with respect to reservations and government policy, as well as voting categories through which parties aggregate votes (and scholars analyse them), more consistently than it does the language through which lower castes in fact apprehend their lives and circumstances. Both categories are divided internally, not only by class and occupation, but also by ritual status which governs marriage rules, inter-caste dining, and various customs. In general, OBCs are seen as occupying a position somewhere between dalits and upper castes (Brahmins in particular), although in Gujarat some Patels (Koli Patels) are also OBCs. Thus, it is with some caution that we refer to OBCs as 'subaltern', particularly as many OBCs have seen their status rise under Bharatiya Janata Party (BJP) rule.[4]

Given that dalits form roughly 7 per cent and OBCs 40 per cent of the population, competition for votes could not but result in some attempt to define and promote a notion of coeval interests with these groups. Accordingly, during the social flux of the anti-reservations riots, the BJP boldly seized the initiative from the Congress Party, and employed a crucial articulation strategy of resignifying caste conflict into a religious one. Thus, by employing the politics of Hindutva, the BJP reasserted the primacy of the upper caste–class groups while *reincorporating* the lower castes through a new cultural politics that de-emphasized caste and made religion the salient fault line. Such attempts at integrating backward castes had a longer history in the form of the Swaminarayan movement, which employed a sanskritizing mode by asking those lower in the caste hierarchy to adopt the customs and values of the upper Brahminical castes. As Ghanshyam Shah (1994: 58) notes, Gandhi also adopted a similarly ambivalent view of caste, simultaneously seeking to eradicate social distance while placing the onus of reform upon the lower castes to improve their lifestyles.

A more contemporary version of this attempt is evident in the way that the concept of 'development' or *vikas* has been discursively interwoven with Hindutva to create a sense of common identification between various Hindu castes. A key aspect of this is the organization of such an identity around themes of stability, order, and progress. Since 1992, the BJP has ruled uninterruptedly in Gujarat, and Chief Minister Narendra Modi occupied office from 2001 to 2014, covering three successive terms—a historical feat yet to be accomplished by any other politician. The Hindu right under his leadership in particular consolidated a hegemonic project centred on the notion of Hindu supremacy, which is conjoined to a modern, technologically driven and entrepreneurial self and society. Thus, although religion is central to the social cement—Hindus seeing themselves as radically distinct from Muslims and Christians—the inflection of Hindutva with development signifies a notion of progress, rather than a conservative backlash as some commentators have suggested. As an ideology, the conjoined elements of Hindutva and development suggest a forward-looking and modern sensibility, which enables people steeped in provincial and outmoded identities to reinvent themselves as individuals and collectivities. Indeed, Modi has taken this message to the national level more recently: 'No one can feed India's youth the poison of caste anymore. The youth of today only understands one language—only sings one mantra—has only one dream—vikas, vikas and vikas. The state should only rule in order to push development forward.'[5]

In seeking to probe the extent to which such ideologies have become hegemonic among subordinate castes and classes, we asked the families we visited to speak about what 'development' or 'vikas' meant to them, which part of their lives had been touched by it, and what its resonance was for understanding the major transformations in their lives, such as work, marriage, children, change of residence, etc. Given that the hegemony of the ethnically inflected neoliberal project is partly enabled by seeking the consent of these groups, what could the emerging subjectivities tell us about the reception of the hegemonic project? In other words, is this discourse hegemonic?

In probing this question, I was aware of the possibility that the long history of weak associationalism among the working classes and poor in Gujarat may have facilitated their assimilation into hegemonic ideologies. Yet the dalits we spoke to often referred to the work of the Dalit Panthers during the 1970s, citing influences that have been critical to a pan-national dalit identity, such as Ambedkar. Lack of political organization thus did not automatically translate into cultural or political assimilation, that is, hegemonic ideologies, for dalits. Instead, the effects of weak political organization among dalits are primarily institutional; in other words, dalits have been unable to extract reforms of the economy, police, and welfare that would alter their subjection to precarity and violence. During our fieldwork, there were two separate incidents where dalits in rural Gujarat were shot by police, adding to the growing number of atrocities against dalits amidst the relative impunity of police officers (Gagdekar 2012). Everyday forms of tyranny thus define the lives of many dalits in urban and rural Gujarat. However, the key point here is that, rather than conceptualizing dalits' efforts to grasp and redefine their subjection in terms of 'hegemony versus resistance', it became increasingly clear that dalits employed the signifier of 'development' in several ways so as to enable them to conceptualize emancipation *through* development rather than against it. In partaking of but redeploying the hegemonic concept in this way, dalits (and OBC men and women, as I will describe) could not but be simultaneously imbricated and oppositional.

I discuss this dual aspect of their subjectivity in a processual sense by drawing on the concept of 'chains of equivalence' borrowed from Laclau and Mouffe (1985). They argue that subject positions are developed through a process of articulating (and partially fixing) floating signifiers into a meaningful chain that draws together various subjects into a broader identity. Chains of equivalence are organized around a universal signifier such as 'freedom' or 'equality', which in effect sutures separate demands that might otherwise have remained at the level of the particular. For example, drawing together individual and isolated demands for food, water, and electricity into a 'chain of equivalence' can create a common subaltern identity against an identifiable elite with specific attributes—Brahmin, English-speaking, and so forth. As Laclau and Mouffe argue, every discourse is constituted as an attempt to dominate the field of discursivity by expanding signifying chains which partially fix the meaning of the floating signifier. The privileged discursive points which partially fix meaning within signifying chains are called 'nodal points' (Laclau and Mouffe 1985: 113). It is critical to note the emphasis here on the *partial* fixation of meaning; indeed, this is what renders articulations inherently unstable and open to resignification.

The political events of the mid-1980s were the moment when new political articulations were forged and new chains of equivalence constructed. The dominant castes used ongoing anti-reservation riots to inflict violence on dalits, who were seen as eroding their power through access to the state (Shani 2005). Over time, however, the BJP and its assorted organizations such as the Rashtriya Swayamsevak Sangh (RSS), which had been particularly active during the riots, gradually created a broader coalition of Hindus against Muslims—a chain of equivalence organized around religious cohesion—who now became the target of violence. A new form of 'social peace' based on the identification of Muslims as the enemy was gradually forged, while dalits were offered the possibility of integration into this new political formation.

Our interviews identified two distinct aspects of the articulation of dalits and OBCs within the hegemonic construction of the BJP's new social order combining Hindutva and development. These were: (a) disassociation from the 'old order'; and (b) resignification of the new, through a form of contemporary, cultural sanskritization in which association with the BJP signified 'moving up' in the new order of things. First, the identification of these groups with the Congress Party was problematized as part of an archaic and corrupt order. The disassociation was made possible, particularly as our interviews suggested, among a younger generation of men and women born during the late 1980s–early 1990s. While their parents expressed a certain loss—both of meaningful work with the mill closures and a sense of respect—their children were more likely to express support for the entrepreneurial sensibility implied in the BJP's pro-market rhetoric. Within this rhetoric, the mobilization of religion seemed to function as a language for improving oneself and one's community. As one OBC respondent put it:

> The conjecture is that the BJP is related to the upper class and the Congress to the lower class... . All the OBC think that if they support the BJP they will be known as the upper class... . You know the Swaminarayan religion? The Patels didn't have a religion. Therefore they joined the Swaminarayan religion, so they automatically came into a high position within the caste frame. We are also trying to do that. If you join the BJP you are trying to go up. These are just the thoughts though, not the reality... . If I say I am supporting the Congress then people will say 'Are you a dalit? Are you lower caste?'

As B, an OBC former college student, now unemployed, stated: 'The Congress Party is the party of the poor. But association with the Congress Party brings with it the stigma of being poor, of needing the support of [affirmative action]. Even though we benefit from it, we don't want to be seen as such. Supporting the BJP is a way of telling others ... we are not poor!'

Dissociation from the Congress was coupled with some distance from the *political* idiom of 'caste' (primarily because of its association with the politics of reservations), which was seen as primordial. This despite the fact that, as the interviews revealed, caste determines almost every aspect of life such as residence, marriage, occupation, and social networks, to name a few. Yet some of our respondents revealed that for them, the articulation of progress with religious nationalism offered a potentially new grammar of politics. As MD, a casual labourer of the Devipujak (OBC) caste in Shahpur locality stated: 'During the Congress era we had no status. Nobody knew us... . People did not count us... . Narendra Modi gave us a name, gave us a place in society, the name Devipujak. He gave us respect.' He and his wife Laxmi were at pains to explain that after their inclusion by Modi in 'society', caste did not really matter; the distinction between upper and lower caste had all but disappeared. It was Muslims, they argued, who continued to call them by the derogatory former name, Vaghri (which was considered a criminal tribe during the colonial period). Similar sentiments were expressed by M and S (M's daughter-in-law), members of the Rabari caste whose primary occupation was tending cows in the village-like enclosures of the city. As M put it in a logic that inverts the scholarly consensus on the issue: 'The BJP is for us poor people and the Congress only listens to influential people. The BJP does not listen to the influential people. Hindutva is unity, where we are all one. We have unity within Hindus, but we cannot have that with Muslims. Because they are different. And will remain different.'

The construction of a Hindu–Muslim antagonism in Gujarat has a long history, but its more recent manifestation, especially since the pogrom of 2002, has created two 'truths' that almost all our Hindu respondents vocalized. First, to them the 2002 violence signified the start of a long era of peace that had never been achieved under Congress rule. For this Modi was credited in no uncertain terms. And second, 'development' was linked to this form of peace in which social (religious) homogeneity and order co-constituted one another. Thus, as M, a dalit casual labourer put it: 'Since the BJP came there have been no more riots. We live in peace... . It is not as it used to be. There is progress everywhere....

It seems that it has become like America now. It all seems like a dream.' KRD, also a dalit labourer, stated: 'Development needs society to be organized. Organization needs stability. Stability is not possible in mixed communities.' As one dalit and former mill worker (T) stated:

> The benefit of [Hindutva] is ... [t]he Muslims they are very aggressive. Their children pull out a knife even on the smallest matter ....
> After the mills closed down where I was working, I was a security guard .... During that time the BJP came into power. At first Keshubhai was [BJP] minister. Keshubhai's regime was very good. You know that encounter that happened at that time, I personally think what happened was good. Those were the times. That was a fake encounter, but what went on happened for the best. They were not good citizens were they? We couldn't go into their streets.

These fragments of the interviews possibly come closest to the meaning of hegemony as the appropriation by the subordinate of the thoughts and worldviews of the dominant classes, which in turn results in consent to being ruled by those who appear to be ruling in the interests of all. Yet, the interview with T was replete with contradictory stances about politics, which represented the ambivalence we found among our respondents. T expressed deep cynicism about democracy, and suggested that dalits were effectively better off under princely rule: 'I just went to Rajasthan two days ago. There I learnt about the monarchy, and I felt that that was better than democracy... . If we are not getting food twice a day then what is the point of all the other facilities?' As he claimed (a claim we heard repeatedly from other respondents): 'What's happened in elections nowadays is that, close to the elections, they give everyone Rs 200–500; they give alcohol and take their votes. That's it. This is what happens in a democracy.'

It was indeed difficult to find either resistance or consent as predominant themes in the subjective expressions of dalit and OBC respondents. Instead, what emerged was ambivalence. One interview with two dalit co-workers in the nearby Arvind Mills was significant, in part because they offered a clear gendered perspective, albeit from the point of view of precariously employed workers. The subjective perception and experience of exploitation was something that they clearly articulated, apprehending development differently in this case, as a linear process of technological modernization and the growing surveillance of work. As C said:

> Before when my parents used to work, the reel was inserted directly into the machines which produced loops of thread. And then as modernization occurred, the reels were replaced by knots. When further modernization occurred, automatic machines were introduced. After that there was further modernization and the machines were computerized. As the computerized machines series came about our stress at work increased. Because you see there are 60 spindles in the machine so if one spindle stops then it takes time to get there because the spindle is further away from us. So the computer instantly detects that the spindle has been stopped for two or three minutes. When the boss comes he asks straightaway why this spindle stopped for three minutes, what were you doing and where were you? So our stress increases. The computer is a machine, we aren't!

She went on to say: 'You have to know what is going on around you. If you make a mistake in the manufacturing of the ball thread then your mistake is shown in the final stage. The ball is viewed inside and outside by the computer.... . We are exploited more.'

However, when I specifically raised the question of 'development', that is, vikas under Modi, both expressed a unanimous view: 'There are good changes and Ahmedabad has become very beautiful. There has been a lot of improvement on the other side of the river. A lot of places to see, a lot of places to eat, places for fun. A lot has been built.' I asked them: 'Do you think you can take part in these improvements and changes that you see?' C replied: 'Yes, we are a part of all these changes. To have fun and wander around ... there is nothing like that anywhere.' Both women felt that they were more free of dalit oppression in the city compared with the village. As C said: 'In the village there is still discrimination against dalits and other castes. This untouchability still exists. Not in the city.' In this way they expressed a sense of substantial improvement in their lives over time, a sense that they were indeed participating in the formation of Ahmedabad as a 'world-class city'.

If the view that Hindutva and development were associated with improvement in their lives came out rather clearly among our Hindu respondents, the view was expressed rather more obliquely by a Muslim self-employed welder. Most Muslims that we spoke to in the ghettoized areas of Juhapura and Jamalpur had suffered huge losses during the 2002 violence, and tended to be highly critical of Modi and the idea of development. However, several Muslims who had employed the social and economic capital of their middle-class origins, and saved money after 2002 to rebuild business and livelihoods, were keen to put those events behind them and look to the future. For them, not only was the economic boom (on the other side) hugely profitable, but the gradual accommodation of some Muslims in the life of the city and politics had created new political subjectivities that were distinct from those of their more deprived and ghettoized counterparts. Rafik, the welder, spoke of his fortunes in ways that clearly reflected the forward-looking and entrepreneurial sensibilities of the Hindutva–development ideology. Thus, when asked why so many Muslims were still out of work, he said: 'There is work everywhere but they are lazy and there are alcohol addictions… . Those who really want to earn find a job.' Honesty, hard work, and responsibility were the key to finding a job, and his view was that 'it had nothing to do with the government.'

Ambivalent Subjectivities

With such evidence of identification with dominant ideologies, the process of hegemonic capture of subordinate class subjectivities might seem fairly well accomplished. However, as Stuart Hall (1996: 446) has suggested, subordinate groups experience deep ambivalence regarding their identification with dominant class concepts and ideologies—there is inevitably 'inexpressible envy and desire' involved with such identification. Identification, Hall argues, is not something that is structured around a fixed self; consequently, there is both 'identification and otherness which is more complex than we had imagined' (Hall 1996: 446). Indeed, Ortner (2005) captures this essential division in the concept of subjectivity itself, which is simultaneously a 'reflection' of prevailing socio-cultural formations and the private thoughts and beliefs that are unique to individuals. Subjectivities are thus complex structures of thought, feeling, and reflection that, as Ortner argues, 'make social beings more than the occupants of particular positions' (Ortner 2005: 8). This complexity arises not only due to the idiosyncratic and particular nature of individual experience, but also because prevalent cultural and political formations and discourses appeal to subjects in a variety of positions. This is what makes discursive formations—or articulations—so open to change, especially at certain moments when there is a crisis in the prevailing system of signification.

The interviews revealed very clearly this 'otherness' of identification, a sense of anger and despair that remains unassimilated into the subaltern's identification with dominant class concepts and myths. For GBJ, who works in a cloth shop, privatization under the BJP had led to a new form of oppression of the poor, and he appeared deeply nostalgic for the days when government jobs were freely available. He had suffered a major accident at work and had been relocated to make way for the new bus rapid transit system (BRTS) that cuts across the city. As he put it: 'There is development ... that is why we have been dumped here. It is because of progress that we are suffering. Development has nothing to do with us.'

MSCJ, a dalit worker, similarly said: 'We have nothing. We are struggling to earn money. This is the situation of my children and me. There is no water, medicine ... we live a dog's life here. Nobody comes here to check whether we are alive or dead.' Yet later he expressed a different sentiment when asked about development: 'Earlier there were small roads... . Now there are 132-foot wide roads. Now traffic can move around smoothly... . Whenever you want to travel there is no difficulty. But you need to have money... . Poor people who did not have facilities for their shelter, they are slowly getting support. We had a hut, but we will get houses tomorrow.' When asked why the BJP was so popular, he stated: 'Whoever is in power has to be respected.'

K, a retired dalit mill worker, keenly expressed the dilemma of the precariously employed, having seen his salary effectively drop through the years as a mill worker, and a rise in exploitation as a result of mechanization. For him, work had effectively ceased to become a means of escape, as it had been for the earlier generation who had escaped rural poverty to become mill workers. As he put it: 'The middle class is in difficulty now. In Gujarati we say that "they are prosperous," the ones with wealth who can buy anything, even at a high price. The others are beggars who beg and get food. Only the middle-class suffers.'

The fact that sentiments of support and admiration could be expressed within the same interview with anger, cynicism, and despair reveals the complexity of identification and attendant political subjectivities. This suggests that reducing hegemony to consent is problematic, for it is difficult to classify these subjectivities as consensual. Neither are subaltern groups repositories of oppositional consciousness in some unproblematic way, that is, akin to James Scott's peasants capable of exercising counter-hegemonic actions through hidden transcripts and everyday forms of resistance. I agree with Derek Sayer's contention that 'to abstract out, reify, and monolithically counterpose "hegemony" and "resistance" is to misunderstand both' (1994: 377). But I argue that attention to subjectivity allows us to understand how hegemonic processes operate—not merely as 'the intellectual equivalent of the emperor's new clothes' (Sayer 1994: 377), but as a partial truth. Each interview revealed the contradictory ways in which hegemony operates among the subordinate—as a dynamic force that simultaneously constructs and erodes the stability and order that is inherent in everyday life, and is simultaneously implicated in the very act of being ruled. Indeed, the hegemonic construction of stability and order is a central dynamic of the passive revolution; it is premised on a slow, molecular articulation of chains of equivalence between different subject positions through the 'inverted spectral distortion' of the notion of freedom. Hindutva and development have offered such notions of freedom particularly by accentuating 'friend–enemy' distinctions between Hindus and Muslims while extending the promise of liberation from caste subalternity to dalits and OBCs. On the other hand, because such development is premised on, rather than a challenge to, precarious work, embedded at the heart of this claim is the material contradiction that all our respondents saw with great clarity. This is not false consciousness. It is the simultaneous truth of the material-discursive formation that is Gujarat's developmentalism under the BJP. Within conditions not of their own choosing, subaltern low-caste workers in the harsh and precarious conditions of everyday life employ existing hegemonic frames to transcend their position, rather than passively acquiescing to, or actively resisting this frame. In turn, this dynamic erodes and thus destabilizes these hegemonic claims, because when subalterns emphatically believe that their children's lives are likely to be worse than their own, such claims appear only partially true—if true nevertheless.

Notes

1. The interviews were conducted by myself (PI) and Dr Indrajit Roy, Research Fellow, during August–December 2012 as part of a Leverhulme Research Project Grant (2011–13) titled 'Beyond Identity? Markets and Logics of Democratization in India, 1991–Present'.

2. As Arrighi (1994: 29) states: 'The claim of the dominant group to represent the general interest is more or less always fraudulent. Nevertheless, following Gramsci, we shall speak of hegemony only when the claim is at least partly true and adds something to the power of the dominant group.'

3. For Chatterjee, in the post-1991 period, corporate capital has emerged hegemonic in civil society, where the urban middle classes seek congruence with the normative models of bourgeois civil society (2008: 57). This site is split from another one, which he calls 'political society'. Here the largely urban and rural poor, marked critically by their informality, have entered into governmentalized relations with the state, through 'temporary, contextual and unstable arrangements arrived at through direct political negotiations' (Chatterjee 2008: 57). Reminiscent once more of the structural split that defined the older subaltern school project, Chatterjee's argument is that this latter form of democratic politics has not come under the sway of the 'moral-political leadership of the capitalist class', that is, hegemony. This newly constituted passive revolution does not operate through the absorption of popular protest, but rather through state instruments of welfare designed to reverse the effects of primitive accumulation.

4. Jaffrelot (2013) argues that there is an evident pro-BJP shift among OBC, neo-middle-class voters when they migrate from rural to urban areas. For example, the Koli Patels tend to vote for the Congress Party when they are in a rural context (53 per cent), but vote for the BJP when they shift to an urban context (65 per cent), which indicates a shift from caste-based voting to class aspirations and upward mobility. Our interviews, in fact, revealed a high degree of animosity between dalits and OBCs, with the latter seen as aggressive and violent towards dalits, while for the OBCs, dalits were the undeserving beneficiaries of state welfare. Nevertheless, OBCs have only recently been incorporated within the BJP's project, and the method of articulation has been similar to dalits despite the friction between them, which in effect constitutes a major fault line in the construction of Hindu unity.

5. 'Development Is the Only Solution, Not Caste Division and Reservation', http://www.youtube.com/watch?v=DQhcjQPphLc (accessed on 15 March 2013).

3

Recovering Caste Privilege

The Politics of Meritocracy at the Indian Institutes of Technology

AJANTHA SUBRAMANIAN

Anthropologists today are skilled at demonstrating the historicity and instability of identity. However, we are typically more adept at showcasing the nuances of subaltern affiliation and manoeuvre than at deciphering the work that goes into the reproduction of privilege. Even when anthropologists train their sights on elites or experts, the dialectical relationship between privilege and oppositional politics often slips out of view. In part, this is due to the considerable influence of the Subaltern Studies project which, for all its merits, pays little attention to the reproduction of hegemony. Perhaps due to the assumption that subalterns exist in an 'autonomous domain' where elite power is experienced as 'dominance without hegemony', the work that goes into the maintenance of power gets short shrift. Instead, rule appears more as an inert structure that is a negative presence but not relationally constituted vis-à-vis subaltern lifeworlds.

By contrast, my work considers the dialectic of caste reproduction and transformation through the lens of Indian technical education. In particular, I look at how the notion of 'merit' has serviced the reconstitution of caste privilege in the face of subaltern political assertion. While in some ways formal political arenas and even the broader cultural sphere have witnessed the entry and even ascendance of backward castes, elite education and the expanding private sphere both within and beyond India have serviced the reconstitution of caste privilege by other means. In this sense, we might think of elite and private domestic and transnational private arenas as spaces of upper-caste flight and retrenchment away from the pressures of low-caste politics. However, this upper-caste flight from the state into the domain of capital is not simply an offensive manoeuvre that pre-emptively secures their power and seamlessly reproduces structures of inequality. Rather, it is an ongoing 'war of manoeuvre' (Gramsci 1971) that propels the dynamics of the hegemonic process.

Within the universe of Indian technical education, I look in particular at the dynamics of meritocracy within the Indian Institutes of Technology (IITs). Deemed 'institutions of national importance', the IITs are directly administered and financed by the Indian central government. In the name of ensuring 'merit' as the only basis for admission, they were also initially exempted from the backward-caste quotas applied by several regional governments. As a result, the IIT student body has been strikingly male and upper caste, even when compared with the next tier of colleges. Over the past 40 years, the IITs have also become stepping-stones to transnational mobility, at their peak sending approximately two-thirds of every graduating class to the United States.

Within Indian and, to a lesser degree, American public discourse, the IITian has become an exemplar of intellectual merit, someone seen as naturally gifted in the technical sciences. While the IITian's profile is now global in reach, understanding the process by which the IITian's merit has been naturalized requires moving between regional, national, and transnational scales of analysis. One of my arguments in the project as a whole is that the meaning of merit, and its relationship to social identity and economic opportunity, has to be situated within multi-scalar histories of caste and capital. Only by illuminating the historical production of caste, and the way it has intersected with colonial and postcolonial political economies of education and employment, can we understand the fetish of the IITian's intellect. For reasons that I detail presently, my own study focuses on the state of Tamil Nadu in India's southeastern region, and on IIT Madras, located in Tamil Nadu's capital city of Chennai.

This project on the making of the IITian's merit addresses a pressing need for scholarly work on the dialectics of high- and low-caste politics. From the mid-1970s, scholarship on caste shifted from its modernist treatment as an outmoded form of social organization and affiliation rooted in the Hindu ritual order, to its consideration as a historical formation that is inherently political and integral to the dynamics of Indian democracy. Scholarship on caste now highlights the transformative effect of low-caste political mobilization on various arenas of life, including parliamentary democracy, social movements, civil society organizations, status conflicts, and forms of embodiment (see, for instance, Bayly 1999; Dirks 2001; Jaffrelot 2003; Jeffrey et al. 2008; Rao 2009). Not just scholarship, the media's portrayal of caste is also now informed far more by low-caste challenges to the social and political status quo. Whether celebratory or hostile to the spread of low-caste rights politics, these perspectives increasingly share a consensus view on caste as a subaltern formation. The postcolonial present thus appears to be one where non-elites have caste while elites have class and other more 'cosmopolitan' affiliations.

While it is undoubtedly true that non-elites have embraced caste as a vehicle of empowerment, and collective mobilization for low-caste rights in both formal and informal political arenas has changed the contours of Indian society and politics, this only underscores the need for work on how caste operates at the other end of the spectrum. This is the case across India, but especially so in regions like Tamil Nadu where the rise to political power of middle and low castes has obscured the workings of upper-caste privilege. Indeed, it is particularly productive to think about how and in which contexts such privilege is reconstituted within the larger milieu of backward-caste political ascendancy. How do 'elite revolts' (Corbridge and Harriss 2000) against low-caste assertion seek to reproduce the conditions for hegemony? As Nilsen and Roy, following Gramsci, remind us in the Introduction to this volume, our conception of hegemony must be supple enough to accommodate its processual, contested character. The context of my own study, where state capture by erstwhile subalterns is complicated by the neoliberal reorganization of accumulation, demands such suppleness. As I hope to show, IIT Madras and its transnational diaspora illuminate the role of merit in reconstituting upper-caste symbolic and economic dominance in the context of democratic transformation and the globalization of capital.

The Politics of Meritocracy at IIT Madras

Founded in 1959 through bilateral co-operation between the Indian and West German governments, IIT Madras was the third IIT established after the institutes in Kharagpur (1951) and Bombay (1958). The student body of IIT Madras is drawn from across India, although a greater percentage is from the four southern states, with students from Tamil Nadu and Andhra Pradesh now comprising the two largest groups. Its location in Tamil Nadu state, home to the ethno-linguistic Dravidian, or Self-Respect, Movement, has made IIT Madras a lightning rod for debates over caste and merit. As a central government institution long exempt from regional state policies of caste-based compensatory discrimination, IIT Madras is seen by its detractors as an extension of Brahmin caste power into non-Brahmin Tamil Nadu, where claims to intellectual superiority have strong caste overtones. The institute is even sardonically referred to by some in the vernacular press as 'Iyer Iyengar Technology' (Azhagi 2012), referencing the two Tamil Brahmin subcastes.

While such popular critiques of the IITs do implicate them in the consolidation of a caste elite, what is less considered is how these institutions operate as a critical site, not for the expression of an already consolidated group identity, but for the very constitution of Tamil Brahminness and upper-casteness. In other words, there has been very little attempt to understand upper-caste identity formation as itself a dynamic process, even a politics.[1]

To what extent can we speak of the IITs as a social formation that underwrites the cultural and economic capital of upper castes while avoiding the 'taint' of caste? How have the technical sciences functioned as a key site for the reconstitution of caste? The role of caste in the definition of intellectual worth is especially striking when one considers the technical sciences within Tamil Nadu. The south-east was one of the first regions where caste quotas in education and employment were implemented in 1921. The reservations system has expanded steadily to the point where, now, most regional engineering colleges in Tamil Nadu reserve up to 69 per cent of their seats for those designated as 'backward castes'. These measures have had considerable success at changing the caste composition of regional colleges from the days when Tamil Brahmins monopolized over 70 per cent of seats (Fuller and Narasimhan 2008). The proliferation of private engineering colleges from the 1980s with increasing numbers of students from across the social spectrum acquiring degrees, and employment opportunities opened up by an information technology sector able to absorb huge amounts of technical labour, have further democratized access to occupational niches once monopolized by upper castes. There is a certain dissonance, then, between the discourse of exclusivity and practices of exclusion around the IITs, and the very real dispersal of social capital among other castes. Part of my task is to understand the consolidation of upper-caste symbolic and economic dominance within and beyond India against these ongoing transformations.

For the remainder of this essay, I turn to the making of the Madras IITian as a uniquely meritocratic individual at the crossroads of regional, national, and transnational dynamics. I focus in particular on two constitutive elements of the IITian's merit—autonomy and mobility—and show how each underwrites the claim to caste exceptionalism and the commodity value of an IIT education. In analysing the place of autonomy within IITians' self-representations, my essay complements others in this volume that advance a critique of subaltern autonomy and argue instead for a relational approach to subalternity. However, instead of interrogating the analytical purchase of autonomy, I show that the notion of autonomy operates as a powerful discursive trope and political strategy through which IITians place themselves in a position of exteriority to the state and its low-caste publics. This sense of autonomy, coupled with the claim to mobility, underwrites IITians' notion of merit as a universalistic value even as they perform a rear-guard action to deny merit to other social groups (on the politics of exclusionary universalism, see also Sinha in this volume).

Autonomy

After independence, the ruling Congress Party's First and Second Five Year Plans conceived of a strong industrial base as a precondition for development. The Second Five Year Plan invested heavily in industry, dam construction, metallurgy, and the railways, with expertise in civil and mechanical engineering identified as a particularly urgent need. Towards meeting this need, the government highlighted technical education as a key growth area.

Beginning in 1956, the Indian government began to set up massive steel industries with foreign collaboration. An added dimension of these partnerships was the transfer of technical knowledge. The foreign partners insisted that this transfer of knowhow should occur within autonomous technical institutions where freedom from the bureaucratic structure of the emerging university system would foster the spirit of research. Prime Minister Nehru constituted the Sarkar Committee under the leadership of Nalini Ranjan Sarkar, then chairman of the All India Council of Technical Education, to facilitate the process. The Sarkar Committee Report recommended the establishment of the IITs as higher technical institutions devoted to engineering education and basic and applied research, along the lines of the Massachusetts Institute of Technology (Leslie and Kargon 2006). The Institutes of Technology Act of 1961 declared them 'institutions of national importance'.

The IITs were founded on the premise of 'autonomy'. In terms of governmental oversight, this placed them wholly within the purview of the central and not of the regional state governments. Second, they fell outside the structure of affiliation to universities, giving them greater say in institutional functioning, faculty hiring, and curricular development. Third, their place outside regional education allowed the IITs to take students from all over

India through a centralized examination. Finally, as national institutions, the only forms of compensatory discrimination originally mandated were the central government quotas of 15 per cent for Scheduled Castes and 7 per cent for Scheduled Tribes, although this changed in 2006 when the Supreme Court mandated 27 per cent reservation for Other Backward Classes in all government-funded institutions including the IITs.

While the notion of autonomy translates procedurally as the right to self-governance, it has also become a key 'folk category' for IITians to distinguish their institution from the 'educational mainstream'. Older IIT Madras alumni, both those from the 1960s who continued the late-colonial pattern of entering the Public Works Department as state engineers, and those from the 1970s and 1980s who came to the US for PhDs, spoke of autonomy much more in terms of dynamics internal to the institution. This included the absence of political influence in faculty hiring and student admissions, the lack of moral policing on campus, as well as freedom from family norms. 'Here', one IIT Madras 1975 alumnus told me, 'not even a powerful politician can use his influence to get his child admitted.' Another who graduated in 1968 maintained that, while a student, he 'had no idea what the caste or religion of my classmates was. It just didn't matter like it does in the wider society.'

The representation of the IIT as a space apart links to another striking overlap of opinion that cuts across early cohorts about an IIT education as a process of national citizen formation. Many from the 1960s and 1970s generations spoke of the transformative effect of meeting students from across the country and coming to think of themselves simply as 'Indians'. One alumnus even confided that a hazing ritual during the late 1970s involved 'training' incoming students in who they were expected to be: 'not Bengalis or Tamils, not Hindus or Muslims, but Indians'. This nationalist sensibility was not simply a by-product of interpersonal dynamics. For the first generations of IITians, the institutes were experienced very much as part of the state-led drive to create both industry and citizenry through technological development. That many of them were themselves children of Indian Administrative Service personnel who were part of an internal diaspora further enhanced their sense of being national rather than regional subjects (I elaborate on this further in the next section).

For both early and later generations, the IITs as spaces of *national* citizen formation seem to be as much about not being *political*. Many of these alumni spoke of their nationalism as transcending the 'parochialisms' of region, religion, and caste, with national belonging standing in for a kind of apolitical bearing consistent with their sense of themselves as 'technical men'. Many contrasted IIT campuses from others where student politics are very much aligned with party, trade union, and social movement activism. 'Our campuses have the best record of working days in a year,' one 1985 alumnus said to me. 'No matter what was happening outside, we never interrupted our studies just to protest.'

However, there is also a perceptible shift between earlier and later articulations of an IIT education as an 'antipolitics machine' (Ferguson 1990). For earlier generations, technical merit involved transcending cultural particularism to forge an unmediated link with the nation. It also meant a strong association with the state and its developmental projects, a link between the engineering profession and the state that dates back to the colonial period. David Gilmartin notes that those inducted into the colonial engineering services experienced a new public identity fostered through association with the state and with scientific expertise. Through his training, the professional engineer was predisposed to identify with the imperial state and be brought within the framework of colonial administration and bureaucracy (Gilmartin 2006: 86). The alliance of state power and engineering science that underwrote the professionalization of engineering, Gilmartin argues, elevated public works to imperial scale and invested engineering with an aspiration to mastery over nature, land, and people alike.

More recently, however, technical merit has acquired a new valence as the transcendence, not just of subnationalisms or cultural particularism, but additionally of the state and the public sector more broadly. Although IITians from as far back as the mid-1960s migrated out of India for education and employment, in the process leaving public sector employment behind, the antipathy towards the public sector is a more recent phenomenon. Several of the alumni from the past 10 years made a clear distinction between the public sector 'as it was' when their parents were employed in the state administrative services, and the public sector 'as it is'. One 2004 graduate put it to me this way: 'Employment became based on interest group politics, on politicians making appointments to build vote banks, and not on individual merit.' This idea of the public sector as having become an extension of 'vote bank politics' where your group identity matters more than your merit must be placed in the context of the increasing influx of low castes into the bureaucracy and other public sector enterprises. As I show later, the discrediting of the state bureaucracy also underpins a new logic of national development, one that delinks the nation from the state and links it instead to transnational actors and private capital investment.

This more recent sense of inhabiting a circumscribed, autonomous sphere of merit unconnected to the state and its associated publics is further reinforced by a dramatic shift in the career trajectories of recent graduates. Most now would find it laughable to even consider public sector employment, a trend that has escalated since the Silicon Valley boom of the 1980s when several IIT alumni made it big. Their stories have circulated both in India and the US, solidifying the equation between an IIT education and financial success in the private sector. Now, however, even the 1980s model of going to the US for an advanced degree and then branching out into either academia or industry is no longer the prevalent one. More and more, IIT graduates are finding lucrative jobs in India and foregoing the option of a higher degree, at least in engineering, altogether. While many go on to get degrees in management to enhance their industry status, fewer and fewer are even interested in keeping the door open to research and education.

The annual event of the institutes' job recruiting drive makes big news in India. In the last 10 years, the number of private corporations that recruit on IIT campuses has increased exponentially. Now, IIT graduates join companies like Schlumberger, Shell Oil, Microsoft, McKinsey, Tata Consultancy Services, Infosys, or Lehman Brothers before its demise, for starting salaries that are considerably higher than what their parents earned at the end of a lifetime of work. This is inter-generational social mobility at its most dramatic. The majority of IITians come from families of bureaucrats, schoolteachers, and other public sector employees. These are families where capital has long been held in education. Within a single generation, many of these families have gone from modest middle-class incomes to the hundreds of thousands of dollars earned by corporate executives.

The impressive salaries garnered by newly minted IIT graduates have been glossed in the Indian media as the realization of 'Brand IIT'. The term has spread like wildfire. For instance, in a 2006 article, Shashi Tharoor, former United Nations Under-Secretary General for Communications and Public Information, wrote in the *Times of India*: '"Brand IIT" has shown the way. In 2007, we must start to scale this up to the point where one day "Brand India" becomes synonymous not with cheap products or services but with the highest standards of scientific and technological excellence' (Tharoor 2006). This reference to an IIT education as a brand that has shored up India's comparative advantage in the global marketplace situates the IITs and IITians as the forerunners of a future Indian modernity.

Despite the munificence of their patron-state, IITians have been at the forefront of challenges to state-led developmentalism. A quote in a 2000 *New York Times* article (Dugger 2000) from Kanwal Rekhi, an IIT Bombay alumnus and one of Silicon Valley's most successful entrepreneurs, is emblematic of this disavowal of the developmental state. In the article, Rekhi says that he left for the US after getting his IIT degree so that his 'brain wouldn't go down the drain in socialist India' (quite a twist on the notion of a 'brain drain'). Significantly, the liberalizing Indian state also actively fosters its relationship with the IITs as a way of trumpeting its own disjuncture with a past of state-centred development and its embrace of a new model of development with native capital as a key component. At the 2008 pan-IIT alumni conference held at IIT Madras, then prime minister Manmohan Singh gave the inaugural speech and launched a study on the societal impact of the IITs: 'I believe it is India's destiny to become a knowledge power', he said, 'and the IITs have contributed handsomely in the country's efforts to realize this destiny.' Once again, we see here the unique role accorded to the IITian as the engine of Indian development through whom the country is to achieve its true potential. Even as

Singh is quick to claim the IITian's success as the nation's own, he and other statesmen are typically careful to downplay the debt to the state owed by these 'institutes of national importance'. Rather, the IITian, a key beneficiary of the developmental state, is lauded for transcending Indian conditions to attain his accomplishments. The shift from public industrial production to private knowledge work as the basis of national development suggests a radical shift in the imagination of postcoloniality.

So far, I have mainly addressed the perceived disjuncture, first between IITians and what they depict as narrow parochialisms, and then between IITians and the state. At IIT Madras, however, the antipathy towards the *regional* state and its educational institutions has a unique charge, and it is here that the caste underpinnings of the Madras IITian's merit, and the animating force of subaltern political assertion, are best illuminated. Despite the student body of IIT Madras being drawn from a national pool of candidates and the institution being trumpeted as a quintessentially national space, regional dynamics have been key to forging its institutional culture. The students are drawn disproportionately from the southern Indian states, particularly Tamil Nadu and Andhra Pradesh, and among the faculty, Tamil Brahmins are the largest single group. In part because of the backgrounds of students and faculty, the institution is seen both from within and from without as the antithesis of 'non-Brahmin' Tamil Nadu.

While protecting 'Brand IIT' is a more widespread exercise, the history of non-Brahminism and caste quotas in Tamil Nadu has resulted in a particular claim on IIT Madras by Tamil Brahmins, many of whom see the institution as the last bastion of real intellectualism in their 'caste-ridden' state. For many, the founding of IIT Madras was uniquely propitious. Affiliation to an 'institution of national importance' promised some measure of redress for what they perceived as their cultural victimization within the region. At the same time, the caste marking of IIT Madras did not preclude claims to merit. On the contrary, Tamil Brahmins understood the institution as meritocratic *because* of its association with them and its insulation from the pressures of regional low-caste demands.

The sense of IIT Madras as a meritocratic space under siege is most palpable when it comes to relations with the regional government. I saw this in 2008 when the director of IIT Madras issued an invitation to M. Karunanidhi, the chief minister of Tamil Nadu, to be a chief guest at the institute's 50th-year celebration. Karunanidhi is one of the last luminaries of political Dravidianism, a playwright and orator who cut his political teeth in the 1950s and 1960s mobilizing Tamil non-Brahmins against Brahmin cultural and economic supremacy. City lore about his relationship to IIT Madras includes one story where he apparently threatened to cut off electricity to the campus if IITians openly protested the expansion of quotas in education and employment to lower castes. (The protest never happened.) The year 2008 was the first time any Dravidianist politician had been invited to IIT Madras, and it was met by significant, if ineffective, opposition from faculty who worried that this augured 'the end of institutional autonomy'.

What remained unstated by his detractors was the *reason* why Karunanidhi was issued a special invitation. Just prior to this, IIT Madras had received a land grant from the regional government of 11.5 acres of prime real estate in the heart of the city to build a research park. The park announced a new 'synergy' between academia and industry that was expected to give a shot in the arm to science and technology research. In a striking departure from past jabs at IIT Madras as an illegitimate Brahminical institution on Tamil soil, Karunanidhi, like many of his other regional counterparts, has embraced the presence of a 'centre of excellence' as a key attraction for domestic and foreign capital investment in the state. Regionalism has come increasingly to mean staking a region's comparative advantage in the competition for capital investment. Despite this transformation in the meaning of regionalism, however, regional politics continues to be characterized by IIT faculty and students in terms of low-caste nepotism inimical to the building of a meritocratic society. Ironically, both Dravidian politicians and IITians continue to rhetorically deploy their opposition to one another even as their differences have been bridged by a shared commitment to bringing education increasingly in line with market demands.

Just like Karunanidhi's reworking of regionalism in neoliberal terms, the research park has come to mean new things for IITians. The park has received overwhelming support from students, faculty, administrators, and diasporic alumni. Despite the national and regional governments significantly underwriting the venture, IITians largely speak of it in terms of a long-sought parity with private research universities in the US, with MIT and Stanford topping the list. Indeed, in most conversations I had about the park, the state was written out as a partner altogether, and the park stood in simply for national achievement, indicative of India's arrival on the stage of global technological modernity.

Significantly, another anticipated structural shift received equal amounts of *negative* attention: admission quotas for backward castes. This proposal was almost uniformly condemned as the first step to the demise of autonomy and its kin term, merit, both values that supposedly distinguish IIT Madras from Tamil Nadu's other academic institutions. In fact, at the time, a counter-proposal circulated among US-based alumni to set up an alumni endowment in place of state funding for IIT Madras that would allow the institution more leverage in opposing reservations and preserve its autonomy. It is on *this* issue that state 'intervention' was most openly discussed, while the ever-present role of the state as patron is hardly ever mentioned.

Yet, even as the state appears to be receding in value and virtue for IITians, in other ways, a statist sensibility is very much present in how IITians articulate their sense of social mission. Many of them echo the ideals of nation-building that are typically associated with state developmentalism. Both Indian and diasporic alumni are intent on proving their nationalism by 'giving back'. As one IITian put it to me, 'We are reversing brain drain with trickle back.' Significantly, their debt is framed very much in terms of giving back to the *nation*, once again forcing their patron-*state* into the shadows. This is particularly striking given the key role of statesmen, such as erstwhile Prime Minister Manmohan Singh and Home Affairs Minister P. Chidambaram, in conscripting the wealthier parts of the Indian diaspora into a revised national development project. Nation-building was the central theme of the 2008 pan-IIT alumni conference which was organized around six tracks that corresponded to six potential sites of alumni involvement: research, innovation, education, infrastructure, entrepreneurship, and rural transformation. The IIT alumni version of nation-building has them taking the place of the state as engines of development. As with state developmentalism, IIT development discourse envisions a vanguardist role for a technocratic elite, except this elite now comprises national and transnational capitalists and not government bureaucrats.

While this 'rule of experts' (Mitchell 2002) is characterized by many as a convergence with a global technocracy, others choose more culturalist terms of analysis. An IIT Madras faculty member, who runs a project to extend telecommunications to rural India, spoke to me about the role of elites in Indian society:

> Indian society always found a very special place for elites, such as in Nalanda and Takshila [ancient Indian Buddhist centres of learning]. The reputation of these institutes was that they were very protected places. The best teachers, the best students went there, and the maximum amount of material resources were provided to them. Even in wars these places were not starved, they were not touched. In famine they were still given enough. India always had that tradition—and now we see it in the IITs.

This resort to an age-old cultural logic sidesteps the democratic commitment to parity in education even as it leaves unmentioned the role of institutional authorities in securing the social capital of some at the expense of others. Instead, we have 'Indian society' acting to protect merit at all costs.

Autonomy at the IITs, then, is both structural and discursive. The IITs' status as 'institutions of national importance' hinged on their structural position outside and above the wider educational system. IITians themselves have come to see the schism between the IITs and other educational institutions as that between excellence and mediocrity, merit and politics, and increasingly non-state and state spaces. Across the board, but especially in Tamil Nadu, these distinctions are at once caste distinctions. Caste difference constitutes IIT Madras as a Brahminical space where merit is a form of caste virtue. With economic liberalization and the rapid expansion in private sector employment, this upper-caste claim to merit was only reinforced by the further consolidation of Brand IIT as a valued commodity within the global marketplace. The enhancement of Brand IIT's commodity value effectively makes merit into a form, not only of caste virtue, but of caste property.

Mobility

In a conversation with an IIT Madras faculty member, himself an alumnus who spent a decade in US industry before returning to teach at his alma mater, he fretted about the 'negative brand effect that quota students with their poor English and their regional aspirations' would have. 'For cultural reasons, fewer of them go abroad', he explained, 'and this will definitely mean a decline from those days when 70 per cent of Silicon Valley companies had Indian—and mostly IITian—names on the board.'

The expectation that the IITian should be a mobile subject does not arise simply from a generic, or recent, claim to global cosmopolitanism. It reflects the historical production of a native intelligentsia who were members of an internal, pan-Indian diaspora. In this section, I locate the IITian's mobility within a regional context of occupational stratification, secondary education, and backward-caste assertion. I show further how mobility itself becomes an index of merit juxtaposed against the 'immobile' low-caste subject.

The earliest sociological study of an IIT conducted in 1968 (Rajagopalan and Singh 1968) corroborates my own interview material on the social backgrounds of IITians: a significant proportion are the children of personnel in the Indian Administrative Services. While such families come from a range of upper castes, in Tamil Nadu the central government services have historically been overwhelmingly Brahmin. In the precolonial period, Tamil Brahmins as a priestly caste accorded divine legitimacy to native sovereigns, in exchange for which they were typically granted land. As rural landlords, their wealth, education, and cultural refinement depended on freedom from work in the fields. While disdain for manual agricultural work was true of most landed castes, within British colonial sociology, Brahmins in particular were identified as an intellectual elite without any organic connection to the land.

More concretely, colonial rule actualized Tamil Brahmin independence of locality through induction into the colonial bureaucracy and the professions. By virtue of their literacy, Tamil Brahmins entered the colonial state apparatus as accountants overseeing the imposition of British land settlements. Many also moved to urban areas for education and employment. By the early twentieth century, Tamil Brahmins dominated all grades of the bureaucracy, law, and education in the Madras Presidency, which was an immediate cause of the rise of the non-Brahmin movement. In response to rural anti-Brahmin hostility and an urban politics of caste rights that forced the state to implement caste quotas in education and employment, many Tamil Brahmins left for other cities, such as Bombay, Bangalore, and Delhi, to work in the central government services, where the only applicable caste quotas were for those at the lowest rung of the administrative typology (Fuller and Narasimhan 2008, 2010; Ludden 1985).

As should be apparent from this schematic history, the overlap between a sociology of caste and governmental imperatives facilitated Tamil Brahmin economic and geographical mobility. Most of the professions that Tamil Brahmins dominate—including law, administration, and management, as well as medicine, engineering, and computing—are nominally governed by modern conceptions of knowledge and rationality, with secular educational qualifications as the sole stated criteria for recruitment. Yet, as I will show, educational choice and stratification have been strongly informed by caste difference.

A significant proportion of Tamil IITians are the children of central government personnel. Most attend the central government's Kendriya Vidyalaya schools that cater specifically to them, guaranteeing a place regardless of frequent inter-regional transfers (in fact, the school located on the IIT Madras campus is a Kendriya Vidyalaya). Other Tamil IITians who are the children of upper-caste professionals attend a wider range of private schools, such as the Dayanand Anglo-Vedic (DAV) and Padma Seshadri schools. These too follow the curriculum set by the Central and not the State Board of Examiners. All of these Central Board schools explicitly state as one of their key missions, 'to develop the spirit of national integration and create a sense of "Indianness" among children'. In addition to the national orientation of these schools, within Tamil Nadu, the divide between Central and State Board education maps quite clearly onto that between upper and lower caste.

The assumption that the Central Board curriculum produces 'thinking students' who are better suited to intellectual life in general and the IITs in particular was conveyed to me across a wide swathe of interviews with Central Board teachers, administrators, and students. Person after person distinguished the Central Board's 'conceptual training' from the 'rote learning' in the State Boards. It was this training, they argued, that made their students a natural fit for the IITs. But it was not merely the elective affinity between the Central Board curriculum and the IIT Joint Entrance Exam (IIT-JEE) that made these feeder schools for the IITs. The principal of the DAV Boys' School, for instance, told me that his school sent an average of 15–18 students each year to IIT Madras. This was no accident. The school specifically tailored their Central Board exam preparation in such a way that it dovetailed with the JEE curriculum. Both DAV and Padma Seshadri also offer JEE coaching classes on their premises, making it almost a given that the vast majority of their students attend them.

I conducted group interviews with students in several JEE coaching classes in Chennai and found that the overwhelming majority were upper castes who went to Central Board schools, where there was a common-sense assumption that students would take the exam. Apart from peer and family pressure, there is another reason why most students from these schools opt for the IITs. Their sense is that the reservations system in Tamil Nadu makes it virtually impossible to gain admission in regional colleges where backward-caste students taking the State Board exam are far more competitive. Using this calculus, they navigate what they perceive as a two-track system: backward castes take the State Boards, get into regional colleges, and remain within Tamil Nadu; forward castes take the Central Boards, get into the IITs, and leave Tamil Nadu. What was intriguing, however, is that most planned *not* to leave Tamil Nadu for one of the other IITs, but to strive for admission in IIT Madras. When I asked why, they explained that it was a better fit because of its proximity to home and family.

I would argue further that these students' link to IIT Madras is an expression of what it means to be upper caste in Tamil Nadu, where they are often constituted as not-belonging. Their affective link to IIT Madras allows Tamil Brahmins in particular a claim to regional belonging that they feel was taken from them by the politics of Dravidianism. On the one hand, their association with IIT Madras symbolizes the transcendence of region through a direct link to the national government. On the other hand, their place within a centre of excellence *in* Tamil Nadu shores up their sense of themselves as exemplary of meritocratic value, especially in comparison with other regional educational institutions where, as they see it, caste trumps intellect.

The role of IIT Madras in shoring up a sense of Tamil Brahminness was conveyed eloquently to me by Venkat, an IIT alumnus who graduated in the late 1990s. His parents were both officers in the central administrative services, and his family had spent many years in Delhi and Mumbai before returning to Chennai, where he attended the DAV Boys' School. Venkat described the school as a bubble within the city where the vast majority of his classmates were Brahmins or other upper castes. Gaining admission to the IIT was the singular goal of his peers. He recollected that his school sponsored annual prayers for their students on the eve of the IIT entrance exam and as part of the ritual culmination of three years of study, and that those who gained admission to the IITs were treated as school heroes.

His stories of studying at IIT Madras make clear that the sense of 'arrival' for Tamil Brahmin boys was twofold. He talked about the comforting sense of homecoming that he felt upon entering the campus gates, where he could stop de-Brahminizing his Tamil and slip back into the Brahmin vernacular spoken by his family. He also spoke of an intimacy between Tamil Brahmin boys and their professors, the cultivation not just of shared intellectual projects, but of a form of caste kinship.

IIT Madras did not just produce forms of caste kinship between Tamil Brahmin students and professors; other Tamilians were also assumed to be Brahmin simply by virtue of being at IIT. The conscription of Tamil IITians into Brahminness was strikingly conveyed to me by Gopi, an IIT Madras alumnus who graduated in the mid-1990s. He was changing his clothes when his roommate inquired into the whereabouts of his *poonal*, the sacred thread worn by Brahmins. 'When I told him that I don't wear one, he paused and then followed with, "Doesn't your mother get upset?" It never struck him that I was backward caste. In fact, I think he still assumes that I'm from a particularly liberal Brahmin family.' That merit was the property of upper castes, and that they properly belonged in the IITs, was also conveyed to me in the course of another interview with Srikanth, a 2007 alumnus now doing a PhD at MIT. He responded to my question about the value of the IIT classroom by confiding that the quality of teaching was quite uneven. 'Some of our profs were quite bad', he told me, 'especially those who were reservation hires.' When I pointed out to him that the IITs don't have caste quotas in faculty hiring, he paused briefly and said, 'Oh ... well, that's what everyone said.'

Far more than to faculty, however, the assumption of low-caste intellectual inferiority applied to fellow students. In fact, even as they insisted that outside social divisions ceased to matter on campus, many IITians admitted that the one category of student that stood out was 'the SC/STs' (Scheduled Castes and Scheduled Tribes). When I probed into how they were singled out from among the other students, I heard a number of explanations, from their own self-segregation to their poor academic performance. Indeed, the same 'C' grade was interpreted entirely differently depending on who earned it: 'open category', or non-quota, students got poor grades because they were too busy having fun, while 'SC/STs' did because they couldn't cut it. One alumnus referred to an upper-caste 'C' as a 'gentleman's C', by which he meant that it by no means undercut the student's actual status as a man of value. That those who gain admission through the reserved category suffer routine slights and indignities has been graphically revealed by a spate of suicides and attempted suicides by Dalit students across the IITs (V. Kumar 2007; Mukherjee 2009).

The equation of upper caste with merit, and merit with the IITs, is reinforced by the JEE entrance exam. While examinations structure the highly competitive system of secondary and post-secondary education in India as a whole, the IIT-JEE is the most mythologized of them all. It is widely perceived as a near-perfect measure of merit, in part because the pan-Indian scope of the exam is assumed to filter only the best out of a vast pool of applicants. In the past 10 years, coaching for the JEE has become a veritable industry. With key outposts in the south-eastern state of Andhra Pradesh and the north-western state of Rajasthan, coaching centres now admit students from as early as the seventh standard, who then spend up to five years mastering a single exam. That families with relatively modest household incomes are willing to invest the money to send children to coaching centres speaks volumes about the expected payoff. As a consequence, the profile of students at IIT Madras has slowly shifted over the past decade to include those from families without as much educational or cultural capital. Their arrival, however, has not been met with equanimity.

In a newspaper interview about the proliferation of coaching classes, IIT Madras's former director, M. S. Ananth, clarified that he was 'looking for students with raw intelligence and not those with a mind prepared by coaching class tutors. The coaching classes only help students in mastering pattern recognition skills. With this, you cannot get students with raw intelligence' (D. Kumar 2008). This notion of 'raw intelligence' places the ideal IITian outside institutional, or even social, formation as a naturally gifted individual with a native capacity for technical knowledge. In conversations with Ananth and other IIT administrators, I heard their concerns that the coaching industry undermined the ability of the exam to test for those who were truly worthy, in the process admitting students who would eventually dilute the brand of the institutions. When pushed on who 'the coached' typically were, I heard that they were from less urban, professional, and English-speaking backgrounds, those who went to schools where rote learning was the norm and where the IIT merely represented 'a paycheck and a local job for life'.

It is indeed strange to hear IIT administrators bemoaning the economic instrumentality of 'the coached', when one of the hallmark features of the IIT pedigree is its market value. What, then, is at stake in this contrast between the approaches to education and employment of 'the gifted' and 'the coached'? It seems to hinge on a perceived relationship between non-market and market value, or inalienable and alienable forms of knowledge. 'The coached' are deemed illegitimate because they are seen as gaining admission to the IIT, not through their innate abilities, but because they paid money for coaching classes. They are pure creatures of the market, further evidenced by their instrumental leveraging of an IIT pedigree into 'a paycheck and a local job for life'. The way 'the coached' buy their way into education is thought to dilute the brand value of the IITs. By contrast, 'the gifted' have intrinsic merit that is reflected in their performance in the exam *and* in the market. However, their inherent value, or 'raw intelligence', is irreducible to market value. As with the prized art object that, precisely because it is invested with a value *transcending* the market, gains value *within* the market, the 'true' IITian's value is inalienable and, because of this, legitimately exchanged in the market. Moreover, the true IITian's innate intelligence bestows a non-market aura on their academic and career ambitions. As a result, when they play the market, as they do remarkably well, unlike 'the coached', they enhance the value of Brand IIT. To go back to the quote that began this section, 'the coached' were students whose 'regional ambitions' were representative of circumscribed spatial and social worlds.

The forms of extended caste kinship at the IITs have facilitated the spatial and social mobility of IITians, not just within India, but also to the US. In the US, older alumni are hugely influential in facilitating the induction of newer alumni into university campuses and corporate businesses, and securing their privileged access to IITian angel investors. The commodity value of an IIT education is perhaps most evident in the role of US-based alumni in facilitating Indian entrepreneurship. The Indus Entrepreneurs, a network started by IIT alumni in Silicon Valley in 1992, currently boasts a membership of 13,000 spread across 57 chapters in 14 countries. Its list of mentors includes the most well-recognized Indian names in the corporate sector, both in India and the US. Its set of achievements include, 'largest pool of intellectual capital anywhere', 'economic wealth creation estimated at $200 billion', and 'influenced liberalization of key economic sectors in India and Pakistan'. Both senior mentors and junior members of the organization confirmed that the entrepreneurial ambitions of IIT graduates are the most actively cultivated. Unlike those of other Indians, IITians' proposals are almost guaranteed seed funding. This is transnational kinship at its best, an affective, institutionally generated bond that underwrites an IIT pedigree as a form of capital.

Even as collective membership in the IIT family is a clear means to education and financial success, entrepreneurial ideologies of risk, initiative, and profit-making have contributed to the image of IITians as self-made individuals with portable knowledge whose successes are owed entirely to their own acumen. It certainly helps that caste has not carried over as a meaningful category in public discourse in the US where the entrepreneurial successes of IITians are most pronounced. Here, the IITian stands in simply for a form of Indian genius that is not further specified sociologically. On the other hand, when these understandings of technical capacity as innate racial talent travel back to India, they reinforce rather than obscure a logic of caste. In India, caste is not quite as easily displaced as a marker of social and individual identity. When combined with diasporic and increasingly domestic notions of the entrepreneurial individual, it becomes possible to associate whole castes with the capacity for producing certain forms of value.

In India as well as the US, alumni have worked not only to promote the commodity value of Brand IIT, but to protect it from dilution. Across India, the siege mentality produced by demands for democratizing caste access to the IITs has only hardened the equation between caste identity and intellectual ability for alumni. The threat to Brand IIT posed by the entry of low castes is expressed, not just within India, but equally in the diaspora. In 2006, as the Indian Parliament was debating the extension of backward-caste quotas to the IITs, alumni staged a protest in Silicon Valley against reservations as an 'attack on meritocracy' and 'brand dilution', thus seamlessly integrating liberal and neo-liberal values in defence of their alma maters (Chadha 2006).

In this section, I have shown how histories of caste, state, and institution have underwritten the spatial and social mobility of upper-caste IITians who now work to actively protect merit as a form of caste property. The elaboration of this dynamic beyond India scales up this 'possessive investment' (Lipsitz 1998), making caste into a transnational formation. Looking at the scholarly literature on the Indian diaspora, one might assume that caste vanishes as a social category. I have argued otherwise: far from disappearing in diaspora, caste has been further consolidated as a form of capital. Indeed, the diaspora has become a key space for retrenching caste privilege beyond the purview of low-caste rights.

* * *

In post-independence India, new patterns of caste stratification and consolidation have emerged through the very process of democratic transformation. Rather than the gradual erosion of caste, what we are seeing is the leveraging of merit by high castes in order to secure new arenas of expertise and accumulation against low-caste rights. Upper-caste claims have been strengthened by transnational mobility and the enhanced value of technical know-how within the late twentieth- and early twenty-first-century 'knowledge economy'. Rather than just subaltern identitarianism, then, the leveraging of caste must also be seen as an upper-caste politics that attempts to forestall democratic progress and derives its legitimacy from the global commodification of knowledge.

What does this suggest for our understanding of postcolonial democracy? In some ways, these upper-caste strategies only harden the divide between modernity and democracy (Chatterjee 2004), although now modernity is framed, not in the terms of mid-twentieth-century civic universalism and national developmentalism, but as private accumulation and global achievement. Rather than discrediting the 'improperly political', this most recent iteration of modernity negates the value of the political altogether. On the other hand, other tenets of modernity have come within the purview of subaltern politics. Even as elites evacuate public arenas and make explicitly identitarian claims to private spheres of accumulation, it is subalterns who articulate universalistic commitments to equality, wellbeing, and rights.

In this sense, what we are witnessing is a muddying of the distinction between elite civic universalism and subaltern communitarian particularism. Much recent work on subaltern politics, my own included (Subramanian 2009), has taken its cues from the political language and manoeuvres of subalterns to interrogate received wisdom about republican democracy. Such analyses of subaltern politics have provoked a reappraisal of democratic politics to include forms of political agency previously seen as pre-political, non-political, or non-democratic. Despite these ways of rethinking democracy, however, there has been less effort to understand how the political imaginaries and tactics of the powerful are shaped by those of the powerless.

What I have tried to show in this essay is how upper-caste privilege and the conditions for accumulation are reconstituted in a context of ongoing subaltern claims to democratic expansion and equal citizenship. By trumpeting 'merit' as the only legitimate basis for intellectual worth and professional advancement, IITians maintain their self-representation as universalistic subjects who have transcended a past of naturalized hierarchy. Moreover, they attempt to delegitimize low-caste mobilization as a parochial, corrupting expression of 'vote bank' politics. At the same time, they conflate ascription with achievement by making merit into a form of high-caste property, a move that mirrors a broader neoliberal affirmation of identity as capital. These manoeuvres—universalistic on the one hand, identitarian on the other—must be understood, not in terms of the stable reproduction of hegemony, but as part of a broader dialectic of high-caste dominance and low-caste rights elaborated on a transnational scale. The story of making merit at IIT Madras thus illuminates hegemony as a process and a politics, and elite and subaltern subjectivities as relationally constituted.

Note

1. One exception is work on Hindu nationalism that addresses its role in mobilizing a Hindu identity against the threat of low-caste rights. Even in this literature, though, we get more of a sense of Hindu nationalism as the instrumental politics of a fully constituted social group than as a process of upper-caste subject formation.

II

Imagination, Faith, Affect

4

Representing the Adivasi

Limits and Possibilities of Postcolonial Theory

This essay examines how the figure of the adivasi appears in postcolonial (literary) theory as one that embodies the limits of representation as the limit horizon of modernity itself.[1] The failure to adequately represent adivasis is understood as symptomatic of the failure of democracy itself, a key feature of modernity. Through a critique of postcolonial theory more broadly, the essay provides a way to reconceptualize subaltern politics via the problematic of representation. A critique of this theoretical work can shed light on the ways in which the adivasi subject of politics (standing in my essay for the subaltern, the purported topic of this volume of essays) has in fact been rendered *apolitical* and thus outside the domain of politics. But I show that such a critique may actually constitute a first step in reconceptualizing the adivasi as the proper subject of politics.

Forged as an oppositional project of criticism within the Anglo-American academy in the first instance, postcolonial theory set out to right the wrongs of an imperialist formation of literary studies. A self-consciously radical theory, employing and flourishing on the resources of the then ascendant poststructuralism of the 1980s, postcolonial theory sought to counter the blind spots of hegemonic literary criticism (exemplified in the veritable absence of Europe's others in its discourse and practice) with two related projects. The first consisted of giving voice to the silenced subaltern by recovering literary traditions, historical traces, and popular sources to construct an alternative presence in the dominant/colonial canon/archive. The second and often less scrutinized aspect consisted of the assertion of the unrepresentability of the other, the subaltern. This entailed a deep suspicion of representation itself, such that in itself, representation was understood as an act of violence (Lazarus 2011).

In this, the figure of the adivasi is ironically one who is simultaneously the unrepresentable par excellence, and one whose marginalized and abjected subjectivity is seen to naturally collude with the operations of invisibility, which is the constitutive dimension of the unrepresentable. Using the literary as a frame and as a productive site for thinking about representation, I argue that this preoccupation in postcolonial theory with the limits and (im)possibilities of representing the adivasi elides the ways in which literary practices are invested in grappling with the singularity of the figure of the tribal and in representing the adivasi across the full spectrum of literary genres, albeit with differing aesthetic strategies. What is therefore vexing about the persistence of the dominant postcolonial theory approach is the entrenched orthodoxy of reading literary works (from before and during the period of decolonization and later) that narrate how the adivasi provides an enabling 'fiction' for the expression of postcolonial Indian modernity, even if it is as its constitutive other, as somehow always and already inadequate attempts at grasping the radically different consciousness of the subaltern. But once we set aside such a commitment to an absolute incommensurability of elite and subaltern worlds, we see that far from excluding the adivasi as unrepresentable, what one finds in a number of literary texts is the presence of a complex set of representations that belie theoretical protestations of elite incapacity to represent the subaltern.

It is this purportedly unbridgeable gap between postcolonial literary studies, their institutionalization in the 'global academy' as a radical project, and the political and aesthetic possibilities within literature and literary practices that are achieved through narrative, that I am interested in exploring in this essay. I do so by offering a reading of three different texts—Mahasweta Devi's long short story 'Pterodactyl' (1995), originally written in Bengali; Gopinath Mohanty's Oriya novel, *Paraja* (1997); and Upamanyu Chatterjee's novel in English entitled *English, August* (1988). In each case I examine how the writers use a range of narrative techniques to grapple with the problem of representation in ways that point to the limitations of postcolonial theory and the political impasse generated by it in thinking about subaltern politics.

A literary critical perspective such as mine may perhaps seem like a counter-intuitive approach to reconceptualizing subaltern politics when the topic is most typically conceived as empirically grounded or theoretically and practically aligned directly to social reality. I would like to contend, however, that my turn to literary texts to explore this subject is to show that critical ways of reading cultural and literary texts not only present ironic analogies with analysing the social ground in empirical ways, but more importantly engage the assumptions behind the volume's two key terms—'subaltern' and 'politics'.

Subalterneity and Representation

One of the most important critical voices within postcolonial studies in terms of theorizing the literary subaltern has been that of the literary and cultural theorist Gayatri Spivak. In this essay, I primarily focus on her formative contribution to what has come to be understood as postcolonial theory, although elsewhere I also engage the critical work of Ganesh Devy, who analyses adivasi literary production as requiring salvage from what he calls 'forced aphasia' (Devy 2002).[2] For those familiar with Spivak's work as part of the Subaltern Studies project and as translator of the Bengali writer Mahasweta Devi, it is her writings on sati or widow immolation as the site where female agency is erased that have become the best-known sources of theoretical writings on subalterneity and the impossibility of representation. In this essay, however, I want to foreground the figure of the adivasi woman who, I argue, has been the exemplary figure of subalterneity in Spivak's work. In a range of different essays with overlapping concerns, Spivak draws on literature to elaborate her notion of the gendered subaltern through an avant-gardist and critical literary postcolonialism. In her engagement with Devi's work, we see that it is to fiction that Spivak (2000b: 333) turns, in a move that involves what she calls 'learning from the singular and the unverifiable'. Aligned with this use of the resources of the literary is the concept of subalterneity that in Spivak's work has not just stood for social, economic, and political subordination, but has constituted a position of radical, and indeed an irretrievable, alterity, one that has profound implications for the politics of representation. Although Spivak's theorization stems from her critique of positivist conceptions of representation, it is specifically deployed against what she perceives to be a key aspect of the project of Subaltern Studies historians—a search for lost historical origins and sources and for a pure subaltern consciousness as the proper subject of history. But for Spivak, the origin is always already contaminated, such that to retrieve it is a theoretical and practical impossibility. In particular, Spivak has elaborated on the problematic of representation in at least two senses of the term as a way to grasp this impossibility: to represent (*darstellen*) as in to re-present (assumed to be the domain of literature and art), and to represent (*vertreten*) as in to stand in for another entity, one that is supposedly without voice or direct presence (understood to be the domain of politics). In her famous essay 'Can the Subaltern Speak?', Spivak (1988a: 288–9) writes: 'To confront them [subaltern others] is not to represent them (*vertreten*) but to learn to represent (*darstellen*) ourselves.' Here we see that there is a taken-for-granted inaccessibility of the subaltern to the investigator and intellectual, transmuted into the presumably elite collective 'ourselves'. Spivak reads the intellectual's role as having engendered an epistemic violence such that the subaltern subject cannot speak, is muted. By using the concrete experiences of the marginalized, the intellectual only consolidates the international division of labour between theory and practice, North and South, intellectual and subaltern, 'a gesture that often marks poststructuralist political theory' (Spivak 1988a: 272). Instead, she writes, what we have to remain attentive to is how 'the staging of the world in representation—its scene of writing, its Darstellung—dissimulates the choice of and need for "heroes", paternal proxies, agents of power—Vertretung' (Spivak 1988a: 279).

One key feature of Spivak's project of literary criticism is that she presents Devi's work as enabling 'a critique of our academic practice' (1995: 199), which we can take to imply a criticism of the ways in which certain Third World texts are 'trafficked' within the Anglo-American academy. In terms of the presence of the Indian adivasi in the curricula of the global academy, Spivak's translation and critical work opened up new ground insofar as the term 'indigenous' had operated as an ill-defined binary opposite of colonizer, such that 'tribals [only] emerge into history in the perspective of the drama of colonialism' (Spivak 2000b: 329). In seeking to translate a Bengali writer into English, Spivak performs the role of interlocutor, native informant, translator, and poststructuralist critic all at once. In *Imaginary Maps*, Devi's stories are bookended by Spivak's interview with the author and a 'Translator's Preface' in the beginning, and her own 'Afterword', both exemplifying the ways in which Spivak translates the literary project of Devi into a kind of manifesto of postcolonial theory about the necessary impossibility of representing the adivasi. In Spivak's translation project we have an exemplary instance of how the figure of the adivasi operates within the global academy (enabling 'our academic practice') as a vehicle for a politics of difference and thus of representation itself. Although in a moment of ironic self-reflection, Spivak herself points to the complicity of the Third World bourgeoisie and First World migrants—in what she calls 'the traffic line in Cultural Studies'—it is through her virtuoso act of translation, one that is linguistic, literary, cultural, and political all at the same time, that the figure of the tribal enters the global academy as a refusenik in the project of representation; as a figure of resistance to globalization; as the embodiment of an alternative modernity; and as the carrier of a transnational ethics.

However, I would argue that there is an interesting and productive dichotomy between how Spivak reads literature in ways that remain strangled in narratives of incommensurability and radical alterity, even as she purports to undo the 'myth of pure difference' (1995: xxiv), and her writings about her 'political' work with rural schooling among adivasis and the poor in Bengal that aims to bring some of the most marginalized Indians into the terrain of national citizenship through education, into what she calls 'citizenship without history' (Spivak 2012). In other words, Spivak's own work demonstrates both the ideological pull or divide between darstellen and vertreten, between re-presentation and representation, and the mutually constitutive yet tense relationship of the two. In Devi's work, Spivak names this '"folding back upon" one another—re-flection in the root sense' of Devi's writing and her activism, between her 'literary text and the textile of activism' (1995: xxvi).

Myth and Analysis

Let us now explore this issue of postcolonial theory's assumptions concerning the adivasi by looking at Devi's short story/novella 'Pterodactyl' from the collection entitled *Imaginary Maps* (1995). The story consists of two overlapping narratives. The one that Spivak, the translator, calls the 'frame' narrative is the story of Puran, a journalist based in provincial Bihar, who travels to remoter villages and districts in the state to report on issues of caste violence, government corruption, natural disasters, and famine. A widower who is unable to commit himself in a proper relationship with his love interest, he uses the opportunities his job affords him as a journalist to escape to remoter areas to confront what seem to be, in his view, the larger, more public concerns of social and economic deprivation and backwardness, especially among India's 'scheduled tribes'.[3] On invitation from his friend Harisharan, a district-level bureaucrat, Puran travels to Pirtha, a famine-stricken, back-of-beyond tribal village settled on barren land whose inhabitants are dying of starvation. Puran hopes that through his reporting of the famine, he could aim to 'put Pirtha on the map', and by so doing enable his friend Harisharan to get the government to bring some amount of relief and aid to the villagers.

This 'frame' narrative of Puran's intellectual commitment and personal alienation is interwoven with the story of the strange sighting of a pterodactyl in the village. When Puran arrives in Pirtha, the tribals are in mourning and have retreated from all communication with the outside world. Just preceding Puran's visit, some mysterious cave drawings have come to light, and although it is not clear if the engravings are ancient or contemporary, at least one of the drawings has been made by Bikhia, a local adivasi boy. The drawing is that of a 'large creature', whose 'wings are webbed like a bat's, body like a giant iguana, four clawed feet, no teeth in the yawning terrible mouth' (Devi 1995: 128). Harisharan hopes that a report on these cave drawings will help bring attention to Pirtha's plight, as the paintings seem deeply mysterious and difficult to interpret. For the residents of Pirtha, Bikhia's painting heralds the return of their ancestral soul, as it must have been traumatized by the contemporary predicament of Pirtha residents.

The appearance of this prehistoric creature in one of modern India's isolated outposts offers an intellectual and ethical challenge to Puran and his group of urban bureaucrats and social activists who are there to bring aid to the miserable villagers. The core of the story then lies in the mysterious nature of this 'event'. Does it imply continuity with adivasi traditions of myth and magic, or is it something radically disruptive of community? For one thing is certain—the appearance of this creature defeats all rational faculties and secular understandings of adivasi cultures. As the subdivisional officer (SDO) puts it to Puran: 'How will I make you understand that it is not possible for those tribals to think reasonably, to offer explanations? You will understand them with your urban mentality? You will fathom the Indian Ocean with a foot-ruler?' (Devi 1995: 104). It is this lack of communicability that the SDO expresses here that is celebrated or at least valorized as representing the irreconcilability of subaltern and elite understandings and worldviews that the project of subaltern history, for instance, has also upheld, an intellectual challenge that in Spivak's terms is both 'impossible but necessary' (Spivak 1995: 200). It is used to underscore an emphasis on a radical alterity, to which no language or form of communication can possibly offer a solution. This also seems to be the premise that both the SDO and Puran seem to adhere to. When Puran learns that 'there are no words for "exploitation" or "deprivation" in the Ho language', we are told that there was 'an explosion in Puran's head that day' (Devi 1995: 118). The absence of words (and by extension of concepts) such as 'exploitation' or 'deprivation', words that saturate the experiences of tribals, from their language establishes a vast abyss between the tribal and non-tribal worlds.

But Devi's fiction, I want to argue, has been typically misread as standing testimony to this apartness. And indeed if the story had not moved in a very unexpected direction towards its close, one could have agreed with such an analysis. The unexpected turn consists of the creature from the drawings actually taking form and becoming material in the stone hut where Puran has come to stay. After the arrival of the creature in physical form, Bikhia, the boy who has made at least one of the drawings, also comes to stay there, in order to guard the deity-like creature. Throughout the time that Puran and Bikhia stay under the same roof, there is no verbal communication between them, as the two do not share a language, as they don't seem to share concepts and worldviews.

Yet, what does bring them together is a common struggle to grapple with the meaning of this event. While the tension surrounding the appearance of the creature is palpable, the story's conclusion draws together the idea that myth (the story of the creature) can function as analysis (story of adivasi exploitation): 'Looking at Bikhia's tawny matted hair, freshly shaven face, he understood that they were being defeated as they were searching in this world for a reason for the ruthless unconcern of the government and administration. It was then that the shadow of that bird with its wings spread came back as at once *myth* and analysis' (Spivak 1995: 193).

The deception carried out on India's tribals is so massive that it belies explanation on the human scale, a scale that surpasses reason and empathy, justice and logic. The narrative voice tells us that 'from now on they will wait in their suffering and in evil times for that shadow, *otherwise this deception cannot be humanly explained*' (Devi 1995: 193, italics mine). Read attentively, the key phrase here seems to be 'otherwise this deception cannot be humanly explained'. Here we see Devi bringing the supposed supernatural aspect of the sighting of the pterodactyl into the human frame. This is hardly illustrative of an embrace of the impossibility of representation, nor a rejection of humanism; rather, Devi's fiction posits possibilities inherent in the ideological fault lines opened up by representation, both for this gigantic deception, as well as for offering explanations that are within human grasp, explanations that have to do with structures of power and the systems of inequality built into them.

It is important to note here that the narrative voice is not the same as Puran's. It establishes distance between Puran the intellectual and Devi the writer for whom, as Spivak puts it in a statement that ironically does not register in her own critical assessment, 'the tribal and the non-tribal must pull together, both in the nation, conjuring against the State' (1995: 204). If postcolonial theory has theorized endlessly the impossibility of grasping subaltern consciousness, Devi's story offers a strong riposte. Puran may be the alienated, small-town intellectual, but Bikhia is the subaltern artist, and they are both involved in the political project of representation. It is their encounter with each other, their visioning of the creature as a form of mystery that is also a solidarity, that opens up the limits of the politics of representation. Bikhia as the artist of the cave drawings and as keeper of the deity resists the state-led or capitalist appropriation of tribal art—in restoring magic, in making primitive art precisely not collectable (there are lines in the story about art as a possible venue for tribals' economic subsistence), in questioning the boundary of the artisanal object and of primitive art as magical, Bikhia emerges as the adivasi artist who can best challenge the politics of representation in postcolonial India. His refusal to explain his drawings, the magical materialization of it in bodily form that is subject to death, can be read as a refusal not necessarily of representation but of commodification, a gesture that is of a piece with the generalized mourning in the village and its collective refusal of state-led dispensations. Bikhia's art then is also suggestive of art as the labour of a collectivity. As the narrative voice records: 'Now something has happened that is their very own, a thing beyond the reach of the understanding and grasp and invasion and plunder of the outsider' (Devi 1995: 193). But Puran's love for Pirtha (a love that stands as the antithesis of 'invasion and plunder of the outsider') means that he 'cannot remain a distant spectator anywhere in life' (ibid.: 196). Although in the end, 'A truck comes by. Puran raises his hand. Steps up,' we can envision the change that Puran has undergone in his consciousness and in his solidarities. And the tribals of Pirtha have successfully mobilized myth as a critique of postcolonial rapacity, as historical explanation.

Manoeuvre and Critique

Paraja, a novel written by Gopinath Mohanty in Oriya in 1945, is set in colonial India in the years immediately preceding independence. Although 'Pterodactyl' and *Paraja* are set widely apart in terms of historical time, Devi and Mohanty as writers could very well be regarded as near contemporaries. Gopinath Mohanty, besides being a dominant figure in Oriya letters who wrote several novels and non-fiction work on tribal society in Orissa (now Odisha), had also worked as a state civil servant in his home state. His literature of social commitment like Devi's in the case of Bihar and West Bengal, comes out of his lived and shared experience among Orissa's adivasis.

Mohanty's novel is rendered in an epic scale, centred on the individual tragedy of Sukru Jani, a Paraja patriarch, and his personal loss of family and land. Equally, it can be read as a long narrative meditation on the extended collective tragedy of the Parajas, the tribe to which Sukru Jani belongs and after which Mohanty has named his novel. It is veritably a record also of the tragedy of the commons set off by colonial rule, and of the slow and steady degradation of tribal life in general, set against a marauding ideology of modernity and progress. The powerful narrative that interweaves the individual and collective consciousness of the various Paraja characters with a biting social commentary on the exploitation of tribals by outsiders—the money-lenders and the tax collectors birthed by a savage colonial system—can be read as a severe indictment of colonial modernity. In its historical setting, then, *Paraja* both chronologically precedes Devi's story, but also anticipates the ways in which the postcolonial state was to reproduce the social and economic marginality of the adivasis.

It should be said at the outset that Mohanty's novel has not garnered the same attention within postcolonial studies as Devi's work has, and the reasons can be garnered from the discussion of Spivak's intervention earlier in this chapter. However, Mohanty's text has been widely circulated in literary circles in India, winning the prestigious Jnanpith Award. But the ways in which it has been framed within that dominant literary circle presents its own set of different but related problems. In his translator's note, Bikram K. Das (1997: vi) writes that 'the choice of the tribal canvas, whether by accident or design, becomes singularly appropriate to Mohanty's theme: the primeval consciousness of his tribal protagonists reflects perfectly the situation of the archetypal human being; their stark joys and interwoven anguish embody the complexity of the human condition.' Das's comment is of a piece with his deeply poetic rendering of Mohanty's prose; it is also symptomatic of the ways in which literature by and about adivasis is appropriated from the specific to the general within mainstream criticism (or relegated to ethnographic interest), such that the 'primeval consciousness' of Mohanty's tribal protagonists comes to stand in for an 'archetypal' human condition. The underlying idea here is the supposed anteriority of the adivasi, the 'primeval', as standing in for the 'archetypal'. Earlier, the Jnanpith Award citation in 1974 had stated that 'in Mohanty's hands, the social is lifted to the level of the metaphysical', once again representing the specificities of adivasi and dalit societies as being lifted on to a metaphysical scale when present in a work of art that is judged as having literary merit.[4]

It is this buried and subsumed specificity of the adivasi experience within the singularity of literature, especially in 'Indian' literature, with all its regional unevenness, that is an issue that I hope to develop in what follows. What I also want to develop further is an examination of the narrative consciousness in Mohanty's novel as well as the methods by which, through manoeuvre and critique, it enters into solidarity with the adivasi characters. Thus, far from failing at representation or narrativizing its limits, the novel narrates the process by which 'other' consciousnesses can be grasped. Thus I hope to show that Mohanty's materialist critique of the adivasi worlds is at odds both with the official appropriation of Mohanty as a novelist of metaphysical proportions, and with postcolonial theory's disavowal of representation itself.

Landscape and Vision

The novel's opening paragraph introduces a crucial omniscient perspective of the landscape that seems to prefigure the social and material violence that the novel records. The expansive view offered by the 'winding road on the fearsome mountain-pass in the Eastern Ghats known as the Dharam-Dooar—"The Gate of Truth"' registers the scene as one of 'violent struggle', a 'landscape of hills fighting ... in two rows facing each other ... wrestling for a foothold' (Mohanty 1997: 1). The narrative vision then focalizes on the tiny hamlet of Sarsupadar where Parajas, the adivasis, and the Dombs, an untouchable group in Hindu India, exist in varying degrees of immiseration. Here, we are told, Sukru Jani, a 50-year-old widower with four children, lives contentedly and in peace. As readers, we follow the lineaments of the narrative as it sweeps us further inside into Sukru Jani's view. We now see that he 'sees a bewildering mass of hills and forests and, above them, a sky so big that he cannot see where it ends. But he does not feel lost in that limitless expanse; he can still find himself whenever he wants to, and he feels that he lives' (Mohanty 1997: 2–3). We hear the authorial voice authoritatively telling us what Sukru Jani sees and what he cannot see, but also how he feels, thus rendering the gap between the author and the protagonist as both very narrow (so as to be at times indistinguishable), in that the narrator can see what Sukru Jani sees, or that the narrator sees through Sukru Jani's eyes, or we see what Sukru Jani sees through the narrator's self-consciously transparent eyes, and very wide because of the ideological manoeuvre involved here in setting up Sukru Jani's consciousness of his 'bewildering' surroundings and their 'limitless expanse' as one in which he does not feel lost, in fact as one in which he 'feels that he lives'. I reference the passage in detail here and in what follows to register the closing of the gap between narrative voice and the protagonist, a manoeuvre that is singularly that of literature itself.

Specificity versus Typicality

There is also the issue of the specificity, as opposed to typicality, of Sukru Jani as a Paraja man, the specificity of which is drawn not from references to a kind of 'primeval' consciousness, but in the consciousness of a deeply limited, meagre, and depleted material, social, and life experience. It is also to the point that part of the process of depletion that is recorded in the novel is also resisted by both an inner subjective consciousness as well as bodily reserve to carry on, as well as a still robust adivasi culture of ritual and festival, of making meaning of an increasingly exploitative world. We are told how 'for Sukru Jani it was different: the land to him was not merely a patch of earth—it was part of his body. He knew every contour and depression in the land; every thorn, every ant-hill had a history. He had watered the land with his sweat and nursed the seedlings with the warmth of his own body' (Mohanty 1997: 193). Who was it different from for Sukru Jani is a question that this paragraph provokes and opens up. Here again we see the narrative attempting to delineate a specific historical and material relationship of the adivasi body and knowledge with the land, one that is not reducible, or is at least resistant, to commodification or accumulation of wealth as well as to appropriation as the same in the history of capital. If there is a certain sentimentality that is evoked here in which land is tied to memory and family attachments, it is attenuated by images of thorns, anthills, sweat.

The fine nuance and sensitivity with which Sukru Jani's characterization takes place, one that underscores his individualism that is both specific and singular while also marked by history, by being adivasi, deserves to be noted. Sukru Jani's memories, love, and pining for his beloved wife Sombari, his sense of betrayal by his daughters, his growing befuddlement at what is happening to him, are recorded in detail: 'Sukru Jani lay tossing on his straw bed all night, smoking his cheroots endlessly.... He felt betrayed by his daughters, and thoroughly confused. All his experience was confined to the land: he knew how to plough, dam a stream, clear jungle; for what was happening now, he was simply not equipped' (Mohanty 1997: 209–10). Here there is the sense of something larger that is called for—something that exceeds the imposed social definition of Sukru as a peasant toiling on the land. He is also a man, a father. The narrative voice establishes here a tension between the social realism that would 'confine' him to his land and to his work, and a larger sense of his emotional world that exceeds socially scripted feelings.

Yet, this suffering world of Sukru Jani is not one of unrelenting victimhood. The novel resolutely eschews romanticism of any kind: 'Sukru Jani knew nothing of soil conservation or the danger of destroying forests... . He was concerned with the present and with his personal interests' (Mohanty 1997: 23). The felling of jungles for more land signals a pre-environmental consciousness, where land and forests are claimed for use and for survival. Further, the Paraja community is not depicted as an ideal one, standing in for an alternative to those communities in the grip of modernity. Race and class distinctions and discriminations abound within the tribe. Kau Paraja, one of the poorer Parajas, is seen by other Parajas as hideous, his features distinctly simian (Mohanty 1997: 132). Neither is the village community a space of easy solidarity. People of the same tribe betray and cheat one another, and it is the Dombs, the outcastes, who report Sukru Jani's son Mandia Jani's illicit liquor brewing to the forest authorities, an event that sets off Sukru Jani's ruination.

Mediation

Elite mediation can of course best be seen and noted in the overall discourse of social realism that the novel employs. But its social realism is precisely what enables the elite standpoint of the author to dovetail with the subaltern positioning of the characters. The novel's commitment to narrating the full scale of adivasi life under conditions of increasing immiseration is evidenced in the ways in which the characters and the reality they inhabit and create are presented. Thus, we are told in one highly evocative passage that Sukru Jani's older son Mandia

> gazed at his rice-field ... a legacy from his ancestors. Generations of his fore-fathers had laboured on that land and the touch of their

hands had made the soil smooth and soft. To Mandia, it was no mere piece of land, but a record of the history of those past generations, of their bygone tales of sorrow and rejoicing and of tradition and change. (Mohanty 1997: 63)

Here we see Mohanty's attribution of complex thoughts to an adivasi, of a whole understanding of human history in terms of tradition and change, words that evoke a distinctively modernist sociological vocabulary. But the specific materiality that this passage evokes, of the smoothness and softness of the soil, of a consciousness of the labour involved in getting it to be that way, belongs very much to that of an adivasi peasant. Mandia's 'gaz[ing] at his rice-field' is an act of recuperation, of salvaging an 'ancestral legacy'. In fact, Mohanty's sharp social realism pervades the dense descriptions of the world of hard, back-breaking labour—'their backs and waists ached with pain and the blood sang in their ears' (Mohanty 1997: 22), but there is also a larger sense of how the imprisonment of adivasi labour belongs to a degrading colonial world in which not only is each day the same for a *goti* (bonded labourer), but all work in the feudal/colonial order is goti work (Mohanty 1997: 46).

Further, the systematic use of the third person narration offers a way into the dovetailing of interior and outer consciousness, in addition to the overlapping of elite and subaltern viewpoints and positions:

And thus it was that in this land of hills and forests, in an unmapped corner of the wide world, luckless men and women who lived on castaway mango stones and hid their nakedness in bits of rag huddled together under the torrent of misery pouring down on their heads, and wept.

Their tears soaked the earth but were powerless to melt human hearts. And their gods laughed. (Mohanty 1997: 37)

Here we have a strong voice that is the narrator's that takes an ethical position, and proclaims the moral bankruptcy of a greedy, avaricious modernity. The sense of marginality evoked here, through the geographical metaphors of 'unmapping' and the figure of hungry, naked people, pierces through the human heart, precisely what the text tells us does not happen in the real world. Yet, through the power of the image, the text, at least indirectly, does melt our heart, or at least sears through it, transforms it.

Another aspect of mediation can be evidenced in the places in the narrative where a deliberate distance is established between the perspectives of the narrator and the subaltern characters. This is most sharply evidenced in the comment on the internalization of degradation among the Parajas, who both unwittingly but also uncritically participate in the dispossession of Kondhs from their lands: 'The gotis felt elated at their own bravery, even though it benefitted only the Sahukar. Their degradation was complete' (Mohanty 1997: 198). Who understands their 'degradation' to be complete? The elite narrative voice steps outside the frame of the immediate story to make this comment, because the gotis cannot/are not able to see that their participation in the dispossession of the Kondhs (also adivasis) only benefits the sahukar. The gotis do not possess a structural understanding of exploitation that the narrator does. Later, when Sukru's daughters, along with other young tribals, are forced to migrate to Assam to work as daily wage labourers, the narratorial voice comments: 'No one thought of what lay ahead; they were happy to have shaken off the dust of old habits' (Mohanty 1997: 208). Once again, we see how a deliberate distancing from the eye of the subaltern experience in fact succeeds in deepening solidarity with their predicament.

The last word in the novel fittingly belongs to Sukru's son Mandia, who finally performs the ultimate act of resistance by murdering the sahukar who had instigated the material and physical ruination of the family.

'Fate!' Mandia shouted angrily. 'I don't believe in it! There is no justice! I don't want to hear about your Dharmu! Keep him to yourselves; we don't need these things. We are peasants and we've only one way of keeping ourselves alive—by tilling the soil. The case may be dead but the land is not dead; nor are we. Who can deny that the land is ours? I shall have one last word with the Sahukar. Let him take his money and return the land; and if he does not agree, let him do what he likes! But I will *never* leave the land.' (Mohanty 1997: 368)

Desiring Tribal

In the last section of this chapter, I want to turn to a novel written in English in order to assess whether postcolonial theory's
assumptions about the impossibility of representation receive
more traction in the more intensely elite field of Indian writing in
English. In an essay entitled 'How to Read a "Culturally Different"
Book', Spivak (1994: 126) argues that the inclusion of 'global
English' in the college curriculum has led to 'dubious results'. For
her, this has particularly amounted to an 'erasure of the tribal'
as Indian writing in English seeks to project, hegemonically and
as part of the 'neo-colonial traffic on cultural identity', a univer-
salizable 'Indian cultural identity' to which the adivasi cannot be
adequately assimilated. Spivak argues that although Indian writing in English is not 'popular' (as English remains a language of
elites and of the middle classes) and draws on discourses of global
cosmopolitan identities that are upper class, upwardly mobile, and
'reterritorialized', it still depends on a 'generalized terrain of India'
that blocks off subaltern and minority identities. This then has led
to what she calls the 'erasure of the tribal' in the service of a cosmopolitan identity in contemporary Indian literature in English.

In a related vein, the critic Tabish Khair (2001: 159–60) writes
that although 'the tribal is definitely more in evidence in some
regional language fictions—written by both aboriginal and non-
aboriginal writers', there is also 'the almost complete absence
of those unacknowledged Indians, the non-Sankritised tribes' in
Indian English fiction. He goes on to argue that

> it can actually be shown that the tribal in general has been even
> more obscured in Indian English fiction than in Anglo-Indian (colo-
> nial) fiction. In the latter, the tribal sometimes appeared (most com-
> plicatedly in Kipling's fiction and poems) as a combination of the
> 'noble savage' and the 'true Indian' and was often used to denigrate
> the 'cowardly' and 'untrue' (in both senses) colonial Babu. (Khair
> 2001: 159–60)

While both Spivak and Khair are right in pointing to this lacuna, the
absence of the adivasi in metropolitan Indian writing in English,
or, in its more conscious form, the erasure of the tribal, needs to

be read symptomatically. Elsewhere I have argued that, contra Spivak (and Khair), recent writing from India, with its obsessive focus on modernity and national development, has in fact recuperated the figure of the tribal, constructed it anew, and mapped on to it new anxieties and desires about the future of Indian identity in a globalizing world economy (Varma 2002). After all, the tribal has been a focal point of reference within development discourses and national culture, which in turn have been key ingredients in the postcolonial state's attempts to gain hegemony. Thus, far from erasing the figure of the tribal, if we were to expand the field of contemporary Indian writing and political discourse in general (including World Bank discourse, the discourse of NGOs, of corporate social responsibility, and social entrepreneurship), we would note how this set of discourses makes productive use of the tribal in order to appropriate the figure as part of a dominant neoliberal economic and social agenda. We can, therefore, see precisely how, through strategic silences and lapses, but also through figuration, the adivasi emerges as a constitutive subject of Indian modernity.

English, August by Upamanyu Chatterjee, a member of the elite Indian Administrative Service and a highly regarded writer, was published in 1988. The novel narrates how the young and urbane Agastya Sen spends his days in a remote, nondescript district in central India called Madna, training to be a bureaucrat. His work is boring and tedious, consisting of signing meaningless files and approving fruitless development projects. Fighting this unrelenting boredom in the district, Agastya bides his time by masturbating, smoking marijuana, and reading Marcus Aurelius!

While much of the novel's narrative seems to consist of mimicking these days of spiritual boredom and official malaise, the story takes a somewhat dramatic turn (however understated that drama is) when Agastya is posted to the drought-prone tribal village of Jompanna for further training (a village not so different from Devi's Pirtha). A posting there is 'a tremendous opportunity to learn' (U. Chatterjee 1988: 189), a fellow bureaucrat puts it to him. For Jompanna is a forested adivasi area where development has come belatedly: 'Government had come to Jompanna but recently—three years ago it had merely been one unremembered outpost of the district of Madna' (U. Chatterjee 1988: 201).

It is here, then, in the drought-ridden adivasi village where tribals are exploited by forest contractors, politicians, and government officers alike, where Naxalites have found a constituency to build ground-level support against the state by simply attempting to try and get the tribals 'to think' (U. Chatterjee 1988: 192), that for the first time in the novel we are given any inkling of Agastya's political and ideological leanings. For on his very first visit to Jompanna, 'it seemed then [to him] that the to-each-his-own outlook was inadequate—some people were compelled to intrude in the affairs of others, sometimes just to remind them that they too had minds' (U. Chatterjee 1988: 198).

Agastya's first impressions of the tribals in the village typify the objectivizing gaze of his class and gender. He sees them as 'vaguely erotic', 'startled-eyed and black-bronzed', 'graceful and open-mouthed', possessing a 'bestial grace' (U. Chatterjee 1988: 209, 211–12, 258). But this objectifying gaze of the young and spoiled elite man is challenged in his very first encounter with Para, an adivasi woman from Chipanthi, a central tribal village in the district. At one level, Para is clearly represented as eroticized and sexualized—Agastya is at first turned on by her 'strong, veined forearms' and 'aquiline nose', even as her 'lined tragic face', her 'eyes darkened by a contemptible life', and the smell she carries of 'years of squalor' present a deadly cocktail of the erotic and the political, such that the tribal woman's sexualized body is already inscribed with a history of exploitation (U. Chatterjee 1988: 254). In fact, the entire scene of the encounter between Para and Agastya is presented as a bleak parody of the sexual exploitation of adivasi women. But one significant way in which Chatterjee's narrative departs from the long and bloody archive of colonial and postcolonial domination is the way in which Para is not just represented here (in a literary sense), but has come to represent her people (in a political sense). Thus, the proverbial twist in the tale occurs when Agastya and the reader learn that Para is an activist in her village of Chipanthi. Caught in the double bind of tribal patriarchy and postcolonial imperialism, Para had been held back by the men of her village from taking on a political role. In spite of that, she travels to Jompanna to appeal to the new officer for bringing water to her drought-ridden village.

At her pleading, Agastya travels to Chipanthi. Para's resistant body and her political consciousness are set off against a mute village. The novel evokes a Blakean scene of nightmarish hell as Agastya inspects children who have fallen and been wounded in the dry well in their attempt to draw out the last drop of water. It is an absurd tableau of complete social desperation and immiseration and of official depredation in which lust for adivasi women offers a pathetic antidote to a pervasive sense of disconnection and alienation.

It is in Chipanthi, too, that Agastya learns of a colleague, a conservator of forests, whose hands have been chopped off by the men of the village who suspected him of having abused the honour of the adivasi woman who cooked for him. Although it is unclear if the conservator had indeed been raping the woman or whether it was consensual sex, for the Naxalites and the radicals, there was no possibility of the latter—'sex was part of the larger exploitation' (U. Chatterjee 1988: 262). This position disgusts Agastya, who finds the act of the chopping of hands to be barbaric. Focalized through his consciousness, we can see how the novel in the end eschews such a radical position as that of the Naxalites as fraught with its own gendered contradictions. After all, the radical non-tribal intellectual Rao thinks nothing of the fact that his mistress Para is made subservient in political discussions, even as the only person who is seen to act and confront the drought is Para.

In the liberal conclusion that Agastya reaches, he thinks:

> If you are teaching them to distrust the world outside this forest, why don't you also teach them to be self-sufficient. They fear exploitation, and they are all illiterate, but they can walk miles to catch a bus to see a Hindi film on the video at Jompanna. Yes, yes, I know, self-sufficiency is not easy and neither is thinking, but both are more valuable than anger. (U. Chatterjee 1988: 263)

In the end, for Agastya, liberal common sense and practicality hold a stronger promise of change than revolutionary fervour and anger. The entire 'tribal episode' of the novel ends with the expected tableau of a tribal dance that takes place in his honour; at the same time, tankers of water roll in to provide some relief to the thirst-ridden adivasis. But in spite of this moment of aesthetic and political redemption, Agastya knows that nothing substantial will change. 'For two months he saw these things, unchanging except for the angles and intensity of light, and they gradually became for him the enduring contours of under-development' (U. Chatterjee 1988: 250).

What I want to highlight in this reading of this novel in English is that it does not refuse representing the adivasi, even as the figure of the adivasi is rendered through the elite consciousness of the central characters, in the idiom of an urban Indian English that is made to fabricate a distinctive Indian modernity in ways that are fraught with contradiction and paradox. And although, with the exception of Para, very few adivasis are given speaking positions, in a sense the novel seems to thematize and enact that silence, a silence that is the very ground of a radical politics of representation. The novel offers a critical rendering of such a position as emblematized in dominant postcolonial theory by eschewing romanticism (after all, the tribals do walk miles to the video store to watch the latest Bombay film!) as well as the notion that representation can ever be unmediated.

* * *

Both Devi and Mohanty are engaged in narrating the shattered history of the adivasi, and the tragic destruction of the old order that gives way to a deformed new social existence. They do so by exploiting the full spectrum of literary possibilities, through highlighting generic discontinuities (frame and core narratives of 'Pterodactyl'; social realism and ethnography in *Paraja*; satire and existentialism in *English, August*) and drawing attention to temporal and spatial unevenness that produces a differentiated modernity in the postcolonial world in the settings of their fictional projects. But what they do not allow their work to do is to withdraw from the political project of representation. This comes out most strongly in Mohanty's novel, but it is also true of Devi's, although, as I have suggested, the reading of 'Pterodactyl' is typically produced in the shadow of postcolonial theory, at least when read in the 'West'. Mohanty shows us, in the case of the Parajas, how a traditional society is dramatically transformed and deformed by imperialism. The peasant adivasi community of Parajas and the adivasis living in Devi's fictional Pirtha are all existing in conditions of subservience to feudal caste society. They lack class consciousness as well as the political resources to become agents of change. Chatterjee's *English, August* shows the limits of elite and official mediation in terms of representing adivasi conditions of under-development, although at the same time the narrative leaves an opening for resistance to come from subalterns themselves. However, in the ending of all three stories, the subaltern social group is shown as developing a consciousness of exploitation, although in very different ways, and there is perhaps also the possibility of coming together as a class, as ongoing adivasi politics in contemporary India would testify.[5]

In conclusion, I want to return then to the problematic of representation that is posed in postcolonial theory, that both forecloses the possibilities of representation but also in its deconstructive gesture opens up the contradictions of re-presentation and representation. I have shown in this essay that through the thematics of myth and analysis, through manoeuvre, critique, and mediation, writers and intellectuals on the one hand, and subalterns on the other, can forge projects of solidarity such that the subaltern does not remain mute, but speaks through his or her political voice and transforms into a proper political subject.

Notes

1. The Indian word 'adivasi' is now the most commonly used and accepted term for referring to India's tribal or indigenous citizens, who constitute roughly 8–10 per cent of the country's population. Throughout this essay, depending on the context, I will use the words 'adivasi' and 'tribal' interchangeably. I also use the idea of the 'figure of the adivasi' in order to examine the layers of ideological meanings that have accrued on the historical and material bodies and lives of adivasis.

2. A longer version of this argument about the adivasi in postcolonial theory, including a fuller engagement with Devy, appears in my forthcoming book, *Modern Tribal: Representing Indigeneity in Postcolonial India.*

3. Roughly 645 tribes or indigenous groups are listed or 'scheduled' in the Constitution of India. This means that these groups have official recognition as distinct tribes.

4. The Jnanpith Award is among the highest and most prestigious awards for contributions to Indian literature. Presented by the Bharatiya Jnanpith, the award was inaugurated in 1961.

5. Spivak (1988a: 276–9) makes productive use of Marx's theorizing in *The Eighteenth Brumaire of Louis Bonaparte* on the formation of class as a political entity.

5

Can the Subaltern Be Secular?

Negotiating Catholic Faith, Identity, and Authority in Coastal Tamil Nadu

In his opening remarks to the workshop for this volume, David Arnold noted that, in its original conception, the Subaltern Studies project failed to take religion seriously in its own right, seeing it chiefly as a useful glossary for understanding subaltern 'mentalities' on the one hand, and on the other, equating it solely with religiosity, which it was reluctant to explore in the belief that the 'excessive religiosity' of Indians was an Orientalist construct. In the few texts of classical Subaltern Studies that deal with religious events, we see a focus on the magical and mytho-poetic, and on subaltern sects and movements unsupported by national and transnational institutions. On the one hand, secular political events like the coming of Gandhi acquire magical and mythical properties (Amin 1989), and on the other, new sects and movements, despite their apparently excessive religiosity, are really vehicles for secular political ends, such as

* I would like to thank Luisa Steur, Subir Sinha, David Arnold, Srila Roy, and Alf Nilsen whose comments have helped improve this chapter.

caste mobility or social reform (Dube 1992; Hardiman 1984; Pandey 1983). The legacy of Subaltern Studies in the study of religion, then, as in other areas of culture and politics (see Ludden 2002a), is a conception of subaltern religiosity as distinct and autonomous from the larger religious institutions and movements such religious practice may be part of, and equally, a sense that subalterns engage in politics or social reform through the idiom of religion, rendering them outsiders to the secular politics of the elite.

Although there has been little explicit attention to the subaltern in recent scholarship on religion and politics, preoccupied as it has largely been with the 'crisis in secularism' (Needham and Sunder Rajan 2007; Tejani 2008), the figure of the subaltern lurks at the heart of these discussions. In pointing to the crisis of state secularism in India, both Ashis Nandy (1998) and T. N. Madan (1998) have argued that state secularism has failed to check the rise of communalism in India because there is no commensurate secularization of society. While this assumption of a necessary relationship between secularism and secularization is increasingly being criticized as sociologically and historically unfounded (Bhatia 2013; Gorski and Altinordu 2008; Iqtidar and Sarkar 2013; Kaviraj 2013), my interest here is in the tension it gestures to between democracy and secularism: as the inadequately secularized 'masses' enter more broadly into politics, the tenets of a secular polity are threatened. In this account, as in early Subaltern Studies, secularism is largely an elite enterprise. In a contrary explanation for the crisis, Hindu communalism in particular is seen as a reaction to growing lower-caste assertion within both religious and political spheres (D. Menon 2007). Lower-caste assertion is due in part to the opportunities offered by electoral politics, but also to the critique of religion itself by dalit and anti-caste reformers, such as Phule, Periyar, and Ambedkar (Geetha 2011a; Ilaiah 2005), for whom Brahmanical 'Hinduism' gave legitimacy to subaltern oppression. Here, religion is a medium of hegemony, and Hindu re-assertion an elite reaction to the growing secularization of the subaltern castes.

These questions of religion, secularization, and subaltern assertion are made more complex when the subalterns concerned belong to a 'minority' religious group. Rajiv Bhargava's (2007) treatment of the specificities of Indian secularism is helpful in illuminating these complexities. Bhargava argues that secularism in the Indian constitution represents an attempt to strike a careful balance between communitarianism and individualism, and as such must be understood in at least three senses. In its most cited sense, it refers to equal distance from each community (*dharma nirpekshata, sarva dharma sambhava*). The second aspect involves social reform—particularly of the majority community—in the form of bans on caste discrimination in religious practice (for instance, temple entry) and reform of the Hindu civil code. This aspect of social reform is related to the third constitutional meaning of secularism—as defence of the individual's right to conscience, and to protection from oppressive religiously sanctioned social customs. These social reformist elements of the constitution do not apply in equal measure to religious minority communities, however, because of their constitutionally guaranteed autonomy. That this aspect of social reform does not apply to 'minority communities' is part of the meaning of secularism as non-intervention or pluralism, and is, of course, the basis of the charge of 'pseudo-secularism' by the BJP (see Bhatt 2001; Jaffrelot 1996).

The arrangements that make up what Bhargava (2007) calls India's 'contextual secularism' pose a particular problem for subaltern (women, lower castes, lower classes, youth) struggles for social reform and individual freedom from religious authority within minority religious communities. As Subramanian (2003) notes in the case of the Catholic Church and Christian communities, religious institutions or authorities are taken to represent the entire community, seen as outside the secular mainstream. Within the context of growing communalism and 'competitive deature-ization', subaltern members of minority communities need the support of the religious establishment for resources, protection, and patronage. But they also struggle against these establishments for freedom from religiously sanctioned hierarchies and discriminatory practices. This dual positioning gives their relationship to religion an especially complex character, as Mosse's (2013) work on dalit Christians in Tamil Nadu shows so vividly: while denied scheduled caste status and its attendant benefits on grounds of having converted to a religion where caste has no doctrinal sanction, they find themselves subject to a range of discriminatory practices within the churches, embedded as they are in a society ordered by caste.

This chapter draws on the case of the Catholic fishing communities of Kanyakumari district, Tamil Nadu, to think through these questions of secularism, secularization, democracy, and subaltern assertion within 'minority' religions, adding to a growing body of work that explores these questions (see Ahmad 2012; Geetha 2011b; Mosse 2013; P. Williams 2012). I argue that, far from being an autonomous and self-enclosed sphere, subaltern religiosity must be read within the context of changing political economies, caste, national, and even geopolitical shifts. This is firstly because the religious and the secular are themselves not dichotomous. Official secularism, with its subcontracting of several state functions to the Church, has meant an articulation of the politics of the Church to the politics of the state. The Catholic Church draws on the same tropes of development, nationalism, and uplift as the state, and the shifts in ideological orientation within it mirror those in other contexts, both international and national. Secondly, as intellectuals and functionaries, diocesan clergy straddle and mediate the spheres of Church and state, and of elite and subaltern. Thirdly, it is precisely the promise of equality through membership in a common church that gives religion its power. This promise of equality makes religion itself a zone of contestation, but also provides the grounds from which to critique the secular political order. Kanyakumari villagers draw on religious resources and idioms to make secular demands; rather than taking away from some abstract universal identity, it is the local church that makes it possible for them to participate as citizens. Fourthly and importantly, however, subaltern struggles for recognition and representation within parish associations are citizenship struggles (see Iqtidar and Lehmann 2012) that transcend the particular ways in which official secularism has subcontracted authority to religious leaders within 'minority' communities. Subalterns draw on the resources provided by a liberal-democratic state and the secular politics of citizenship to transform the religious order itself, confirming Kaviraj's (2013) argument that liberal ideals of 'equal treatment' have become a kind of Gramscian common sense of

Indian political discourse, whether religious or secular (see also Chandhoke 2010). Finally, by bending the institutions, resources, and teachings of the church to the specifically subaltern politics of livelihoods, social reform, and political participation, subaltern actors contribute actively to the secularization of the public sphere.

I begin with a focus on the institutional Church, and its negotiation over the centuries with changing forms of political authority and social-cultural order. The Church's dominant, but contested, position among the fishing communities, its status as a minority institution, albeit a powerful one, within India, as well as theological and other shifts that have taken place within the global Church, have frequently led it to articulate a secular, even radical, politics as its primary mode of religious engagement. I then go on to examine the role of diocesan clergy, many from fishing backgrounds, who act as both organic and traditional intellectuals in the Gramscian sense, thus occupying an ambiguous and shifting place between the elite and the subaltern spheres. Finally, I examine villagers' participation in Church-generated associational spaces, and their use of state institutions and secular political idioms to challenge religious directives. Attention to these multiple institutional layers and actors allows one to see within subaltern religiosity a long history of negotiation with national and transnational imperatives around modernity and development, and the transformation of this religiosity through practices of political participation, democracy, and citizenship.

The Fishing Communities of Kanyakumari

The empirical core of this chapter draws on field work conducted in seven fishing villages in Kanyakumari district of Tamil Nadu over a year in 1994–5 and more briefly in 2004 and 2012. Kanyakumari district borders Kerala and has a sizable Christian minority, though not all of it is Catholic. According to the 2001 census, 44.5 per cent of the district's population identified as Christian, compared to 6 per cent in Tamil Nadu, and 2.3 per cent in India. At the southernmost edge of the district are the 42 coastal fishing villages which are the focus of this chapter. The inhabitants of these villages are all Catholic, and the villages themselves are really parishes, geographically distant and socially distinct from the revenue villages of which they are part. Kurien (2000) has noted that the fishing villages in Kerala prove an aberration to the 'Kerala model' of high literacy and social development; this is equally the case in Kanyakumari, as it is globally (Bene 2003). The fishing castes—Mukkuvar and Paravar—that make up these villages are both categorized as 'Other Backward Classes' for purposes of affirmative action. Despite their traditional economic and social marginality, however, these fishing communities have a strong sense of their own identity, stemming from their independence from everyday ritual submission to higher castes, pride in their difficult profession, awareness of their long lineage in the region, and membership in the Catholic Church since the sixteenth century. They are also shaped by a variety of intellectual, social, and political influences made possible by their closeness to the district headquarters of Nagercoil, as well as to Thiruvananthapuram, the capital of Kerala; the constant flow of tourists to Kanyakumari; the international flows of people and ideas facilitated by the Catholic Church; the fishermen's mobility, both across the country and to the countries of the Persian Gulf; and the villagers' steady consumption of films, television, and now, the internet.

The Catholic Church in Kanyakumari:
A Political History

An overview of key moments in the history of the Catholic Church in Kanyakumari district reveals institutional structures and practices that have been moulded, through adaptation or resistance, to the needs of fishing people and patterns of village life. Equally, local religiosities have been structured by wider institutional and theological shifts within the universal Church, which themselves are linked to changing global and national political contexts as much as to the predilections of individual popes.

A relationship of accommodation and collaboration for mutual benefit was established between church personnel and the state from the Catholic Church's very beginnings in the region. The Paravars converted in 1536 in exchange for Portuguese protection of their independence in the pearl trade (Bayly 1989: 323–5; Fernando 1984; Schurhammer 1973–82: 259), while access to the Mukkuvars was the price of Portuguese support for the Venad king against the Pandyas in 1544 (Narchison et al. 1983: 12). Given the tactical nature of the conversions (Bayly 1989: 328), religious identity, faith, and authority developed in complex syntheses with existing religious practices, social structures, and the specificities of an economy organized around the fishery. The emerging religious tradition was syncretic in nature, with the growing cult of St Francis Xavier taking on features of Sufi saints' biographies and of the region's warrior cults, and the retention of oral traditions relating Paravar rituals to the great Hindu temples of southern Tamil Nadu (Bayly 1989: 330–58; Mosse 2013). It was further shaped by the vagaries of fishing work, and the poverty and marginality of the villagers. Even up to the present, institutional attempts at strengthening a more doctrinal Catholicism against forms of popular devotion, such as visits to shrines of St Antony and other saints to cure possession and other ailments (see Ram 1992), have been largely unsuccessful. Equally, the belief derived from the unpredictable and often dangerous nature of fishing work in the power of Kadalamma, or 'sea mother', to cause feast or famine, and the need to propitiate her to ensure a good catch, may only recently have been moderated, with new technologies such as trawlers, powerful engines, GPS, and echosounders, reducing the unpredictability of a day's work.

A similar accommodation was achieved with caste. In order to attract higher castes to the Church, the Jesuit Robert de Nobili argued early on that caste had no religious implications, thus 'secularizing' caste (Mosse 2013) by relegating it to culture and freeing it of doctrinal meaning. This received papal assent in the early 1600s, while later Popes overturned it as a religious sacrilege. In practice, separate churches were constructed for the inland Nadars and the coastal Mukkuvars and Paravars; in some churches, a wall separated seating for the higher and lower castes (Roche 1984; Subramanian 2009: 49–50).

Parochial governance relied on the fusion between the group's caste institutions and their identity as Roman Catholics. Xavier and subsequent missionaries used the village leaders as a kind of moral police against drunkenness, idolatry, and other transgressions; the Portuguese colonial authorities further used them to recruit and discipline Paravar divers and others necessary to a productive fishery (Bayly 1989). This layer of caste notables, whose power was entrenched by the Church, belonged largely to the *mejaikarar* or non-fishing families. These lay officers were maintained, the bulk of the churches constructed, and, in later years, the priests supported, through taxes on the fishery in each village. Given the variety of levies imposed, the Portuguese priests were commonly referred to as *kuthagaikkara samigal* (levy priests) (Sivasubramanian 1996), and the collection of these levies was increasingly resented by the fishing families that were its chief contributors. In 1930, a new Diocese of Kottar was formed from the southern and Tamil-speaking villages of Travancore, and entrusted to indigenous diocesan clergy (Villavarayan 1956: 34). Following sustained campaigns by fishing families, intra-village divisions between pro- and anti-levy factions, and the conversion to Hinduism by a group of anti-levy Paravar in the adjacent diocese (Sivasubramanian 1996), the Diocese eventually began to collect levies from all households regardless of occupation (Villavarayan 1956: 52), though it was only in the 1990s that non-fishing families were finally displaced from parish leadership.

The politics of post-independence India impacted the institutional Church in new ways. While the principle of secularism in India's constitution was largely welcome in its sense of equal respect for all religions, less welcome was Nehru's thrust toward the greater secularization of society, given that opposition to secularization was a key principle of the Church's involvement in politics across the world, along with opposition to communism (Houtart 1984). In the first few national and state elections, bishops asked Catholic electors not to support parties which were against religion, morality, and the sanctity of family life, such as the Communists or the social reformist Dravida Munnetra Kazhagam (DMK) (Narchison et al. 1983: 94–5, 115–16). The Catholic Church chose to work closely with the Congress government, expanding its institution-building in education and health (Wilfred 1981: 829).

By the 1960s, this consensus was destabilized by developments within the global church. The election of Pope John XXIII in 1958, and the holding of the Second Vatican Ecumenical Council in 1962, marked a major change in the Catholic Church's understanding of its role in the polity. While historically, society, church, and state were considered organically interlinked, with political authority seen as ultimately derived from God, Vatican II expressed an acceptance of religious, social, and political pluralism (Hehir 1993: 22). Locally, this meant greater lay participation, both in parochial administration and in the liturgy, to be facilitated by new structures of administration, such as the parish councils, and new pastoral strategies, such as the Basic Ecclesiastical Communities. The council sparked new theological reflection, as in the liberation theology of Latin America and the contextual theology of South Africa (Lehmann 1996: 49; Littwin 1989), and the idea of social ministry understood as social activism gained growing adherence.

As in Latin America and other nations of Asia and Africa (Lehmann 1996: 13–14), the ideas of Vatican II interacted with indigenous movements and currents of social reform. Theologians such as George Soares-Prabhu (1929–1995), Sebastian Kappen (1925–1993), and M. M. Thomas (1916–1996) developed an Indian theology of liberation (Kappen 1986: 305). This was cross-pollinated by Gandhian tropes of indigenous development; in the early 1970s by the ideas of Naxalbari and the Jayaprakash Nararyan movement, which challenged, albeit in different ways, the class bias of the Indian development model; and by the emergence of a voluntary sector (G. Shah 1988). However, Indian liberation theology was unique in being forced to grapple from the outset with India's multi-religious society. Here, the true community of Christ, if it was to transform social structures, had necessarily to go beyond the Christian community to society at large (Kappen 1986), thus militating against the compact of official secularism, under which 'minority' religious communities were represented by their religious leaders and considered discrete from the national mainstream.

In Kottar, these innovations, some of which had already been prefigured by the work of Belgian priest James Tombeur, who established the Kottar Social Service Society (KSSS) in 1963, began to be taken up widely following Vatican II (Tombeur 1990). They took the form of: liturgical renewal; emphasis on Bible reading and catechism; inculturation, through the mass now being said in Tamil, and other local elements of worship added to the liturgy; lay participation in the mass and in ministry; and new structures for pastoral administration and social involvement. Leading diocesan priests influenced by liberation theology expressed a growing sense that even developmental works might not be radical enough:

> The developmental works of KSSS, commendable though in themselves, are they not still becoming unwittingly agents of alienation? Do they not deflect the Church from raising fundamental questions about the condition of the society and the structures of injustice at work? The strength of the developmental work can well become the weakness of the Church in Kottar, in the sense that they can make the Church insensitive to the real causes of poverty and underdevelopment and blunt the Christian conscience of its social responsibility. They can make us forget that as Church we are called upon to be catalysts and agents of change in society. (Narchison et al. 1983: 229–30)

A pastoral letter issued by Bishop M. Arokiaswamy in April 1986 traces the problems of the people to the unjust socio-economic structures of feudalism and capitalism and speaks of the danger that religion might legitimize them. Describing various flawed Church models adopted in the past, the letter recommends a new approach, the 'Radical Church' model, guided by the gospel vision and aiming to bring radical change in all spheres. The action plan laid out on the basis of this model (Jeremias 1989: 203–5) calls upon the Kottar Church to take a stand in support of people's movements active in the district, rally around progressive parties and trade unions, and engage with Marxist ideology and movements as sharing a common concern with human liberation. Strategies that involve violence are not condemned out of hand; rather, structures that oppress people are seen as violent in themselves. The action plan calls for priests and lay people to work together as equals, and for youth and women to be involved. Political awareness and involvement is seen as a Christian duty, with priests responsible for fostering it among the laity.

The election of John Paul II as Pope in 1978 saw a retreat from the principles of Vatican II (Della Cava 1992; Houtart 1984). This was reflected in the Indian Church, which also exercised greater caution about questions of social justice, a greater emphasis on spirituality, and a re-separation of the notions of development and evangelization. Within Kottar, even though the startling radicalism of the approach outlined in the Bishop's 1986 letter suggests the persistence of these principles for far longer, 'liberationists' had at no point been the majority of the clergy. Rather, their influence appears to have been due to the leadership of key bishops and other clergy. However, insofar as there was a clear shift away from liberationist positions by the end of the 1990s, the impetus for this was not the outcome of internal contestation, but of the need to respond to external threats: the rise of Hindu nationalism as a significant political force, and the growing popularity of Protestant evangelical churches, even among the Catholic masses.

Although their influence in Kanyakumari has never reached the proportions it has in Latin America (see Lehmann 1996), many Catholic villagers began to be attracted from the 1990s to the new Pentecostal churches (see also Mosse 1994, 2013). Their practices of 'sharing' life histories and 'bearing witness' to the moment of revelation were recognized even by radical clergy as providing the individual catharsis and psychological healing that post-conciliar Catholicism, with its emphasis on social change, had turned away from. In response, Pope John Paul II encouraged a charismatic movement which borrowed evangelical elements such as catchy music, prophetic preaching, and collective cathartic participation.

The growing political strength of Hindu nationalism posed a problem of another kind, in this case for the Catholic community as much as for the Church as an institution. Relations between the Catholic fishing communities and their Hindu and Muslim neighbours in coastal Kanyakumari had not been markedly conflictual, with a few conflicts escalating when political parties inflamed local quarrels in order to secure electoral majorities (see Chiriyankandath 1993). The rise of Hindu nationalism in the early 1980s was reflected in two watershed events in the district: the government-supported construction of the Vivekananda Rock Memorial on a site claimed also by Catholics as a spot where

Xavier had meditated, and an incident at Mondaikadu village in 1982, in which rumours set off a spiral of retaliatory violence between Hindus and Catholics, leading to massive injury, loss, and destruction in the coastal villages (Mathew 1983: 417). The BJP's rise to power nationally in the 1990s, and the rising tide of attacks against minority communities across the country in the decades following, has contributed to a growing sense of besiege-ment. This has hardened identities to a great extent, but has not done away entirely with syncretic practices, or with villagers' bargaining with the Church hierarchy. For instance, in the mid-1990s, when expressing frustration with the local priest, or the Diocese more generally, more than one fisherman voiced to me in private a threat (usually rhetorical) to convert. More significantly, in 1995, Catholic trawler owners voted as a group for the BJP, upset that the radical politics of the diocesan church had led it to favour the small-scale fishermen in conflicts between the two groups (Subramanian 2009: 228–34).

By the turn of the century, as a result of the conjuncture between the need to demonstrate patriotism in the face of Hindu nation-alism; gradual conformity with the global Church in its retreat from Vatican II; and the changed understanding of 'development' as market-led growth after India's economic reforms of the early 1990s, the Diocese had reverted to older priorities. These included establishing educational and medical institutions, and develop-ment work, such as microcredit groups for women and training programmes around hygiene or computer literacy. Nevertheless, 'power from below' and 'breaking the yokes of injustice' remain two of the four pillars of the diocese's stated vision (Diocese of Kottar), suggesting either that liberationist values remain deeply held by many diocesan clergy, or that they remain important to invoke.

The Diocesan Clergy: Between Elite and Subaltern?

The priest in the coastal parish is called upon to fulfil a variety of functions, unlike in an inland one, where parishioners are more comfortable dealing directly with the civic administration

(Narchison et al. 1983: 138). In the fishing village, the priest is leader, judge, problem solver, liaison with government, sole representative of the village, preacher, counsellor, and guide (Ram 1992: 40). The work of the priest is not only concrete and practical, but also, as Gramsci (1971: 5–16) famously observed, 'intellectual', that of generating social and political hegemony. There are, increasingly, other intellectuals in the villages, such as social workers, political activists, and NGO staff, but the priests are still the best educated as a group, and, by virtue of their historic pre-eminence and institutional base, the most authoritative. Distinguishing between two types of intellectuals, Gramsci (1971: 5–16) describes organic intellectuals as those who arise as a part of every social group or class to give it 'homogeneity and an awareness of its own function not only in the economic but also in the social and political fields'. Traditional intellectuals, in contrast, are those who have always performed the role of intellectuals in society, such as state functionaries, scholars, scientists, and philosophers; by virtue of their uninterrupted historical continuity as a group and their special qualifications, they consider themselves autonomous of every social class.

Of priests, Gramsci (1971: 7) writes that 'the category of ecclesiastics can be considered the category of intellectuals organically bound to the landed aristocracy,' and further that, unlike other social groups, a person of peasant origin who becomes an 'intellectual' (priest, lawyer, etc.) generally ceases thereby to be organically linked to his class of origin, and functions as a traditional intellectual. This Gramscian schema cannot be transposed directly across time and space (see Arnold 1984; Davidson 1984), given that the Indian Church does not share an organic relationship with the landed classes and the state, and is further vulnerable in the face of rising Hindu chauvinism. Nevertheless, it is a powerful and wealthy institution, with a history of working closely with the state in various areas. Ram (1995: 293) thus concludes that the clergy of the Kottar diocese function as traditional intellectuals, sharing with the state 'a commonly understood vocabulary of reform, rationalism, development and cultural nationalism'.

I argue for a different reading. The common use of 'weapons of the weak' against the priests, such as rumours of financial corruption, or intimacy with women, and ridicule about their soft hands and clean-shaven faces, suggests a hegemony that is unstable at best, as it was in earlier days when the priest also managed the parish funds, and factions and court cases against the priest were common. Further, although there may be certain common tropes underlying both religious and secular attempts at social transformation, the ideological content of these tropes matters. I draw here on Lehmann's (1996: 13–14) description of *basismo* in Brazil—an influential social current of belief that the people, the 'grassroots', have a distinctive culture and outlook and that political and religious salvation necessarily involves listening to them and gaining empathy with them—which came out of the cross-fertilization of liberation theology and other movements for democratization in Latin America. Just as *basismo* represented a new respect for the subaltern, and thus a challenge to the more authoritarian and elitist traditions of Church and state in Latin America, so different currents within the Kottar Church must be seen as existing in some tension and contradiction with each other, and with the state. For instance, although the idea of modernization informed both state fisheries policy and the interventions of the diocesan KSSS, the former resulted in large-scale mechanization initially accessible only to a handful of villagers, while KSSS interventions through appropriate technology and co-operativization had a wider reach.

The 275 or so clergy of Kottar diocese are drawn from the district's Catholic castes: Nadar, Paravar, and Mukkuvar. They hold a range of ideological positions including: (*a*) an exclusive focus on the spiritual aspects of the religion, usually accompanied by works of charity and non-political activities such as youth groups and prayer meetings, family development, and personal 'improvement'; (*b*) an emphasis on development understood as schools, better housing, co-operatives, and community health programmes; and (*c*) an emphasis on political and cultural analysis and activism informed by a liberationist theology. These strands are not always mutually exclusive, and all the priests involve themselves in development works within the village and other traditional parochial responsibilities. There is nonetheless a tension between the first category of priests, concerned to separate religion from politics, and the other two. What distinguished the priests who took one of the latter two positions, but chiefly the third, was that they were intellectuals in the commonplace (non-Gramscian) sense of the term, being highly educated and frequently engaged in research and writing. The diocesan clergy all begin their education in a local minor seminary, where they are formed in matters intellectual and spiritual, and in skills like music, public speaking, and acting, before being sent elsewhere to a major seminary for theological studies. There is also a growing tendency for them to be sent to college between minor and major seminary, or to pursue higher studies, often in secular subjects (Narchison et al. 1983: 211). Of the group I interviewed, almost all had pursued higher studies in subjects they believed would assist them in their role as (organic) intellectuals and leaders, such as group dynamics and management, public administration, law, media and communication, computers, and counselling.

Working in the coastal parishes, these priests had introduced reforms to break existing power structures, encourage lay leadership, reduce violent conflict, and systematize parochial administration. These reforms included the establishment of fishermen's co-operatives to break the stranglehold of the merchants; the initiation of Basic Christian Communities (BCCs) to end factionalism and build leadership capacity; the creation of family cards based on a survey of all parish households; and the application for individual land titles so as to enable bank loans. In the mid-1990s, some 20 of these priests had formed a group called the 'Coastal Analysis Programme' aimed at studying and strategizing around social problems in the villages. They thought of themselves as an 'enabling group' within the diocese, providing direction and analysis to other organizations, building up a documentation centre on coastal issues, and carrying out reflection on coastal ministry. They held study meetings around issues such as the Indian government's deep-sea fishing policy, educational backwardness and violence in the villages, and the design of participatory governance structures. At one such meeting, I observed an extensive discussion on a programme of culture for the villages, the understanding being that certain of the villagers' cultural habits prevented their liberation. Many of those present spoke as 'insiders' to this culture, talking nostalgically of old games and songs that had been lost with the coming of television. Although the group disbanded after a few years, its members' interests became institutionalized in diocesan agencies concerned with new media and the revival of traditional cultural forms.

Drawing on this last group, I argue that the reformist clergy are in fact drawn to act *both* as intellectuals of their class, articulating the consciousness of that class, and of the church and state. Their identification as organic intellectuals is illustrated by the opening words to Fr Jeremias's (1989) thesis in pastoral theology: 'The eagerness to search for ways and means to better the conditions of the fisherfolk gushes out of me as I am one who had experienced the stings of poverty from my birth.' In the ideas and aspirations the clergy hold and transmit, and in the variety of pastoral approaches they favour, they mirror the different stages of, and influences in, the universal Church's recent development, its location within the Indian political community, *and its local social and cultural embeddedness.* Located in the shifting space between elite and subaltern, they view the use of religious authority for social reform as both a religious and a civic duty.

Lay Associations: Vehicles of Modernity?

In the 1970s, the diocesan Church began attempting to reform structures of village governance, prompted partly by the directives of Vatican II, and partly by growing popular resentment against the traditional headmen it had backed. The two main organizations introduced were the BCCs and the parish councils.

The BCCs, modelled on the base communities (Communidades Eclesiales de Base [CEB]) which had emerged in Brazil and other parts of Latin America post–Vatican II (see Lehmann 1990; Levine and Mainwaring 1989), were brought to Kottar diocese by Fr Edwin, a Mukkuvar diocesan priest who had grown up in a fishing village. His first parish was rife with violent factionalism, making the idea of cross-cutting, neighbourhood-based units of participation especially appealing as an alternative. Fr Edwin began with house visits and sustained interaction with his parishioners between

1977 and 1979, running formation programmes on spiritual and socio-economic themes, and topics such as leadership and group dynamics. The basic units consisted of 30 neighbouring households each, called the *anbiam*, which in turn sent five people to the general body of the village. For the first time, the village leadership, including the president's post, was in the hands of the laity rather than the parish priest. A whole generation of active youth emerged from this process, but it was also met with a great deal of opposition, with many of the past leaders and strongmen resenting their loss of power, and using the increased visibility of women in public life to denounce the new structures as 'alien to the local culture'.

The BCCs were eventually officially adopted by the Diocese in 1984 as the basic units from which representatives were to be elected to the parish council. However, their most radical element—institutional autonomy from the Church—was tempered by making the parish priest rather than a lay person the president of the parish council. In practice, the scope of the BCCs varies from village to village, depending in part on the interest of the parish priest and the powers he is willing to cede to them: in some villages they discuss village finances, which give them a great deal of power; in others where this financial control is lacking because of opposition from the better-off fishermen, they function almost solely as prayer groups, composed mainly of women and children.

Since the mid-1980s, parish councils have been made mandatory in each parish, making the grant of diocesan money conditional on their establishment. Of course, since the bulk of village monies continue to be raised from within the village, the Diocese cannot insist that these flow only through a parish council. The parish councils act like a village governing body, with rules for membership and elections, the conduct of meetings, constitutional amendments, and representation for different categories of village residents, including women and youth, and for key village associations, such as the fishermen's co-operatives.

Of the seven villages I studied in the 1990s, parish councils had been successfully established in three; in the remaining four they had been prevented from being set up, or opposition to the

BCCs meant that they could not be set up as required through representation from the basic communities; or the councils were set up, but struggled against opposition and then collapsed. In Kanyakumari village, for instance, the establishment of a parish council was resisted, not because of factional differences or the belligerence of previously dominant families, but because they did not want women leaders. It was argued that women could not take the lead on highly contentious issues in the fishery because physical prowess and backing were important in settling these. It was also feared that a parish council would mean that every decision would be subject to review by the Church. Nevertheless, the village committee that governed instead was also elected, and consisted entirely of active fishermen, rather than being formed by nomination from the leading non-fishing families of the village, as in the past. The three functioning parish councils I observed did indeed follow rules of order. Their meetings were held in the parish priest's office, the church, village meeting hall, or school. Matters dealt with by the council arose from a variety of sources: precedence, ongoing projects, and petitions by villagers. A sample list of such matters, drawn from the three councils, includes expenditure and revenues; development and welfare projects; fishing conflicts; intra-village conflicts; relations with other organizations, such as the fishermen's co-operatives; village services; the school; stopping alcohol sales; and collective support in the lean fishing season for families of the service castes (mainly barbers). In 2012, more parish councils were functioning, although some villages still resisted having the parish priest as president.

The BCCs and parish councils were designed under Vatican II to increase lay participation in the Church. The diocesan website notes: 'In the Kingdom where God's will is to reign here on earth as in heaven everybody shares in governing, everybody is taken into confidence, everybody searches together and everybody involves' (Diocese of Kottar). As in Latin America, so in Kottar the BCCs are now thoroughly integrated into diocesan administration. Given this, we may question the extent to which 'this paradox of an anti-hierarchical movement depending for its survival on the hierarchy itself' (Lehmann 1996: 76) has the possibility of genuine transformation of the Church. However, one must look beyond the democratization of the Church to judge the true significance of these organizations. As much as theological shifts and Vatican II–inspired directives, they are the result of socio-economic transformation and a changed political order. Subramanian (2009: 250–2) is right, that villagers' negotiations with the Church, other powers, and the modern state, reveal a long history of claims-making with its own vernacular forms. But more is at work here, I argue. The establishment of liberal-democratic institutions and processes under the postcolonial state has been enormously consequential in generating a new vocabulary of claims-making, as well as new technologies of governance. The associations described here reflect the politics of the reformist Church, but also the deep influence of the ideas of social equality, and democracy as participation in governance, contained in India's liberal-democratic constitution (see also Kaviraj 2013; Mosse 2013).

Within these associations, we see a struggle between the Church, the village community, traditional village leaders, and hitherto marginalized groups such as youth and women, with individual, gender, and class interests emerging to challenge the traditional identity of village and church community. The growing economic clout of fishing families as a result of rising incomes from the fishery, and the fact that the bulk of village revenues came from the fishery, had led to growing resentment against the *pradhanis*, unelected village headmen, who came largely from non-fishing families. Participation is thus directed at democratizing society itself. We also see a widening of the will to self-governance, and the routinization of the procedures and technologies of modern governance, for instance in the insistence that all members of the community have equal claims to participate, and that leaders, even at the village level, should be elected. A self-conscious modernity may also be seen in the manner in which meetings are conducted, with rules of order, minutes, and formal agendas. Various technologies of (self-) governance are beginning to be adopted, such as village censuses and the computerization of village records; family cards indicating membership in the village; and the assignment of individual land titles to land previously held in common in order to allow villagers to apply for bank loans. It may be that, as Lehmann (1996) has argued regarding the Brazilian CEBs, the deeper impact of these associations has been to serve as mediums of modernity.

* * *

For over three years now, Paravar villagers in the neighbouring district of Tirunelveli have been at the forefront of a steadfast non-violent campaign against the commissioning of the Koodankulam nuclear power plant. The premises of the church and rectory of Idinthakarai, a Paravar fishing village, have been given over to the campaign, which also depends largely on regular contributions from the villagers for its funding. While some local clergy are sympathetic to the cause, others have been forced to join because of their parishioners' fervent support of it. The state has responded viciously, with police violence, arrests, and the slapping of charges of 'sedition' against campaign leaders. The state and Hindu nationalists, who see opposition to nuclear power as 'anti-national', have alleged that the campaign is a plot funded by the international Church, and the foreign funding of local Christian NGOs has been thoroughly investigated and restricted. Meanwhile, observers credit the BCCs in these villages with creating the ideological and organizational capacity for a campaign of this strength (*Down to Earth* 2012; *Hindu* 2011). The Koodankulam case illustrates the ease with which the compact of official secularism between Church and state breaks down, and Christians are 'othered' as outsiders when they oppose state projects. More relevant to my argument, however, is the way in which the religiously inspired BCCs become spaces for political resistance, and conversely, how the Church and clergy are drafted into subaltern projects of resistance to the state. The Catholic fishers opposing Koodankulam are actors in a wider public sphere constituted by religious faith, and simultaneously, by the secular politics of democracy and development.

While it may be hard to argue for the presence of a similar public sphere in the sixteenth century, it is clear that even in those earliest times, subalterns did not exist in some alternative and unvarying religious sphere. As members of the global Church, they were drawn into its schisms and rivalries, as much as they were protected by its agreements with local rulers. Likewise in recent decades, villagers have been drawn into larger shifts and debates, from anti-communism in the 1950s, to the social reformist currents of Vatican II and liberation theology, to the more recent retreat to institution building and service provision. Along with wider influences, villagers' religiosity responded to local contexts and their own needs. From the start, allegiances to the new faith, identity, and authority represented by the Catholic Church were shifting and fluid. The new converts incorporated elements of pre-existing sacral systems into their faith and ritual practices. Over the centuries, the faith has deepened, aided most recently by the changes introduced by Vatican II, such as the mass being recited in Tamil and greater lay involvement in the liturgy. But these same changes, along with liberation theology, have infused the faith with new meanings. Villagers also continue to engage in expressions of faith that are not endorsed by the hierarchy, from popular devotions having to do with health and healing, to participation in evangelical churches, even while remaining officially Catholic. If the element of religious identity has remained most constant, and even hardened in the context of growing communalism, mobilization along religious lines has not closed off other identities. Villagers have mobilized as Tamils, or as members of the national fishworkers' movement, or divided themselves along (sometimes ideological) party lines. Equally, individual threats of conversion, or the rare group conversion, as well as the decision by trawler owners to vote for the BJP, indicate that identity too is seen as negotiable, rather than given. What seems visible is a growing freedom from inherited faith and identity, or, in other words, a process of secularization.

Like faith and identity, the Church's authority has always been contested. Most resented were the taxes on the fisheries raised to maintain the Church, the control of parish finances by the parish priest, and the appointment of caste leaders from largely non-fishing families to the village administration. The expression of this resentment in threats to leave the fold, and factions and courts cases against the village leadership and parish priest, led finally to the reform of village revenues in the early 1930s. It was only in the 1990s, however, that more thoroughgoing reform of village administration in the form of the BCCs and parish councils gained traction. This was the result of the confluence between the Vatican II ideals of participation and social justice, the 'habits of the heart' acquired through the politics of liberal democracy (see Sundar and Sundar 2012), and the socio-economic shifts brought about by rising incomes from the fishery and the greater education and mobility of fisher youth and women.

In the vision of Vatican II, BCCs and parish councils were a means of actualizing the 'Kingdom dimension' (Diocese of Kottar) of participation. For the local clergy and for villagers themselves, these associations became spaces from which to challenge the Church hierarchy, to challenge state policies around fisheries modernization, globalization, or nuclear energy, or equally, to further state projects of modernization and reform, as in the granting of individual titles to fishing households, or the encouragement of women's self-help groups. Likewise, religious texts and idioms, such as biblical allegories, were drawn on by both priests and villagers to call for social justice. Thus, living the faith gave rise to acts of citizenship, which came to have meaning as ways of living the faith. As Mosse (2013: 28) has noted: 'while profoundly localized into existing social and representational structures, Christianity nonetheless becomes a source of distinctive thought, action and modes of signification that are potentially transformative', and contribute to distinctive forms of self-making as a Christian in the world.

One might question, however, how distinctive to Christianity these modes of self-making are (see, for instance, Ahmad 2012; Geetha 2011b; P. Williams 2012). The religious participation of the Kanyakumari villagers is deeply influenced by the ideals and technologies of liberal democracy: priests, even if unelected, are required to be accountable to parishioners; religiously derived spaces like the BCCs and parish councils have elected leaders, formal by-laws, records, and procedures to ensure group representation and participation. While subalterns may always have contested Church authority, the establishment of liberal democracy has dramatically restructured the arena and means of contestation, both through its ideals of individual freedom and equality of treatment, and in the procedures it offers for their actualization. Faced with the opportunities, aspirations, and pressures of a rapidly transforming political economy, subaltern groups like the Kanyakumari fishers draw on the resources of liberal democracy to challenge the religious sphere as much as the political. It may be possible to conclude, then, that far from operating in a domain of pure religiosity autonomous of a wider public sphere, subaltern practices of religion are shaped by wider public currents and, in turn, contribute to the secularization of society.

6

Affective Politics and the Sexual Subaltern

Lesbian Activism in Eastern India

SRILA ROY*

In my contribution, I want to ask: to what extent does queer activism in India today contribute to the project of reshaping the way we think and do politics? The expansion of the sphere of the political was one of the original mandates of the Subaltern Studies group in order to include what was ordinarily considered 'pre-political' (religious, traditional, affective). The instance of lesbian activism in India offers several possibilities of broadening our usually employed analytics of activism, resistance, and politics. I focus on the affective dimension of such activism insofar as the turn to

---

* My thanks to all the contributors to this volume, especially Rashmi Varma, for their engagement with this chapter. Thanks also to Dilip Menon for critical comments and Stephen Legg for helpful suggestions. Without the support of my collaborator, Alf Nilsen, this chapter would have not been written.

affect and emotions has already substantially enriched our sense of politics beyond the paradigm of rational action. To this extent, this chapter locates itself in recent and not so recent conversations, not merely about the significant role that emotions and affect (not synonymous with one another, as explained later) play in propelling people to act, but how activism can be thought of as being affective.

Indeed, the activist response to the Supreme Court's recent decision to uphold Section 377 of the Indian Penal Code that criminalizes homosexuality was saturated with affect. Intimate, intense, and moving—as these were often described (see, for example, Ponni 2013)—they spoke against an act of political silencing, of subalternization which could only be resisted through the force of bare, visceral, often inarticulate emotion. Such an emotional repertoire formed the foundation of the activist pledge to continue the fight for sexual rights and equality. Wider political agendas and struggles also have the un/intended effect of containing the affective or emotive force that propelled political change in the first place. This is a key argument that Naisargi Dave (2012) makes in her recently published ethnography on lesbian activism in India, and that I take forward in the ensuing discussion.

The chapter begins with a discussion of the category of the subaltern as mobilized in the context of sexuality. While sexuality might give us new purchase on the well-worn concept of the subaltern, affect, as I argue in the subsequent section, expands how we understand political action besides challenging our presumptions of political agency and action ordinarily centred on the rational male subject. A focus on affective and not merely rational action (and a questioning of the divide between the two) provides a stronger mode of displacing from centrality the normative male subject that has been at the heart of liberal theories of political agency, and of foregrounding, instead, questions of gender and sexuality in ways that the original Subaltern Studies project never managed. The rest of the chapter draws on my ethnography of lesbian activism in eastern India to show the mobilization and containment of affect and the significance of this dynamic for and within the field of queer politics.

Who Is a Sexual Subaltern?

In introducing this volume of essays, we noted the twin agendas of mobilizing the term 'subaltern' both empirically (who is a subaltern?) and analytically (what does 'subaltern' tell us about the functioning of power?). In a dual and inevitably contradictory sense, 'subaltern' is employed both as an identitarian category *and* as a critical lens to study power: that is, to unearth the sites and workings of power. The category of the 'sexual subaltern' can be similarly mobilized on both terrains. On the one hand, and evoking Gidwani's (2009) definition of 'subaltern' (see Introduction to this volume), it refers to persons and groups that are positioned as subordinates or inferiors within relations of sexuality, patriarchy, and gender. On the other hand, 'sexual subaltern' can function analytically to expose the workings of 'sexual normativity' (Kapur 2009: 384), especially through a focus on what it marginalizes and excludes. We also argued in the Introduction for a more expansive and intersectional conception of subalternity to address a plurality of context-specific manifestations of power. With respect to sexuality, as I show in what follows, the urgency and implications of mobilizing a more expansive concept of the 'subaltern' are all the more obvious.

Ratna Kapur's usage of the term 'sexual subaltern' (Kapur 2000, 2005, 2009, 2012; see also Legg and Roy 2013) is the most deliberate evocation of the tradition of Subaltern Studies. She too employs the term in a dual sense: referring, on the one hand, to 'the disparate range of sexual minorities within postcolonial India' (Kapur 2000: 16), and, on the other hand, as a critical lens on the (normative and exclusionary) functioning of heterosexuality. As an identity category, it includes a vast array of minority sexual subjects (gay, lesbian, bisexual, transgendered, queer, hijra, kothis, etc.) as well as sexual practices and behaviours that are specific to the postcolonial context and not sufficiently captured by the acronym 'LGBT' (lesbian, gay, bisexual, and transgender). Kapur (2000, 2012) includes in her definition of the sexual subaltern non-normative sexual identities and practices that may even be heterosexual, such as sex work. Counter-heteronormative movements (Kapur 2009; see also N. Menon 2007) that gained political visibility and confidence in the late 1990s in India also fall under the rubric of 'sexual subaltern', given the postcolonial and inevitably contradictory politics of such groups being imbricated as they are in the politics of class, caste, religion, and gender.

For Kapur (2009), the sexual subaltern—like any other subaltern subject—does not merely occupy a peripheral position vis-à-vis the norm, but also exposes and disrupts dominant norms pertaining especially, but not only, to the sexual. By virtue of her exclusion from liberal rights discourses, the sexual subaltern exposes and disrupts the normative assumptions pertaining to gender, sexuality, culture, and the family that continue to inform the liberal project in a postcolonial context. This is especially true of the lesbian whom Ranjita Biswas (2007: 273) theorizes as the constitutive outside of the category of human in that 'she is not-male, not-rational (by virtue of her sexuality), not-scientific (by virtue of her pathological sexuality) and not-political (by virtue of the illegal status of her pathological sexuality) and therefore excluded from the humanist underpinnings of human rights and citizenship' (see also Salih and Butler 2004). It is because of her (violent) exclusion in this manner that lesbians challenge the heteronormative underpinning of the family, the community, and even the nation-state. Lesbian responses to the right-wing protests around the screening of Deepa Mehta's *Fire*, a film on lesbian love, propelled the issue of lesbian desire into the Indian public sphere for the first time. Declaring that they were part of the nation-state, lesbians asserted their existence and disrupted dominant sexual and cultural norms that relied on rendering them invisible (see Dave 2012; Kapur 2009). Likewise, campaigns for legal rights by gays and lesbians open up an unprecedented space, not merely for rendering such subaltern subjects visible, but for questioning the existing heteronormative order.

While Kapur (2012) is sceptical of the use of the term 'queer' in the Indian context, finding 'subaltern' to be more apposite to the complexities of postcolonial contexts and histories, it is fair to say that in recent activism and scholarship on 'queer India' (Cossman 2012) the term functions in the same manner as does the 'sexual subaltern'. Queer is, in Narrain and Bhan's words (2005), a deeply personal identity and a defiant political perspective. It is rooted in a politics of identity while attempting, at the same time, to go beyond identity to provide a broader understanding and questioning of 'the naturalness, the rightness and the inevitability of heterosexuality' (Narrain and Bhan 2005: 3). Nivedita Menon (2007: 3) similarly uses the term 'counter-heteronormative' 'to refer to a range of political assertions that implicitly or explicitly challenge heteronormativity and the institution of monogamous patriarchal marriage'. Like subalternity, then, 'queer' functions as a position of critique even as it includes and validates a range of non-normative sexual identities and practices.

However, in some recent commentaries (for example, Bose and Bhattacharya 2007), 'queer' is deployed as signifying LGBT identities alone. Cossman (2012) finds Kapur to be one of the only scholars to extend her analysis of non-normative sexualities to include heterosexual forms, attempting to deconstruct the hetero/homo binary in ways that a focus on non-heterosexual subjects alone cannot achieve. While I am inclined to agree with Cossman about the resonances between Kapur's sexual subaltern and queer theory (irrespective of whether the latter mobilizes the term 'queer' or not), a more expansive understanding of subalternity might have more to offer. It might shift our focus from the hetero/homo divide to the intersectionality of class, caste, race, gender, and religion, on the one hand, and nationalist, imperialist, and postcolonial ideologies on the other, as together constitutive of sexual subjectivity in the global South. The idea of subalternity with respect to sexuality also potentially captures, to a greater extent than does 'queer', the relations and politics of subordination, exclusion, and invisibility attached to non-hegemonic sexual identities. Finally, the empirical and analytical function of subalternity serves to name those who are rendered politically unintelligible by sexual normativity, but also their distinct modes of resisting subalternization in discourses and forms of resistance deployed against 'regimes of normal' (Warner 1993).

Sexual Subalternity as Intersectional

To what extent are the subjects of this chapter 'subaltern'? These are educated, largely upper-caste women 'of means', a criterion that

Dave (2012) says determines lesbian activism in India as such, marginalizing non-urban and working-class lesbians (see M. Sharma 2006; Swarr and Nagar 2003). Privilege of this kind, accruing from class-caste status, would place these women outside of the category of subaltern, as elite even. But this rationalization works only if we embrace a narrow, crudely economist understanding of subalternity. When it comes to sexuality, a (false) hierarchy of priorities—or what Dave (2012: 98) after Mindry (2001) calls 'hierarchies of worthiness'—has meant the prioritization of class and devaluation of sexuality in feminist theorizations of and activism around Third World women. Subalternity in the Indian women's movement has come to be located, par excellence, in the poverty-ridden rural woman who cannot at the same time be sexual or desiring (see S. Roy 2014). A more intersectional deployment of subalternity (that we identified in the work of Spivak in the Introduction) would make it possible to understand that a woman can be working class *and* lesbian, and that to pit the politics of class against the politics of sexuality, as the Indian women's movement has repeatedly done, is to 'stifle emergent critiques and practices' (Dave 2012: 122; see also N. Menon 2007; C. Shah 2005).

Whether elite, middle class, or non-elite, lesbian existence in India is marked not just by marginalization but also by invisibility. For Dave (2012: 13), the deeply naturalized aspect of heteronormative life renders the lesbian an impossibility in terms of both experience and identity (see also Akanksha and Malobika 2007). She is different from other subaltern groups, including women who recognize their otherness and oppression through practices of enforced social segregation: 'but lesbians are excluded from all social and cultural recognition, so that even the comfort of collective anger, the possibility of resistance, and the knowledge of what to resist and with whom is unavailable' (Dave 2012: 13). She is thus invisible even to herself, a paradigmatic subaltern subject who cannot speak or be heard.

The subalternity of middle-class lesbians by virtue of gender and sexuality does not, however, obviate the need to pay attention to how the field of sexual subalternity is differentiated by vectors of social stigma and economic power (not to mention differences of caste, gender, and religion). A wider context of socio-economic disparities renders socio-economically marginalized sexual minorities (such as kothis, dhuranis, and hijras) more vulnerable to institutionalized forms of violence and abuse than others. Rights-based queer activism also reproduces the structural vulnerability of lower-class/caste groups by subordinating their localized forms of resistance to transnationally hegemonic formations of LGBT rights activism, as Aniruddha Dutta's (2012) work shows. It is precisely by recognizing these kinds of complexities born out of neoliberalism and the intersectionality of class, caste, religion, and gender that we move towards a genuinely relational and expansive understanding of subalternity in relation to and mobilizations around sexuality.

The women who form the subjects of this chapter are a politically organized group. It is only with the recent advent of the queer movement in India that representation and organization have become possible ways of resisting sexual subalternity for groups such as theirs. But, as argued in the Introduction, political mobilization in no way entails emancipation and the end of subalternity. Even in the face of a very vocal and vibrant queer movement, the sexual subaltern does not cease to be subaltern so long as the root cause of subalternity remains, reinforced in the Supreme Court's decision to (re)criminalize homosexuality in India. The journey from being non-normative to achieving common-sense status or becoming hegemonic (Hall and O'Shea 2013; N. Menon 2004) is a long one and not guaranteed by the attainment of sexual citizenship alone. In any case, given the absolute invisibility and not mere marginalization of lesbian existence—even to themselves—political action centres around the invention of possibilities that did not previously exist, especially the possibility of love and desire in a world that renders 'such desiring impossible' (Duggan and Munoz 2009: 278). Such an activism of invention, as Dave (2012) calls it, is thoroughly affective and not exhausted by the struggle for formal equality and legal rights.

Subaltern Politics as Affective Activism

The interest in the affective dimension of queer politics has to be located in a broader move, first to the role of emotions, and then to affect, in the study of public protest and social movements (I deal with these in turn in what follows). Politics is after all the social realm that is 'most strongly based on the expulsion of irrationality' (Carole Pateman cited in Holmes 2004: 210), the passions being contained if not expunged for clear political reasoning and strategizing.

While the 'turn to affect' is often presented in novel and groundbreaking terms (Pedwell and Whitehead 2012), it has an older history particularly in the study of social movements, where there has been an 'emotional turn' (Gould 2009). Challenging narrow rationalist explanations of political behaviour that excluded feeling and emotion, this turn has been critical to countering the assumed divide between reason and emotion, the equation of emotionality with irrationality, and in bringing into view the social and cultural aspects of emotions besides their biological and psychological dimensions (Clarke et al. 2006; Gould 2009; Thompson and Hoggett 2012). Even in the case of the Subaltern Studies project, Veena Das (1989: 311) observed a Weberian tendency to privilege social action as rational action such that 'affective action becomes a residual category in which all that cannot be explained by the paradigm of rational action is sought to be fitted'. Given the historical association of masculinity with rationality, the privileging of such a paradigm centres the male as the normative political subject, with the female being understood as 'a lack, a deflection from the ideal type' (Das 1989: 312). The non-Western man—especially the subaltern—is equally configured as lack and deviation. Das (1989: 318) finds the inadvertent reproduction of the 'civilized–savage dichotomy' in the work of some subaltern historians a consequence of this uncritical association of political action with rational action.

Conceptions of politics have moved substantially from such paradigms of rational action centred on the (Western) male subject-agent. So much so that it has now become fairly mainstream to include an analysis of the role of emotions in shaping public protest, and as motivating rather than deflecting the behaviour of political actors. Based on the premise that emotions infuse all aspects of social life including political action or inaction (Gould 2002; see also Clarke et al. 2006), a fully rounded portrait of political life is offered which does not attempt to negate either the rationality or the passion of the protestor. Gould (2002, 2009), for instance, found it impossible to study early lesbian and gay AIDS activism in the US without a consideration of the necessarily affective dimension of meaning-making, insofar as movement participants were animated by feelings and not instrumental rationality alone. She argues (Gould 2002) that emotions were central to the sustainability and success of such activism—that the emotion work that movement participants were involved in actually altered how people felt (by transforming grief into anger or shame into gay pride, for instance) and thereby enabled the movement to sustain over time.

Even as Gould aligns her work with scholarship on the 'emotional turn' in social movements, she notes an inadvertent tendency of scholars in the field to 'rationalize' feelings or to stress their cognitive as opposed to noncognitive dimensions as being more conducive to political action. This close (and slightly defensive) aligning of political feelings with reason has the effect of ignoring how feelings 'frequently diverge from our reasoning selves' (Gould 2009: 23). Rationalist understandings of emotions go together with constructivist models casting aside the 'noncognitive, nonconscious, nonlinguistic, and nonrational aspects of the general phenomenon of emotions' (Gould 2009: 23), or what Gould calls 'affect'. Like many who are writing in the now established and influential field of affect studies, Gould draws on Deleuze and Massumi to define affect as an embodied, non-conscious, pre-discursive, visceral reaction, intensity, or force. Emotion can be thought of as affect that is clearly experienced and communicable in language and within the bounds of social conventions and norms. Affect remains, however, an excess; 'there is always something more than what is actualized in social life' (Gould 2009: 21). This 'something more'—an inarticulate and intense bodily force— is what underlies both our rational and emotional lifeworlds and thereby plays a crucial role in political in/action. In the context of gay and lesbian AIDS activism, Gould speaks of the contradictory and ambivalent feelings that were at play amongst activists, but not at a conscious or cognitive level. These nonconscious and noncognitive dimensions of feelings were central to their sense of themselves, the world they inhabited at that moment, and 'their sense of political possibility' (Gould 2009: 26) in ways that both facilitated and hindered political action.

The *sense* of political possibility is what is at stake in Dave's (2012) story of lesbian activism in India. Taking from this Deleuzian idea of affect as possibility and potentiality, Dave asks: how is it that something previously unthinkable comes to be? How is it, in other words, that normatively unthinkable lesbian existence, desire, and identity come to be experienced and lived as a possibility? In being an indeterminate and unstructured bodily force that is not even manifest in language and not yet subject to social norms, affect serves as such a locus of possibility. This sense of possibility is particularly significant for subaltern politics. Dave uses Baviskar's work on the Narmada Bachao Andolan as an example of how this particular instance of subaltern mobilization made certain imaginings possible, such as 'other worlds where adivasis could be powerful and respected' (Baviskar 2004: 279, cited in Dave 2012: 11). The opening up of such possibilities is also, as Dave shows and as I detail in what follows, the closing of others.

The affective nature of lesbian activism in India turned Dave's attention away from matters of political strategizing and organization, or even 'critical events' like the initial activist success in decriminalizing the anti-sodomy law. What get obscured from such a focus, she says, are the everyday and ordinary affective exercises that constitute activism. Lesbian activism is an ethical practice—born out of affect—that includes the critique of existing norms, the invention of alternative norms, and the actualization of these in order to live differently. In foregrounding spaces of ethics and affect, Dave seems to suggest that activism of this kind is born less out of a sense of righting wrongs than out of a desire and need to imagine and institute new spaces and forms of care, relationality, and sociality, *as queers*. It is these 'structures of feelings' (R. Williams 2011) that propel wider political agendas of combating invisibility and marginalization through an assertion of 'rights'. The latter can, however, be experienced by queer activists as a series of limits against and 'within which dreams of possibility are variously kindled and assimilated' (Dave 2012: 10). Fields of possibilities thus have their own limits.

Limits and Exclusions

Both Kapur (2009, 2012) and Dave (2012) find disruptive *and* inventive possibilities in queer activism in India today, especially in terms of its engagements with the state and the law. While Kapur (2009: 384) makes a standard critique of the regulatory and normalizing tendency of the law which diminishes 'the radical potential of sexual subaltern politics' (see also Biswas 2007), Dave offers a richer, more complex story that is common to the making of all political communities. Stories of invention, she says, are always stories of loss. Her ethnography shows what is lost or foreclosed in the journey from ethical and affective activism to the consolidation of political communities, from the imagined to the real, as she puts it. Just as affect is the mobilizing factor of queer activism and the world it attempts to ethically constitute, what is foreclosed—circumscribed or disciplined in the political attempt to materialize such a world—is also affect or the 'affective space of politics' (Dave 2012: 47). Dave locates 'the production and circumscription of affect' (2012: 36) not merely in struggles for formal rights and equality (vis-à-vis the state and the law), but also in the spaces of support and solidarity that activists themselves create. More broadly and beyond affect, Dave's ethnography maps the struggles or 'limits' that new forms of political possibility and belonging run up against, especially in seeking legitimacy from and entry into the norms and institutions of the postcolonial nation-state.

With respect to queer politics in India, Dave usefully plots the three models that have evolved in the course of its short history. First, one that adheres to a Western model of lesbian identity politics calling on women to identify and interpellate themselves not just as 'lesbian' but as part of a transnational political community based on this identification. Second, the sexual minority support group that is also based on identity, but eschews political mobilization in the name of safety and support. Finally, the collective or platform that consciously moves away from identity to undertake advocacy work in which everyone, regardless of sex, gender, or sexuality, can participate. In all three models, Dave shows how affect was the enabling condition for lesbian community formation, but also how this affective transformation was necessarily curtailed in the process. Very briefly, in privileging political competence and dialogue, the first model foreclosed desire and joy, affects that had served to imagine the possibility of a lesbian community and lifeworld in the first place. Desire and joy were also sublimated in the second 'support group' model that emphasized vulnerability and fear for the sake of safety and support, and distanced itself, in sharp contrast to the first, from the realm of the political. The third model returned from that of the support group 'to highlight sexuality as first and foremost political' (Dave 2012: 92). Unlike the first two that rooted themselves in identity, whether politicized or not, the third 'underst[ood] identity as stripped of affect and as a strategic calculus' (Dave 2012: 92). Affect was once again delinked from activism.

The 'limits' that these forms of queer organization encountered are not merely suggestive of the complicated relationship between politics and emotion, but also of the complexities of mobilizing around (sexual) identity. Dave finds problematic both the support group's *and* the activist platform's attempt to take these complexities head-on. It is fair to say that these two models are paradigmatic of queer organizing in India, those that we shall encounter in my own case study of lesbian politics in this chapter. The sexual minorities support group, which now operates under the aegis of non-governmental organisations (NGOs) in most Indian cities, aims to provide a social and 'safe' space for self-identified sexual minorities to share their experiences freely, without fear of violence (Khanna 2007). It embodies an identitarian logic: it is, Akshay Khanna (2005: 101) says in a critique that recalls Foucault's influential theorization of sexual categorization, 'about the naming of oneself, recognizing oneself within certain terms' (see also Biswas 2007). Identifying oneself as this or that also serves to emphasize commonality and obscure difference—differences of class, caste, and religion—under the sign of 'lesbian' (Dave 2012: 94). For Dave (2012: 75), the social use towards which the space of the support group was put was premised on a particular understanding of lesbian subjectivity—as being 'the "raw", unpoliticized Indian woman who simply desires other women and has no ambitions for a politics around that desire'.

In sharp contrast, the activist platform moves away from the support group's identity politics model towards one of intersectionality, the custodian of which is the properly political activist. It includes the likes of Sappho for Equality (discussed presently), and the Delhi-based PRISM that Dave refers to and that Khanna helped found. By virtue of the fact that such platforms are open to all—they are 'identity-neutral' and not 'identity-based', as one of my interviewees put it—they create a collective ownership of sexuality as not simply affecting homosexuals 'with no apparent implications for "other" people', but as affecting 'all of us regardless of our sexual orientation' (Narrain and Bhan 2005: 4). The existence of a platform that includes queer and non-queer people also blurs the boundaries of who belongs and who is the appropriate subject of a queer politics (N. Menon 2007). Dave (2012: 94) is, however, quick to underscore the limits and costs of delinking, in this manner, queer activism from identity, 'the primary shaping mechanism of gay and lesbian life'. She speaks of the discomforts and disquiets that activists expressed with a nonidentitarian platform as circumscribing their vision of politics, which was centrally about affective and ethical ties: 'politics was for them intrinsically about love, care and connection; about using the fact of queer marginality as a reason to invent new ways to be' (Dave 2012: 96).

Both the activist platform and the support group were based on sharp divisions between social and political spaces and those who could and could not participate in a public queer activism. These reflect deeper internal divisions of class and accessibility, suggesting that some sexual subalterns are more subaltern than others in terms of their (in)ability to participate in political process and be intelligible (see also Dutta 2012; Alok Gupta 2005). Such divisions and exclusions—that reflect if not replicate existing social division—are not particular to lesbian activism in India. Central to Dave's point about the necessarily limited nature of such 'organized activism' (Ram 2008) is its differential market value, as determined by local and transnational, community and state imperatives, and that posits particular challenges to sexual subaltern politics as affective and ethical practice (see also Dutta 2012).

Sappho

The (forced) divisions between affect and activism, and correspond-ingly between social and political spaces, are key to the instance of lesbian activism that is the focus of my ethnography. A prominent Kolkata-based lesbian organization and the only one of its kind in eastern India, Sappho was started by six middle-class Bengali women on 20 June 1999 as an 'emotional support group' for sexual minority women (Akanksha and Malobika 2007). While Sappho continues to provide a 'safe space' for lesbian, bisexual, and trans-gender women, Sappho for Equality or SFE was started in 2003 as a registered NGO that functions as a locus of the organization's activism and outreach. SFE fulfils the founder members' belief in the need for the support of the wider (heterosexual) community in its struggle for sexual citizenship, and represents a shift from service provision to issue-based 'activism'. It is the public face of the organization, and through its public awareness-raising pro-grammes, such as running a queer film festival and being a part of one of Kolkata's most prominent cultural activities, the annual Boi Mela or Book Fair, it has become part of the weave of the cul-tural-political life of the city. Members of Sappho are automatically members of SFE, but not the other way round. Several SFE mem-bers are critical to the survival of the organization as a whole, given that it is their voluntary labour that runs a range of activities from advocacy to providing counselling services. The need for a 'safe space' not open to 'non-community' members, however, persists.

Sappho embodies, in this way, two common strands of the queer movement in India—one that links sexuality to identity (the sup-port group) and one that attempts to break this very association (the activist platform). The separation between the two echoes sev-eral of the divides, exclusions, and limits that Dave finds in early lesbian groups and that I detail in what follows. For the moment, let me note that the existence and functioning of SFE is inseparable from that of a transnational, institutionalized queer activism that is contingent on India's globalization and a broader history of neo-liberalism. Unlike comparable platforms like PRISM that eschewed external funds, it is funded by international donors. Its steady but fairly aggressive expansion over a short period of time reflects the manner in which activist worth is determined by the 'ability to penetrate farther and larger realms of influence' (Dave 2012: 29). Several members of Sappho—who invariably use the name as a shorthand for both Sappho and SFE, especially given the majority's belonging to both—inhabit an economically liberalized India, and owe their visibility and activism to the political configurations that this made possible, whether through the international funding 'boom' or the globalizing of the media. Although largely women of means, they are best described as middle or lower middle class and not elite; many come from surrounding suburban areas, and the majority are more comfortable speaking Bengali than English.

The Affective Scope of Sappho

In an article about the 'journey' of Sappho, Akanksha and Malobika (2007: 363), the current directors and founder members of the organization, write of the moment of its inception on a summer day in 1999:

> Two to four, four to six, six lesbians in the heart of the city of Calcutta exchanging laughter and tears—who had thought such a day would come in our lives? When we would be able to speak our minds freely without fear or shame, share jokes with people of a similar mindset? ... The basic urge to meet our social needs led us to getting in touch with another couple in the same city.

As with much of their larger corpus of writing, including a published volume of life stories of lesbian women (and interviews with me), this piece of writing is saturated with affect. It forms part of an emergent archive of same-sex love in this part of the country—'an archive of feelings', as Cvetkovich (2003) calls gay and lesbian archives—which Sappho is proactively building as part of its outreach work. A small part of this archive, the quotation reproduced here serves to voice the 'structures of feelings' (R. Williams 1977)—the inchoate, at times articulable urges, drives, desires, and needs—that formed the basis of lesbian identity formation and community building and eventually, of political mobilization. It articulates, in other words, the affective dimensions of politicization and of political organizing—how individuals felt about themselves, what brought them together and shaped their sense of political possibility (Gould 2009).

What is striking in the quotation is the use of the words 'fear' and 'shame' in relation to speaking openly about same-sex love and desire. The ability to 'speak our minds freely without fear or shame' suggests that an affective transformation occurs when subalterns come together. This is especially significant for subaltern groups, given that the affective underpinnings of subalternity as fear and shame are instrumental to keeping subalterns in their place, on the margins, without voice. Such a transformation is also fundamental to making it possible for subaltern groups to imagine 'other worlds' in which they can be assertive, proud, powerful, and openly defiant of existing power structures. Affective transformations—of shame to gay pride, as Gould (2002, 2009) has documented—can thus act as a major impulse towards the formation of a collective 'we' based on a shared sense of victimization and an emergent sense of political possibility. However, the last line of the quote—'the basic urge to meet our social needs led us to getting in touch with another couple in the same city'—posits affective needs as the most basic impulse that drives sexual subalterns towards building some kind of collective. It voices the need for relationality, care, and sociality that Dave (2012) finds central to a queer politics of invention given the solitude, secrecy, and unknowability within which same-sex love is generally lived.

The support group is, par excellence, the constituted space for affective recognition and transformation. Members explain its functionality through the trope of 'coming out':

> Membership of Sappho itself is a form of 'coming out' for a lot of women. The organization supports and encourages the coming out process. They consider it a sort of mental preparation to put everything at risk—a form of self-consciousness and empowerment. Empowerment does not, however, mean a final declaration but a step-by-step process in coming out of the closet and the mental preparation that is needed to do this. 'Coming out' addresses the internalized fear and homophobia that queer people have. Sappho sees as its first task the development of individual self-confidence

which can then spread on a more mass scale.... . Once more and more girls started to come to Sappho and began to share their life stories then there was a realization that they cannot tackle the root cause by crying on another's shoulders. So Sappho evolved from being an emotional service provider to taking an activist stance [in SFE]. (Interview with Sappho member)

In understanding 'coming to' Sappho as a process of 'coming out', the quote voices the identitarian logic behind the working of support groups, or the manner in which they act as communal spaces for interpellation into lesbian identity. Belonging to the support group is determined by sexual identity; it excludes, as already noted, those who do not identify as lesbian or bisexual, as well as men. The imperative to fix otherwise fluid identities into nameable categories—and thereby reinstate the hetero/homo dichotomy that 'queer' attempts to deconstruct—is the reason why at least two members have chosen not to join Sappho and are only members of SFE. Yet the fluidity of such identities persists in the everyday life of queer activism, observable in the manner in which some members of SFE consequently became members of Sappho. Even as the support group essentializes sexual identity, its actual functioning—especially the stretching of boundaries to include those who previously did not identify with such an identity—conveys the performativity of identities.

In addressing the internalized fear and homophobia that sexual subalterns might have, and in facilitating their transformation into self-confidence and self-loving, 'coming out' is a process that is based on the kinds of affective transformations previously described. Activists at Sappho clearly understand that such emotion work lies at the heart of their political mobilization. It would, however, seem that affect is not considered to be an adequate foundation of a politics that challenges the structures of power that heteronormativity rests on. Affective responses like 'sharing' and 'crying over one's shoulder' are posited, at least in this quote, as inadequate to addressing the 'root' or underlying cause of individual marginalization. With the expansion of lesbian activism—in the entry of more girls—a properly political response is required. Activist politics, in SFE, is presented as an example of

'growth' over the support group model (Dave 2012: 91), of responding to wider, more collective, and more fundamental needs and not
merely emotional or affective ones.

From Private Struggle to Public Emergence: Sappho to SFE

In contrast to Sappho, SFE is imaginatively constituted as the space
for legitimate politics, the custodian of which is the publicly visible activist. The journey from Sappho, the support group, to SFE,
the activist platform, can be understood as one from the private to
the public/political: from the private realm of secrecy and safety to
a realm of public visibility, risk, and recognition. This is the same
story that Dave (2012: 140) tells of the 'public emergence' of lesbian
activism in India post the critical event of *Fire*. This emergence
crystallized at the confluence of two processes—the response to
the backlash of heteronormative hegemony as articulated through
Hindutva, and the increased market value of lesbian activism in
transnational advocacy networks.[1] The attainment of lesbian visibility became a political goal post *Fire*, enabling a new subjectivity
for the Indian lesbian, that of the activist (Dave 2012: 140).

One of the founder members, Akanksha (2009: 2), explains the
rationale for the 'public emergence' of lesbian activism in SFE in
the following ways:

> Just sticking together within a community based support group
> would never sensitize general people to overcome all the hostili-
> ties and hesitations against homosexuals, lesbians in particular. The
> social, legal and political space for a woman with same-sex prefer-
> ence would never be achieved by restricting ourselves to a support
> group. It would only replicate the dynamics of a ghetto. This belief
> led us to create the platform, Sappho for Equality, where anyone
> who supports our cause can join irrespective of gender and sexual
> orientation. Thus a shift from identity based politics to a politics of
> standpoint marked our journey from Sappho to Sappho for Equality.

The expansion and public emergence of lesbian activism is here predicated on a stagist model of political mobilization, as progressing, in

other words, from one model of politics to another. The inadequacy of the support group, most clearly encapsulated in its description as a 'ghetto', necessitates political progression to a universal and inclusive model of queer empowerment. These two models reflect a binary way of thinking about politics and activism—one based on affect and identity with the imperative to change subaltern subjectivity, and another which employs the language of universality in terms of political practice (human rights, equality) and subjects ('everyone'). Finally, the two distinct domains of politics that are carved out in the course of political expansion presume two distinct constituents whose needs they seek to represent and respond to: lesbians who could afford public visibility and manage the risks it brought through political competence and activism, and those who could or would not, preferring to desire the same sex in the privacy of silence and secrecy (see Dave 2012).

In many of my conversations with members with regard to the division between Sappho and SFE, its necessity was explained by evoking these two imagined constituencies. Their distinction was based on various criteria: being closeted or 'coming out', being interested in politics or being disinterested, and being only involved in personal as opposed to public/political struggles. When compared to the publicly visible lesbian activist, Sappho members are rendered 'closeted lesbians', even as their coming to Sappho is described by the trope of 'coming out', as I previously noted. The very formation of SFE, Akanksha says, freed community members 'from the burden of carrying dual identities'. At the same time, the continued existence of Sappho protects those who prefer secrecy to the public visibility entailed in the expansion of lesbian activism. In some—but certainly not all—discussions, closeted lesbians were also identified as *gramer meyera*, rural lesbian subjects, suggestive of a distinct middle-class flavour to this emphasis on public visibility in 'coming out'.[2]

Above all, the distinction between Sappho and SFE was based on presumptions about varying levels of political investment if not competence. As one of the founder members I interviewed explained: 'not everyone does or understands activism'. Another younger member said: 'not all are interested in issues, activism, or in discussing homonationalism. For some, it's more important to work through personal issues than discuss homonationalism.' The personal and the political were clearly sequestered in these conversations about the need for a divide between Sappho and SFE: 'The Sunday meeting is personal unlike Thursday meeting which is political.'

Removed from the realm of proper politics, the space of the 'Sunday meeting' was linked, by these interviewees, to informality, socializing, care, and *adda* (informal discussion), all signifiers of the personal. Correspondingly, the space of SFE or the 'Thursday meeting' (which occupies, in fact, the same physical space as the Sunday meeting) was associated with the attainment of wider public good/interest, subsequent to the personal struggle with the self. Some SFE members spoke of attempts to discipline desire in its everyday functioning as well as anxieties around the excess of desire, expressed in the assertion that we are not a 'sex club' and that the office space is not one for enacting sexual desire. Disciplining desire is effected through the setting up of implicit expectations and norms. The annual three-day residential workshop, where members are taken to a location outside of Kolkata for discussion and debate, is one example. Even though it was acknowledged by members that this might be the first opportunity for some individuals to stay overnight with their partners, it was made clear that the workshop was not a space for romancing. Coupledom, it was stressed in defence, should not take precedence over friendship and community building. This is partly a way of showing sensitivity to those who are single, especially given that many of the core members of at least SFE are couples. It would be too easy to say that the disciplining of desire occurs in an entirely unreflexive manner, especially for such a self-aware lesbian organization that understands the politics of desire as central to its activism. It is perhaps best to express this tension in the manner of one of my interviewees, an SFE member, who says: 'Sappho [used as a shorthand for both Sappho and SFE] does not fully repress the play mode but it does police [it].'

Affective Politics, Through and Through

Even as this instance of lesbian activism provides an expansive understanding of politics—as not being about rational action and strategy alone, but centrally about feelings—its public emergence and expansion circumscribed the boundaries of 'the political' in specific ways. In the organizational speak behind the setting up of SFE as not only distinct from but as an advancement over the support group, politics is understood in fairly normative terms as manifest in public and risky activism, and as prompted by universal ideals and values to which anyone can be 'hailed'. The organizational divide between Sappho and SFE presumes and reinforces a series of other divisions in preserving the boundaries of 'the political'—between emotion and activism, the personal and the political, social and political spaces, closeted and 'out' identities. However, organization members whom I interviewed emphasized and troubled these divisions. Even as they regurgitated the normative view of politics that the organization had made materially available in SFE, they destabilized it by attaching it to the personal and the affective. They reclaimed politics in their own terms, as being about the self, personal feelings, needs, and emotions, rather than the pursuit of some abstract public good. Concomitantly, as I show in this final discussion, divisions between emotion and politics and the personal and the political were also rendered unstable in the everyday instantiation of queer activism within a network of care, relationality, friendship, and desire. Both the practices and processes associated with the political, in Sappho and SFE, can be understood as affective politics, 'through and through' (Dave 2012: 4), even as they are subsumed under normative ideas of activism and politics as being stripped of affect.

While interviewees associated the 'Sunday meeting' with affective attachment, or simply 'emotion', they emphasized how activism was impossible without any kind of emotional investment. Emotion, one said, 'works in movement ... emotion is required for movement'. Another stressed that political and emotional spaces are interlinked, and that 'Sappho needs both as they need Sappho'. 'The political' also became a broader, unstable category in their conversations with me, inevitably becoming something intimate and personal. One interviewee says: 'The facing of personal struggles is also movement. A lot of us would say we are not interested in politics but all of us are involved in politics, at home, in *ghor-shongshar* [household], in office.' Several interviewees explained their politicization in Sappho in terms of the changed nature of their engagement with their personal troubles, such as how to negotiate pressures (of marriage) from the family, how to respond to teasing and taunting in the *para* (neighbourhood), and how to effectively face questioning around gender and sexual identity in paid work. Sappho had provided, they said, a language by which to explain their identity and difference to intimate and not-so-intimate others ('if people look at me in a certain way then I can answer them through Sappho'). Sappho had enabled them to speak, as a way out of sexual subalternity.

What was also obvious in these responses was that such queer politicization takes place as much informally as it does formally under the remit of SFE and the study circles it runs. Indeed, it is the support group that provides the context for informal consciousness-raising amidst adda and socializing, without which an engagement with the wider politics of hegemonic heteronormativity would not be possible. One interviewee explains her first encounter with Sappho as arriving at a Thursday meeting with her partner and being told by an older member to come on a Sunday instead. Had it been the other way around, she says that she would not have understood the language around 'heteronormativity'. She describes the 'urge' to meet others, to understand and to 'get into activism', as emerging from the familiarity and kinship of the Sunday (Sappho) meeting. These changes in her feelings appear to form the bedrock of her engagement with wider and more universal issues to do with subalternization on the basis of sexual identity. But without the former—without the ability to be moved—there would, she seems to suggest, scarcely be any activism or politics at all.

Politicization was also explained affectively in terms of the gaining in self-esteem or self-confidence besides the ability to speak. In facilitating 'comfort' and 'bonding', in the words of one member, Sappho enables self-recognition and ultimately self-transformation; 'that's also activism,' she says. Interviewees plot their narratives as moving from self-ambivalence (if not rejection) to self-recognition, and eventually to confidence and pride in oneself. This struggle with the self takes place through informal and affective practices such as the sharing of feelings, the exchange of stories, adda, friendship, and *prem* (love), and finally, through self-recognition in a community of 'people like me'. It is these affective transformations that enable the fighting of the kinds of private battles described earlier.

So, for 'community members', the political struggle begins in a highly personalized and intimate fashion. But this is true for SFE members as well who may or may not identify as part of the community. In my earliest interviews with them, they centred affect—particularly passion—as the basis of their political involvement. As I have detailed elsewhere (S. Roy 2011), they explained their involvement in terms of 'passion', as that which is motivated from within or 'inside' even as it is directed towards the public good. The articulation of politics as 'passion' given its voluntary nature was also an attempt to distance it from paid or professionalized NGO work. Passion was thus repeatedly distinguished from 'profession'. This expressed affective attachment to activism in SFE suggests the following: that the rise of funded politics complicates divisions between the public and private, and the political and affective, insofar as it affords the possibility of fusing public good and private self-interest. But it is also this wider context of the professionalization of activism under neoliberalism that entails its 'scaling up' from the private/emotional to the public/universal and the circumscription of the boundaries of the political therein.

Finally, the proper work of politics was also recreated through ties of friendship, informality, fun, and socializing. The fact that the 'Thursday meeting is also a space for adda and socializing', as one of my interviewees put it, was quickly apparent in my observations of several of these meetings (I am not able to attend Sunday meetings as I am only a member of SFE and not Sappho). The meetings standardly proceed by discussion around the upcoming events and activities that SFE is involved in, including allocating roles and responsibility for various tasks to those who are present, seated on the floor in a circle. On days when there is no pending event to plan (increasingly rare given the expansion of activities and events), there is indeed discussion of 'heavy' issues, ranging from whether queer politics is a 'lifestyle politics' to those of class and accessibility. Interspersed with political planning and intellectual discussion is much banter, camaraderie, and even flirting, helped by the circulation of chai and snacks which members bring along. One of the meetings I observed included a newly joined young butch lesbian who sat quietly in one corner of the room. Opposite her and right next to me sat one of my interviewees, a pretty young thing, munching on *moori* (puffed rice) and half listening to the discussion at hand and half playing with her phone. For the greater part of the meeting, the two exchanged glances, smiles, and eventually gestures indicating the need for phone numbers. No doubt these silent expressions of desire were fully expressed at the close of the meeting, when members invariably linger on, catch up with their queer families, friends, and actual and potential lovers. The promise of what Dave (2012) calls an 'alternative sociality', key to the inventive practice of affective lesbian activism, is here fulfilled inadvertently, outside of the design and function of the support group.

The thoroughly affective dimensions of the subaltern sexual politics under discussion in this chapter make it an unstable and contingent formation; its effects cannot be anticipated in advance. Subaltern mobilizing around sexuality can be inventive in constituting for sexual subalterns a sense of political possibility or a political horizon, as Gould (2009) calls it. It can equally be normative in directing if not policing the very 'structures of feeling' that enabled this sense of political possibility in the first place. The circumscription of the political in this manner is partly responsive to a wider context of the increased market value of such activism, but also for the sake of inserting sexual subalterns into a normative and hegemonic political project that is rational, universal, public. The constitution of SFE as separate from and an advancement over Sappho responds to these pressures in part through the containment of the thoroughly affective dimension of lesbian activism—its imbrication with subjectivity, intimacy, desire, and care—in a 'safe space'. But this containment remains always already incomplete and contested. In my conversations with organization members and observations of their time at Sappho, affect functioned as an excess interrupting and destabilizing the binary imaginary and organization of activism. It drew attention to deeply intimate, subjective, embodied, and unconscious dimension of such activism which could account for its unpredictable and potentially transformative potential. Most importantly, it centred how politics feels, appeals, moves, and transforms us, without an appreciation of which it would not be intelligible at all. Instead of mobilizing in order to insert sexual subalterns into the political as it exists, this instance of lesbian activism offers a significant site for the expansion and transformation of the political especially through its embrace of affect.

Notes

1. The short history of the queer movement in India is part of the history of neoliberalism in this part of the world and the attendant professionalization of activism in the 1990s. Dave's point about the expansion of the scope of lesbian activism in terms of its market value also explains the transnational funds available for the setting up of SFE and its continual growth and expansion.

2. What such discussions also elide are the forms of sexual subalternity that are always and already 'out', and how public visibility in such instances is a marker of vulnerability and not empowerment. Dutta (2012: 137) mentions, as one example of the differential treatment of elite and non-elite queer subjects, how SFE chooses not to be part of the annual Kolkata Rainbow Pride given the objectification and commodification of queer identities in mainstream media. While he is sympathetic to their reasoning, he draws attention to the fact that many kothis and hijras have used the space of the Pride 'precisely to foreground their embodied difference that the dominant activist discourse seeks to control by relegating it to the realm of personal gender expression'.

III

Caste and Community
in Civil/Political Society

7

Theorizing Thervoy

Subaltern Studies *and Dalit Praxis in India's Land Wars*

LUISA STEUR

> The Secretary of Industry for the Government of Tamil Nadu prom-
> ised to construct roads, schools, even a primary health centre in
> return for our land. But isn't it our fundamental right to be provided
> with such basic facilities? Our land need not be taken by the govern-
> ment in exchange for the delivery of 'welfare schemes'!
> —Public statement by Thervoy Struggle Committee, 14 July 2011[1]

Except to the most neoclassical of economists believing in capitalism as an idyllic balancing act of supply and demand, it is no
secret that 'the methods of primitive accumulation are anything
but idyllic' (Marx 1990: 874). The history of world capitalism
is ridden with the violence of accumulation by dispossession
(Harvey 2003), much of which has centred on land. Without turning neoliberalism into an exception or denying how the seeds of
neoliberalism were already planted by the Nehruvian postcolonial state (Neveling 2014), there is, however, something specific
about the 'land wars' (Levien 2013) in India today. Indeed, land

dispossession also happened under the state-developmentalist 'regime of dispossession' (Levien 2013), but the overriding aim then was that of production and, through it, national development. In neoliberal India, land dispossession happens more deliberately for the market with financial growth as the overriding concern and local development as an afterthought in order to manage the impact of dispossession. A key text in Subaltern Studies that has captured this shift is Partha Chatterjee's 'Democracy and Economic Transformation in India' (2008), which this chapter will draw on extensively. The case that allows us to refine Chatterjee's analysis empirically is that of the Thervoy land struggle,[2] where, as the epigraph indicates, those under threat of dispossession were less than enthusiastic about participating in the neoliberal game of dispossession-for-benefits.

Chatterjee's 2008 article is one of the most recent contributions to the Subaltern Studies project and proposes a framework for the study of agrarian change and peasant politics in contemporary India that both transcends and reproduces the template of the original Subaltern Studies project. Since coming out in India's foremost left-leaning intellectual magazine *Economic and Political Weekly*, the article has inspired a lot of debate and received many critical responses already (most immediately, Baviskar and Sundar 2008; John and Deshpande 2008; M. Shah 2008; see also Sinha, this volume). As this chapter will show, it however remains a text that is productive to 'think with—or against' (John and Deshpande 2008: 83).

This chapter engages with Chatterjee's argument in three parts. In the first section of the chapter, I focus on Chatterjee's analysis of 'peasant society' in India today and how it is changing. Chatterjee analyses how non-agricultural livelihoods have become a major part of rural life and argues that many small and marginal farmers—and all the more those who know the village as a place of caste oppression—have started to want to stop being peasants altogether. Looking at the Thervoy case, I demonstrate the relevance of Chatterjee's analysis of the social forces changing peasant society. I also argue, however, that villagers can politically re-articulate what caste and agriculture mean in village India, and that they are likely to do so as the attractions of city life appear more imaginary than real in neoliberal India. In the second section, I come to the core of Chatterjee's argument about the hegemony of primitive accumulation and the multiplication of governmental technologies aimed at reversing its effects that result in most subaltern politics taking place in the realm of 'political society'. There, peasants compete for state benefits and accuse the government of discrimination but do not affect the logic of the overall system. Chatterjee's argument is useful in capturing the structural logics that Thervoy activists found themselves up against, but also has its limitations. Activists saw the attempted restriction of their claims to political society as an elite strategy to contain their struggle. In practice, therefore, activists often transgress the binary between civil society and political society in search of emancipatory goals. Having argued in the first two sections that it is important to pay more attention to emergent political possibilities, the third section looks at why such political possibility may not come to be realized. In Chatterjee's analysis, there is a shift towards consent in the balance of consent and coercion that forms the hegemony of corporate capital in India. Through governmental programmes, peasants are being given a stake in the neoliberal development path. Drawing on the insights gained by Thervoy activists through their struggle, I argue instead that policy regimes that ameliorate the impacts of primitive accumulation may not be primarily about creating consent, but also about disarticulating and disorganizing subaltern resistance. To develop the argument emerging from the encounter of Chatterjee's analytical framework and the Thervoy land struggle, I end each section with a short theoretical reflection.

With this general argument, let me now offer a brief introduction to the Thervoy struggle. The village of Thervoy-Kandigai lies in Gummidipoondi district on the periphery of 'greater Chennai', about 50 kilometres north of the city. The area around the village is predominantly agricultural, but nearer to the main road there are all kinds of firms, from industrial plants to private educational institutions. The village itself has about 5,000 inhabitants, most of whom are Dalits (Scheduled Castes—mostly Paraiyar). On one side of the Dalit colony there is the large, 1,127-acre area of land that had for generations been commonly maintained by the Thervoy Dalits and used to collect forest products and graze cattle. The forest area also functioned as a water catchment area for the Dalit villagers' agricultural production on land held privately on the other side of the village. In line with Tamil Nadu's 'Vision 2023' policy document calling for 'global leadership' of the 'Tamil Nadu brand' in the auto/auto components industry, this area of land became the target of the State Industries Promotion Corporation of Tamil Nadu (SIPCOT) to establish an industrial park that would host Michelin, the French multinational tyre manufacturer. Thervoy villagers only learnt about these plans when reading about it in 2007 in a local newspaper. From there started a long process of organizing protest against the land grab, in which Dalit villagers used every possible tactic from hunger strikes to petitions, demonstrations, and marches, organizing scientific studies of the environmental and human rights impact of the industrial park, appealing to the collector, political parties, media, the National Human Rights Commission, and other government bodies, and putting the case before the courts. By January 2009, large-scale demolition of the forest at the site started. In May 2009 a stay order on demolitions was issued by the high court, but only for three months; afterwards, construction proceeded as before even though issues of compensation and human rights and environmental impact were still far from settled. In November 2009, the official memorandum of understanding between Michelin and the Tamil Nadu government was signed for what was to become the biggest tyre factory in the world. By August 2010, construction of the tyre factory had started, and Thervoy villagers had started to feel the impact, particularly in the drying up of their agricultural fields. Michelin already planned to officially inaugurate the plant in November 2012, by when indeed the factory building was a fait accompli. By January 2014, four of the six tyre assembly lines were already in operation, and Thervoy villagers were bitterly growing used to seeing the factory as a permanent reality. As they have been refusing to give their official consent (their 'no-objection certificate'), however, the official inauguration of the plant is still being postponed.

I will of course not be able to tell the full story of the Thervoy struggle in this chapter. Instead I focus on three aspects where the praxis of Thervoy activists helps us get a sharper understanding of the political possibility and hegemony involved in India's land wars. Firstly, I describe how, despite the imagined attractions of the city and the desire to move away from caste discrimination that Chatterjee analyses as part of changing peasant society, Thervoy activists managed to reinterpret Dalit identity as a claim to rural belonging and pride in sustainable agricultural work. Secondly, I look at how, despite the way governmental institutions try to restrict them to Chatterjee's 'political society', Thervoy activists break out of this confinement and manage to articulate a vision of local development to confront the hegemony of neoliberal accumulation by dispossession. And finally, I describe activists' experience with some of the 'ethical' mechanisms that Chatterjee sees as part of the maturation of hegemony, where consent becomes more important than coercion to keep peasant society in line with neoliberal development. In fact, activists' experience with corporate social responsibility (CSR) made them even *less* willing to consent to their dispossession. I argue that rather than create consent, CSR's main use for the corporate–state alliance was to undermine the effectiveness of the resistance.

Changing Political Imaginaries of Caste and Agriculture in Village India

Chatterjee's (2008: 53) analysis of economic transformation and democracy in India starts with an important reflection on 'peasant society today' that stresses that the classic model of peasant insurgency, where the peasantry is seen as tied to the land, practising small-scale agriculture, and united in a local rural community by cultural and moral bonds while resisting an external state, is no longer appropriate. This classic model would invoke 'a long tradition of anthropological studies of peasant societies' (Chatterjee 2008: 54) focusing on 'characteristic forms of dependence of peasant economies' and 'forms of autonomy of peasant cultures', as well as Marxist analysis of the inevitable dissolution of the peasantry as a result of the process of primitive accumulation of capital, including Gramscian analysis of the contradictory consciousness of the peasantry (being both dominated by and resistant to elite culture). Chatterjee does not give more specific references here, except summing up that the more classical way in which one could have looked at rural agitations before would be in terms of the analysis provided in Ranajit Guha's (1983) *Elementary Aspects of Peasant Insurgency in Colonial India*. This analysis, however, would be 'inappropriate today' (Chatterjee 2008: 54): the spread of governmental technologies, for instance, means there is no entity external to the peasant community any more, and the structure of agrarian property—and taxation—has changed such that small peasants are not necessarily subjected to an exploitative class in the village any longer, nor to an extractive state. Moreover, with rapid urbanization, many peasants shift to non-agricultural occupations not only when forcibly separated from the land but often as a voluntary choice shaped by new desires and new perceived opportunities. For lower-caste youth, the desire to move away from village India is not only, Chatterjee argues, fed by the disadvantages of class but also by the discriminations of caste, 'compared to which the sheer anonymity of life in the city is often seen as liberating' (Chatterjee 2008: 54). For a majority of agricultural labourers who are from Dalit communities, 'the desired future is to move out of the traditional servitude of rural labour into urban non-agricultural occupations' (Chatterjee 2008: 54).

The desired future in the city does not, however, translate into a linear rural-to-urban migration. In fact, the entire narrative of transition, in which primitive accumulation eventually sunders the organic unity of labour and the means of labour, and where the free labour thus created moves to the cities, does not apply. This is, as Chatterjee argues, because the city cannot productively integrate the rural surplus population, but also because there are a host of government agencies providing welfare and developmental benefits in rural areas.[3] Hence, even though in many Indian states today almost half of the rural population is engaged in non-agricultural occupations, these governmental policies discourage an outright rural out-migration as they become an integral part of peasant livelihood strategies (Chatterjee 2008: 59).

A Dalit Claim to Agriculture

Let us see whether the radical transformations in peasant culture and politics that Chatterjee detects can help us understand how resistance to the industrial park set up on the Dalit communal land of Thervoy took shape. We can start by noting that the village of Thervoy indeed does not fit a classical moral economy type of peasant community. In fact, it never did: since the early twentieth century, there have been strong urban links as many Dalit villagers were labourers in the Chennai port. Today, many Thervoy Dalit youth are highly educated, and one even has a PhD. The Thervoy Dalits also, however, have pride in working the lands around the village, which they themselves own. They generally fused an urban connection with a persistent attachment to land, both in terms of livelihoods and identification.

A certain disdain for rural life and agricultural livelihoods—and a consequent desire to move away from it—had, however, emerged amongst a group of Thervoy villagers (about 10 per cent), who had obtained highly successful jobs in Chennai and who had moved to live in the city. Many of these new urbanites still owned land in Thervoy and maintained a large say in village affairs. It was precisely this urban clique who were most easily convinced by SIPCOT that the industrial park would 'develop' the area and bring the kind of benefits expected from a developmental state—quality education, a road facilitating travel to and from Chennai, and industrial employment opportunities. These 'creamy layer' Dalits were also aware that the industrial park might attract 'satellite' companies to set up near the park, hence making the price of land in the area rise. In anticipation, some landowners around Thervoy had already started demarcating their own lands to offer them for sale to potential buyers.

The communal land that was targeted by the state for the construction of the industrial park had already been signed off by the panchayat president before the members of the *grama* (village) panchayat—the most participatory, direct-democratic local body in the Indian system of governance—had even heard of the project. The panchayat president at the time was someone from the urban 'creamy layer' clique, and had organized the necessary signatures with the story that this was an initiative to resolve long-standing conflicts between Thervoy and other surrounding villages over the distribution of water. It turned out there were also strong political party links involved—the leadership of the Dravida Munnetra

Kazhagam (DMK) (one of the two major political parties in Tamil Nadu) had private interests in the industrial park, and the panchayat president belonged to the DMK.

Chatterjee's analysis of the new culture and politics of peasant society helps us recognize clearly the urban connections and desires and the new political preoccupation with negotiating development benefits that shaped the initial response of Thervoy to the land acquisition. Yet, though Thervoy exhibited many of the features that Chatterjee finds to be typical of contemporary rural India, the villagers were not willing to go down the path of bargaining with the state for benefits in return for giving up their communal land. What changed the scenario is the connection that emerged over time between the Thervoy villagers and the Integrated Rural Development Society (IRDS)—a Dalit non-governmental organization (NGO) based in Villapuram, a district south of Chennai.

In the course of time, many NGOs came through Thervoy, for instance to try to incorporate the Thervoy case into a wider platform to fight against the policy of special economic zones, but also to provide services to entice the villagers to join a project of 'ethical industrialization'. The IRDS, however, connected most organically with the Thervoy villagers, who since the beginning had suspected this was an issue of the state targeting Dalit lands for easy acquisition. As one of the activists pointed out to the media, there was already an industrial park in the district that had been set up earlier and was now lying vacant: 'why don't they open the new companies there which have better infrastructure facilities and a national highway rather than build a SEZ [special economic zone] in Thervoy which does not even boast of proper buses? The main reason is to destroy Dalit villages' (*Indian Express*, 24 January 2009).

Still in line with Chatterjee's analysis, the dominant frame for interpreting what was going on was indeed that of *discrimination*.[4] Though the IRDS's experience (see Nagappan 2012) was mainly with the struggle of reclaiming the *panchami* lands,[5] what appealed especially to the villagers was the IRDS's commitment to uniting Dalit communities in struggles over land. The IRDS activists initially got in contact with Thervoy villagers as there was a common emotional outrage about the fact that Dalit lands were being grabbed by the state—a situation that the IRDS activists

New Subaltern Politics

had become aware of through media coverage of protests that had been staged by Thervoy villagers. Several such local, largely spontaneous protests erupted in Thervoy, for instance in January 2009 when earth-digging machines and heavy equipment were brought into the area by SIPCOT to demolish the forest, and 61 protestors were arrested and held in jail before being released on conditional bail. At one such protest, several IRDS activists also got arrested, which pushed IRDS as an organization to become more closely involved in the Thervoy struggle. It was also felt that a new front had to be opened in the Dalit land struggle to counter the aggressive drive of the Tamil Nadu government to acquire land—and especially communally held Dalit land—to attract foreign investors. Thervoy villagers opposing the industrial park hence found a lot of practical and intellectual support in the IRDS, from legal support, to being introduced to channels to communicate their attempts to safeguard the land of their ancestors to a larger public.

Besides the emotional appeal and practical support, the IRDS's involvement in Thervoy also, however, started the process of re-politicizing Dalit identity, which makes the Thervoy villagers' case deviate from the scenario described by Chatterjee, precisely because of the importance of the connections to urban activist circles. Initially the IRDS had followed the more essentialist, emotive reading of Dalit identity that had existed among the villagers and that had been the trend in the 1990s, creating the necessary confidence and solidarity amongst socially oppressed and ostracized groups. However, IRDS activists had also run into the problem that this interpretation of Dalit identity at times led to the reproduction of caste. In Thervoy, the emotional response of Dalit villagers to the 'grabbing of Dalit land' did not invite solidarity from the surrounding, non-Dalit villages in the area where generally suspicion and vigilance reigned because of a historical conflict over water existing between the villages. Emphasizing the Thervoy struggle as a Dalit struggle was bound to further isolate Thervoy and facilitate a divide-and-rule strategy to counter the mobilization.

The IRDS and the Thervoy Dalits hence started rethinking the ideological framing of the land struggle.[6] Over the course of two years of intense meetings and debates, a shift became clearly observable: IRDS activists started talking of how an overly identity-focused appeal to 'Dalitness' could reproduce a deep-seated caste reflex that they ought to overcome, while Thervoy Dalit activists organized a campaign to reach out to neighbouring villages and discuss issues jointly. Thereby, when the news started circulating in 2012 of yet another, even bigger, intervention in the water levels in the area (in the form of a government plan to redirect the Krishna River), government-sponsored divide-and-rule-type rumours that this was to benefit Thervoy at the expense of neighbouring villages had little local appeal. Instead a resolve emerged amongst the different villages to resist such plans collectively.

Dalit identity was also reinterpreted in terms of what it meant to be Dalit in rural India. What Chatterjee calls the 'voluntary choice' seen amongst Dalit youth today to move away from village India was turned on its head by Thervoy and IRDS activists: rather than being encouraged, in the name of the myth of liberation from casteism, to run after often meaningless city jobs and acquire at most a foothold in some city slum, Dalit youth at Thervoy were encouraged to claim the choice of actually staying meaningfully connected to the land. As the activists put it in their online letter published in *Countercurrents* on 14 July 2011: 'If all rural agriculture land was industrialised what would happen to food and nutrition security? As traditionally we are tillers we were worried about this. Though we are educated in our village, we are interested in agriculture' (*Countercurrents* 2011). Activists hence asserted connection to the land as key to both Dalit identity and sustainable development efforts. And alternative economic ways of linking to the city were initiated, for instance, by combining a turn to organic agriculture with the strengthening of urban demand for organic produce.

As the IRDS chairman framed it in the context of one of the court cases against the industrial park, the Thervoy villagers on whose land the industrial park was planned 'do not want any other type of life'. He proceeded: 'This is the normal feeling of any Rural Indian. In the name of development they do not want their life style to be disrupted. This feeling may not be applicable to few urban educated young people. That does not mean all want to work in factories instead of their own lands' (personal communication, 1 March 2013).

The re-politicization of Dalit identity allowed for a radical reinterpretation of the symbolism of agriculture in the past—and future—of Dalits, from being the source of their oppression to being the core of their 'type of life' and a potential source of pride and emancipation as with 'any Rural Indian'. This re-politicization was driven by connections to urban intellectual-activist debates, connections that the IRDS chairman was the key embodiment of,[7] even if it allowed him to actually criticize the 'few urban educated young people' who were articulating the opposite agenda of Dalit liberation in the city and the necessary link between Dalit oppression and agriculture.

Peasant Community as Ever-Changing Political Association

This reinterpretation of Dalit identity makes the Thervoy villagers deviate from Chatterjee's scenario, and we may wonder why Chatterjee didn't make this possibility of the political reinterpretation of village India more central to his analysis—that is, why did he implicitly take the political narrative of the city as liberating and the village as casteist for a reality? It seems to me that the reason is that Chatterjee (2008: 53) starts his reflections on 'peasant society today' with a consideration of how classical models of peasant insurgency derived from anthropological studies of peasant moral economies or of teleological Marxist interpretations of the role of the peasant in the history of capitalism are 'inappropriate today' (Chatterjee 2008: 54). But obviously they were problematic before today as well. Had Chatterjee turned instead to the intellectual confluence of anthropology and Marxism—to 'Marxian anthropology', as Eric Wolf (1982) called it—he would have found an analytical framework that would have likewise criticized the conceptions of the peasantry that prevailed in the 'familiar anthropological descriptions' and in orthodox Marxist accounts, and that had already suggested theoretical approaches that avoid their pitfalls in the study of peasant societies in transformation. Indeed, from Marxian anthropology, Chatterjee could have developed a more useful conceptualization of peasant community, not as 'a given society- or culture- outside-of-history but as a political association formed through processes of political and cultural creation and imagination ... [in] contexts of unequal power' (Roseberry 1989: 14). And the 'market economy' and its association with 'the city', familiar counterpoints to the peasant moral economy, could then likewise be seen as 'a socially constructed and politically instituted reality' (Friedman 2013).

Though Chatterjee suggests that once-upon-a-time peasant communities functioned according to the orderly dynamic of the classical model, it would be more realistic to see history as always moving—*pace* moral economy theorists—from a 'disordered past to a disordered present' (Roseberry 1989: 58). Chatterjee argues that Dalits now see rural labour as 'traditional servitude' that they want to get away from, as if moving to the city is the only way for Dalits to overcome village servitude. Chatterjee in fact writes of the dramatically changed property relations in village India as traditional landowners have moved away and petty landownership has become more widespread among the rural population. Under these changed circumstances, the discourse of rural labour as 'traditional servitude' is out of sync with the relational make-up of the village. Thereby, far from being the only possible critical Dalit interpretation of village India, the ideological equation of rural labour with caste-based servitude can actually start benefiting those seeking to grab Dalit land. Raymond Williams's (2011) point, that the contrast of the city and the country are central symbols in the interpretation of and political mobilization within the social changes associated with capitalist development, can be recalled here.[8] Hence, rather than starting with tropes of the essential peasant community, a more historically dynamic way of conceiving of agrarian continuity and change is to read the fluidity of urban–rural symbolism and identity formation as shaped by the changing conditions of class struggle.

Accumulation by Dispossession and Governmental Policy

Having decided to resist the land grab that would make their relation to agriculture impossible, a process of political praxis was set in train that would expose a lot about the nature of the power relations that the Thervoy activists confronted. To pinpoint the insights that can be discerned in the fault lines of the struggle, Chatterjee's analytical framework is again a useful counterpoint. Chatterjee argues that corporate capital has a hegemonic hold over the Indian state today, ensuring that the only priority in India's political economy is that of growth, which in the current phase of historical capitalism means a continuous process of primitive accumulation. The framework of electoral democracy in which primitive accumulation unfolds in India however makes it 'unacceptable and illegitimate' for the government to not show itself concerned with the victims of this primitive accumulation—the peasants, artisans, and petty manufacturers who are separated from their means of production and who, if simply left to fend for themselves, may well turn into 'dangerous classes'. For the reality of jobless growth militates against the promises of job creation and makes it unlikely that the victims of private accumulation will be absorbed in the new economic growth sectors.

Hence, there is a constant generation of governmental policies—including by NGOs that carry out governmental functions—'devised to reverse the effects of primitive accumulation' (Chatterjee 2008: 62). The associated benefits are extended to the denizens of 'political society' who are not legally secure enough to not be dispossessed (as those in 'civil society' are), but who are too potentially 'dangerous' to just ignore (unlike some absolutely marginal groups). According to Chatterjee, this whole set-up encourages peasants to engage in a competitive struggle—often organized along caste lines—to gain access to benefits. This struggle does not lead to any change in the legal framework or the overriding logic of governance, as the claims of people in political society are 'a matter of constant political negotiation and the results are never secure or permanent'—'their entitlements ... never quite become rights' (Chatterjee 2008: 58).

Breaking Out of 'Political Society'

This overall scenario and the pressures it exerts on those threatened by primitive accumulation has strong resonances in the

Thervoy case. It was clear from the beginning that the overriding priority of the Tamil Nadu government and SIPCOT was to facilitate primitive accumulation on behalf of private companies. Indeed, the whole process of land acquisition had already started before people in Thervoy had even heard about it, and had it not been for their demonstration of discontent with the project, SIPCOT may not have bothered at all to try and legitimize the land grab according to the public good. The local panchayat president was encouraged to get grama panchayat members' signatures without even revealing to them what it was they were giving their official consent to. Those pushing for the industrial park seemed convinced that providing compensation and benefits would be enough to secure the actual consent of villagers once they noticed what was going on.

Bringing the local panchayat under democratic local control again, and convincing the villagers to act as rights-bearing citizens rather than as denizens who should be content with negotiating benefits for their dispossession, was not an easy process. It was only with the support of the IRDS that the Thervoy struggle started effectively to move beyond the framework sketched by Chatterjee. An active effort emerged to unify the many divisions in the village so as to prevent the government from fomenting a competition for benefits along the lines of existing divisions. For there were certainly divisions in the village: between castes, but also within the majority of Dalits between the urbanites and those in the village, between the client-supporters of different political party patrons, between the majority with access to agricultural land (for whom the water catchment function of the communal forest land was crucial) and poorer villagers dependent on day labour and hence more attracted to working at the industrial site. As the debate shifted, from what to demand from SIPCOT and/or Michelin to recapturing the village panchayat as a truly representative local body and insisting that decision-making power over the project should lie with the local panchayat, however, these divisions started to be overcome. In 2011, the village struggle committee (the 'Sangam', for short) had managed to reclaim the panchayat for local democratic decision-making, and the elected president was now a Sangam representative.

The emerging, more radical vision of local democratic development moreover coincided with the emergence, under the guidance of the IRDS chairman, of the Tamil Nadu Land Rights Federation. This platform was strengthened by the connections made during the Thervoy land struggle and grew further with the resistance to land grabbing for thermal power plants and to the infrastructural and 'land-bank'-related dispossession elsewhere in Tamil Nadu. The platform now brings together Dalit, adivasi, fisherfolk, and other social movements (cum NGOs) involved in land struggles from southern, western, and northern Tamil Nadu who, in a long process of meetings, produced a strategic vision of the land grabbing process affecting these different regions, formulated in a 'Land Rights Manifesto' that came out in 2013.

The 'Selective' Hegemony of Finance Capital

We may conclude that confining subaltern resistance to negotiations over benefits in the domain of political society is a feature of neoliberalism as a hegemonic project, but not necessarily a characteristic of the forms of praxis developed by subaltern groups. I would not be the first, however, to demonstrate that Chatterjee's distinction of political society versus civil society tends to break down in practice. Subir Sinha's contribution to this volume shows how the conduct of the putative members of 'civil society'—India's middle classes and elites—in practice resembles the practices that Chatterjee ascribes to the denizens of 'political society', while Sundar and Sundar (2012) show that subaltern groups are not merely denizens of political society, but also mobilize democratically and as citizens to vindicate their oppositional projects.

Rather than using 'political society' and 'civil society' as concepts referring to pre-eminently divided domains, it is useful, then, to return to a focus on the production of this division, which, under the global dominance of finance capital, has become increasingly salient (Smith 2011). For hegemony under neoliberalism is particularly 'selective', resting on manipulating distinctions among the population (Smith 2014: 194). Hence, public politics *in general* tends to become 'a frantic arena for the negotiation of selection' (Smith 2011), partly driven by the fear of becoming so marginalized as to not even be able to participate in this competition any longer. A platform like the Tamil Nadu Land Rights Federation demonstrates the possibility for subaltern politics, through collective organizing, to go against this general tendency and threaten the distinction of civil society versus political society. It is thereby an attempt to confront the confluence of 'experiences of dispossession and disenfranchisement in the neoliberal epoch' (Kalb 2011: 1)—to confront not just the land grabbing itself but also the accompanying evaporation of fundamental (non-conditional) rights to development and the silencing of collective claims that do not fit the neoliberal paradigm (such as the claim for democratic decision-making on local development).

Coercion and Consent in the Maintenance of Neoliberal Hegemony

Despite the activists' achievements in confronting their disenfranchisement, it seems they were not sufficiently politically experienced to overcome the full spectrum of tactics that the powerful political bloc behind the land grab put in their way. It is here we may consider Chatterjee's argument that, ironically (considering the brutality of primitive accumulation that has become central to the neoliberal development model), the balance between consent and coercion that underlies the hegemony of the Indian state is actually, at least when it comes to peasant society, shifting more towards consent.

According to Chatterjee, the governmental policies designed to reverse primitive accumulation *are* in a way successful: first of all by encouraging more people than before to imagine they have 'a stake, strategically and morally, in the process of governmental power' (2008: 93). But also by making even resistance a much more murky affair, as 'the implication is that even the most fervent activist of the rights of the underprivileged, or the most resolute and incorruptible non-governmental organization, is being deployed, even in its opposition to the state, into a constituent element of the strategic war of position of the passive revolution of capital' (Chatterjee 2008: 93). Considering this logic at work in maintaining corporate hegemony, the bourgeoisie in the neoliberal phase can show itself more ethically concerned: according to Chatterjee, 'present globally prevailing normative ideas' (Chatterjee 2008: 55) disapprove of putting down peasant resistance with violence and find poverty unacceptable.

Discontented Thervoy Activists' Experience with 'Ethics'

As we already saw, Thervoy activists did not conform to dominant definitions of peasant society and their political praxis was not restricted to political society. And still their struggle did not succeed in preventing the construction of the industrial park. No doubt the overriding explanation is that going against the grain of history, as sketched by Chatterjee, is difficult. There were also, however, two types of concrete events that set the struggle back, and, interestingly, both events point in the opposite direction of Chatterjee's analysis of the growing element of consent in the maintenance of hegemony. The first is the simplest: numerous times, when, either spontaneously or in organized manner, Thervoy villagers demonstrated to reject the coming of the industrial park, the response came in the form of coercion. When mass protests erupted, villagers were put in jail and individual court cases were initiated to further intimidate and harass them. Only by criminalizing the protest could the resistance be curbed and physical dispossession proceed. The famous endless delays in the working of the Indian judiciary meanwhile made sure legal routes of resistance would remain ineffective. A perpetual ping-ponging between courts—from the Chennai High Court to the Supreme Court in Delhi, back to the high court, on to the National Green Tribunal, and back—ensured that any clear verdict against the environmental pollution and human rights violations involved in the construction of the industrial park would, even if held in favour of the villagers, come out long after the period when the damage could still be reversed.

The second, more complex type of events that likewise point less to consent than to coercion, however, at first sight appear to actually fit Chatterjee's description. They are about CSR and particularly about Michelin's strong 'ethical' agenda. Indeed, despite the history of the Michelin Rubber Plantation in Vietnam (see Murray 1981: 255ff.), Michelin has a high reputation as an ethical corporation. This reputation concerns not only what the company provides its employees and customers, but also involves organizing a standard of excellence in fields varying from road safety to culinary achievement. Michelin's arrival in India almost looked like something of a 'civilizing mission', and both journalists and academics have been prone to describe it as an example of 'ethical' corporate conduct. Eager to finally secure its foothold in the emerging market in car tyres in South Asia, Michelin even came armed with an elaborate 'common development' vision that emphatically goes beyond philanthropy towards 'partnerships'. This 'ethical' drive turned out to pose a rather formidable challenge for the Thervoy activists.

From the beginning, there were forms of CSR launched by Michelin in the area around Thervoy. These were carried out by the Foundation for Rural Recovery and Development (FORRAD), led by a self-proclaimed 'Gandhian' who had come to realize that industrialization was inevitable and was eager to prove, with Michelin, that it was possible to practice 'ethical industrialization'. The NGO appeared in Thervoy in late 2009 to conduct a survey, it said, to assess people's needs and provide adequate services. With this prospect, youth in the village participated in conducting the survey, not knowing of FORRAD's ties to Michelin. Subsequently, FORRAD produced a glossy survey identifying a host of purported 'needs' in the village that they would help to meet.

The initiatives of FORRAD seem like a rather straightforward example of how CSR seeks to give villagers a stake in the type of 'development' involved in land grabbing, and seeks to transmit neoliberal values via programmes that stress income-generation projects of a kind amenable to the proposed industrial development. Villagers at Thervoy were not so easily charmed by these initiatives, however, and in fact broke all ties with FORRAD as soon as it was discovered that the NGO had been contacted by Michelin to do its work at Thervoy. The main effect of these types of CSR activities was hence not to buy consent but rather to disrupt the growing resistance. It induced a fear of external meddling and a slight paranoia amongst Thervoy activists regarding the many regional, national, and international activists and scholars who passed through the village to offer support. And it pushed for the isolation of Thervoy from other villages in the area that did not refuse FORRAD's services.

An even more subtle way of undermining the resistance through CSR, however, came to light as Thervoy activists decided to participate in an international hearing of the Thervoy–Michelin case before the National Contact Point (NCP) of the Organisation for Economic Co-operation and Development (OECD) in Paris. What was clear from the beginning in 2011, when this possibility was suggested by the French Catholic NGO Comité Catholique contre la Faim et pour le Développement (CCFD-Terre Solidaire), in the phase when the activists' hopes of 'winning' their struggle through other means were already heavily dinted, was that this was a 'soft law' case. At most a negative pronouncement on Michelin would help to put pressure on the Indian courts or to open the public debate in France, which CCFD could not do itself because Michelin has historically been closely intertwined with the same Catholic networks through which CCFD gets its funding.[9] Participating in the NCP process could have opened a window towards transnational solidarity against the twofold dispossession accompanying the relocation of production from France to India. Through the French union Confédération Générale du Travail, a common cause could have been articulated between the Thervoy villagers and the Michelin employees in France concerned about job losses. For CCFD, the clearest aim of participation in the NCP, which it organized and funded, was, however, in favour of CCFD's lobbying department, which sought to expose the limitations of international soft law frameworks—and in particular the OECD NCP procedure—in order to support an international call for hard law regulations for the conduct of transnational corporations.

The initial hearing of Thervoy villagers at the NCP provoked some enthusiasm among the activists, who felt they had managed to make their case with flair and substance—including flying in local villagers who had testified in Tamil through an interpreter paid for by CCFD. Yet activists were stunned to find out that subsequently all their claims were forwarded directly to Michelin, whose executives, rather than having to build their case autonomously, were given ample time to prepare a refutation of each and every argument made by the activists. On top of this, the NCP hearings were chaired by none other than the representative of France's Ministry of Economy and Finance, whose political sympathies were rather easily guessed from his career as a high-ranking French official responsible for the economic expansion of French companies into China, Israel, and the former Soviet bloc. It was stunning to find out, moreover, that because of a 'confidentiality clause' in the NCP, activists were barred from sharing any information about the Thervoy struggle with the general public as long as the NCP process was going on. Activists were even threatened with a letter from the NCP condemning the fact that Nicholas Chinnapan, the IRDS chairman, had talked about the Thervoy struggle in France. With the set-up of the committee of the NCP biased in favour of corporate interests (the NCP president was to decide in case a consensus could not be reached) and with the refusal by the NCP to hear a counter-response from Thervoy, it soon became clear where this was heading: not the exposure of the soft law mechanism as impotent, but rather a verdict by this soft law body entirely in favour of Michelin.

However, the worst of it was not that the NCP verdict would formally deny any violation on the part of Michelin of the OECD Guidelines for Multinational Companies. The worst part of the NCP experience for activists was that in contrast to the care with which they treat any interview with outsiders locally, a great deal of information from their side had been circulated amongst corporates and employers' unions in France, while Michelin's own operations in India remain largely hidden from view.[10] The whole NCP exercise thus mainly helped Michelin's executives to produce further self-justifying narratives and fine-tune future tactics and discursive representations. These narratives certainly have not led to any further 'consent' amongst the villagers. To the contrary, it has only fuelled their anger. What the series of CSR events has done, however, is to complement the police repression in undermining the resistance to the extent that the industrial park and the tyre factory are now a fait accompli.

The Alignment of Ethics and Political Economy

Chatterjee's framework is useful to think about the logic of the relations of power facing Thervoy activists, but if we pose the question of why the struggle ultimately failed to achieve its objectives, the answer does not dovetail with his propositions. Chatterjee's analysis suggests that the nature of the political-economic transformations unfolding in neoliberal India is such that people are increasingly enticed to buy into and consent to the system that is simultaneously orchestrating their dispossession—and that social policy and CSR help to cement this consent. What the Thervoy case shows is that this is not necessarily the case, and that at least part of the maintenance of India's path of 'predatory growth' (Walker 2008) is based not on creating consent but on mobilizing ever more cunning ways of undermining resistance, coupled with the mobilization of state coercion. The actors involved in welfare policies are perhaps more involved in also directly facilitating primitive accumulation than the idea of these two fields operating on opposite—even if connected—logics (primitive accumulation versus its reversal) suggests.

Eric Wolf (2001: 184) makes a distinction that may be useful here between structural power, which organizes and orchestrates settings globally, and 'tactical relations of power' that operate within those settings and control the particular interactions taking place there. 'Primitive accumulation' may be seen as a process driven by structural power—that is, the power of capital—but it still needs to be made to happen through tactical manoeuvring by dominant groups within a particular setting. The set of new normative ideas and social policies (including CSR) that are such a striking part of the neoliberal landscape may, then, not just be the political tinkering with a given political-economic process, but may often be called upon to fulfil the necessary tactical function on behalf of capital of deliberately undermining the actually existing resistance to primitive accumulation.

This interpretation of what social policy and CSR can mean for subaltern politics would lend support to those sceptical of what really goes on concretely behind the rhetoric of corporate ethics and social assistance in India today (see, for example, Harriss

2011b; Pratap et al. 2012). Corporate social responsibility is perhaps intended to 'reverse the effects of primitive accumulation' and thereby sustain the system, but in practice it is actually used to directly help realize primitive accumulation—it is not as brutal a coercive force as the police, but neither is it one seriously out to create consent. It may be useful here to remember William Roseberry's (1994) argument that hegemony is not so much about creating consent (usually backed up, in the last instance, by the possibility of coercion) but about determining the limits within which resistance will take place. Organized violent resistance was a path that the Thervoy activists avoided, and indeed, despite rejecting the land grab and the offers of benefits that came with it, the activists did not reject the legal-democratic framework in which resistance is expected to take place. Perhaps at this level, then, we may detect some 'consent' from the activists, but that consent surely does not concern the larger picture sketched by Chatterjee—rather, it emphasizes their disagreement with the largely illegal and undemocratic way the Indian state actually operates in organizing primitive accumulation in the interest of private capital under *formally* democratic conditions.

* * *

The question that haunts Thervoy activists is why they did not succeed in opposing the industrial park that is now sitting on top of their communal forest land. Small tactical mistakes and the slowness—probably always so with hindsight—with which they managed to take the form and direction of the struggle into their own hands played a role. Chatterjee's analysis of how changes in 'peasant society' reshape the response peasants will have towards the offer of being bought out of their land, and of the tendency for the space of politics to become restricted to competing for benefits, is useful in sensing the enormity of the forces that were pushing the Thervoy Sangam in the opposite direction. The 'success' of the Sangam in politically redefining Dalit identity less in opposition/ competition with other castes and as intimately tied to the land, plus its success in turning the local panchayat into a platform to formulate an alternative democratic vision of development, however, points to why it remains important to read Chatterjee's analysis dynamically and dialectically. It makes it imperative to see the analysis as trying to capture process and trend, rather than as trying to characterize present–past differences or categorize India's economy and politics into two or three distinct fields.

Another trend Chatterjee points out is the growing degree of 'consent' (despite the presence of coercion) in Indian democracy and, related to this, the set of new global norms that make coercion and abject poverty unacceptable. Again, it is clear why consent would perhaps have been likely, but Thervoy activists did not demonstrate much if any consent, including to the CSR initiatives they were offered. They tried all possible legal-democratic means of resistance not because they consented to the Indian state, but because those were the only realistic and desirable means available to them. Most of the CSR activity, though not 'coercive', in fact fuelled the activists' anger and *dissent* precisely as it became clear that the corporate world was using CSR to try and undermine the resistance.

Chatterjee's analysis thus proves productive in interpreting the dynamics of the Thervoy struggle and theorizing the dynamics of India's neoliberal land wars, though I have also suggested refinements to his analysis. These refinements mostly concern the reifications that Chatterjee's concepts run into where he posits moral economy versus capitalism, civil society versus political society, or coercion versus consent. Critiquing these reifications to re-emphasize politicized—and politicizing—historical process, I have often relied on the work of Marxian anthropologists such as Eric Wolf, William Roseberry, and Gavin Smith. This is perhaps a logical step considering how Subaltern Studies and Marxian anthropology started off from some of the same key theoretical texts—E. P. Thompson, and notably, of course, Gramsci. Both bodies of literature are interested in the debates about capitalist transformation and peasant society, the reproduction of hegemony and the creation of political possibility under particular constitutive conditions. Both are moreover clearly wedded to a methodology that moves dialectically between history and theory, is geographically sensitive, and ethnographically informed. As this chapter suggests, there is much to be gained from a dialogue between the analytical templates of the Subaltern Studies project and the theoretical and methodological perspectives developed in Marxian anthropology.

Notes

1. This was part of a statement published under the title 'Tale of a village's struggle for survival' on the activist news website *Countercurrents*. I have slightly edited the text in the epigraph to clarify its meaning (considering English is not the activists' first language). The original text can be found at http://www.countercurrents.org/thervoy140711.htm (accessed 29 December 2014).

2. Research on the Thervoy land struggle is part of the 'Caste Out of Development' project funded by ESRC (RES-062-23-2227). All views presented here, however, are the author's own and not representative of the research team.

3. When compared to other historical national social welfare schemes such as Brazil's *Bolsa Familia*, the National Rural Employment Guarantee Act's conservative logic of discouraging the dispossessed from moving to the city is striking.

4. Interestingly, villages around Thervoy, where other castes form a majority, also claimed there was discrimination involved, but in an opposite way: 'why is the state not offering to buy up *our* lands?'

5. Panchami lands were legally assigned to Dalit communities during British rule but have often been illegally occupied by other castes over time (see Anandhi 1995).

6. This was mirrored in the changing policies of international development donors: from an emotional appeal for Dalit rights, CCFD-Terre Solidaire, one of the main donors of the IRDS, moved towards a strategic 'impact and territory approach' during this period while ActionAid, the other major donor, started focusing on the category of 'the dispossessed'.

7. Nicholas Chinnapan, the IRDS chairman, received his training in the 1970s at the then strongly Marxist-oriented Indian Social Institute in Bangalore (now Bengaluru), and is well connected with national activist platforms, even though his base is rural Tamil Nadu.

8. Kenneth Bo Nielsen makes a similar point about the mobilizing potency of the trope of the 'peasant community under threat' in his contribution to this volume.

9. Criticizing Michelin in public in France is moreover politically risky in the current conjuncture, as the company has become a key national symbol of a bygone golden era of French industrialization.

10. There are strong rumours and credible evidence that Michelin at some point contacted an intelligence bureau to elicit information on the resistance, and that in hastily building the Michelin factory, a wall collapsed killing eight migrant workers. Yet no official body has bothered to verify—let alone acknowledge—these potentially grave 'ethical' violations. Nor has the absolute vagueness about who has the legal responsibility for the land acquisition been clarified: though presenting itself as a responsible company, Michelin in practice continues to be shielded from legal responsibility through SIPCOT.

8

'Community' and the Politics of Caste, Class, and Representation in the Singur Movement, West Bengal

KENNETH BO NIELSEN

The resistance that farmers in Singur in West Bengal put up against the forcible acquisition of their agricultural land for setting up a Tata car factory was one of the most widely publicized incidents in India in 2006. The recently re-elected Communist Party of India (Marxist)–led Left Front government of West Bengal had, in May 2006, singled out 997 acres of prime agricultural land in Singur, which it intended to acquire and subsequently lease out to Tata Motors. Tata Motors would, in turn, build and operate a car manufacturing unit in Singur, in which the company aimed to produce its new Tata Nano, the world's most affordable car. The land was acquired through force and in spite of the resistance of the 'unwilling farmers', as they came to be known. But in late 2008, Tata Motors decided to close shop in Singur, citing the persistent local hostility to the project that made it impossible for them to run the factory in a satisfactory manner. Instead they moved the entire factory to greener Gujarati pastures.

While much has been written on the Singur movement and its implications for political change and development in West Bengal, in this chapter, I use the Singur case as my point of entry to a critical discussion of the notion of 'community' in Subaltern Studies. The idea that the subaltern is embedded in a community has been of significant analytical importance for Subaltern Studies from the outset. It was operative in the foundational structural distinction as formulated by Ranajit Guha, which posited subaltern politics and consciousness as distinct and autonomous from that of the elite. In contrast to the individualistic and 'vertical' nature of elite politics, the subaltern organized his politics horizontally along the lines of kinship and territoriality (Guha 1988: 40). In the words of Partha Chatterjee (1988: 10), the single unifying idea that gave to subaltern and peasant insurgency its fundamental social character was thus the notion and principle of community. Insurgent subalterns, Chatterjee claimed, were tied together by bonds of solidarity that preceded collective action, not vice versa (1988: 10):

> In peasant consciousness ... solidarities do not grow because individuals feel they can come together because of their common individual interests: on the contrary, individuals are enjoined to act within a collective because, it is believed, there already exists bonds of solidarity which tie them together.

Although Chatterjee acknowledges that peasant communities were differentiated and not necessarily egalitarian unities, they were unities nonetheless (Chatterjee 1988: 14). And this 'community unity' would, as Chatterjee (2013: 72–3) has recently reiterated, be 'activated' during 'political struggles' against especially government officials and big landlords. As Chandra (2013b) has rightly summarized, subaltern politics and peasant resistance were seen by the early subalternists as conducted on the basis of pre-existing (communal) solidarities and an autonomous domain of consciousness.

More recently, there has been increasing concern among subaltern scholars about the inadequacy of the original Subaltern Studies framework when it comes to analysing contemporary rather than colonial forms of peasant politics and resistance. Perhaps the most ambitious attempt at a comprehensive and systematic rethinking of the original Subaltern Studies framework has come from one of the original subalternists, namely, Partha Chatterjee, who in a series of articles and books (Chatterjee 2001, 2004, 2008, 2011) has developed the concept of 'the politics of the governed' as an alternative analytical device. To Chatterjee, contestations over land acquisition and industrialization in rural areas in West Bengal like Singur and Nandigram that are the topic of this chapter, were clear indications that the original Subaltern Studies framework for analysing peasant resistance was no longer sufficient. Chatterjee writes:

> If these incidents had taken place twenty-five years ago, we would have seen in them the classic signs of peasant insurgency. Here were the long-familiar features of a peasantry, tied to the land and small-scale agriculture, united by the cultural and moral bonds of a local rural community, resisting the agents of an external state and of city-based commercial institutions by using both peaceful and violent means... . I believe that analysis would be inappropriate today. (Chatterjee 2011: 209–10)

The contributions by Nilsen, Steur, and Sinha in this volume all engage at length with the new conceptual framework that Chatterjee offers, taking issue with how it, amongst other things, appears to reproduce the original 'Manichean' (Nilsen 2012: 254) dichotomy between elite and subaltern domains in the new guise of the civil society versus political society divide. What concerns me here is what the introduction of this new conceptual pair means for the status of 'community' as both an analytical and empirical category.

At first sight, communities seem to disappear when the analytical centre of gravity switches from subaltern politics to what Chatterjee labels 'the politics of the governed'. The political subjects of political society are no longer members of communities, but rather of population groups that are empirically defined by and through new technologies of governance. Singur's unwilling farmers may be seen as one such population group, defined and brought into being by the Left Front's policy of acquiring agricultural land for industrial purposes from several villages in a fertile agricultural region of southern Bengal. But once so defined, a population group may generate its own associations, organizations, or movements to negotiate strategically with governmental authorities, political parties, non-governmental organizations (NGOs), or other actors to further their own cause. Here the notion of community makes a comeback since the political mobilization of population groups, Chatterjee writes, involves strategic efforts to turn an empirically formed population group into a 'moral community' (Chatterjee 2011: 15). Central to Chatterjee's theory is, in other words, the claim that the politics of the governed is a politics of communities that are not given but rather strategically *created* in the course of political action. To illustrate this, Chatterjee uses the example of a group of vulnerable urban squatters whose solidarity is rooted not in a 'pregiven communal form' (Chatterjee 2004: 57) that could easily be activated in times of political struggle. It was rather built from scratch, based on the collective occupation of 'a territory clearly defined in time and space and one that is under threat' (Chatterjee 2004: 58). In much the same way, the workings of the state-led policy of land acquisition created, in Singur, a new category of 'unwilling farmers', defined only by common ties to 'a territory clearly defined in time and space and one that is under threat'.

In what follows, I use the case of the Singur movement to critique the notion of community as it appears in Chatterjee's recent writings, as well as the many questions it raises and leaves unanswered. Firstly, I discuss the process of what Chatterjee would perhaps call 'community formation': how do empirically defined population groups work strategically to become and, more importantly, gain recognition as 'moral communities'? I argue that this process can only be understood in light of the broader politics of representation and contestation that contemporary rural movements are embedded in. Secondly, I examine what such strategic community formation glosses over and silences. Doing so assumes particular importance since, as Gudavarthy (2012: 17) rightly argues, the notion of 'community' in Chatterjee's work appears curiously bereft of internal power dynamics. I argue that social hierarchies rooted in caste and class deserve particular attention in this regard since they, as an integral part of everyday life, potentially fracture strategic 'community formation'. I proceed by giving a brief background to the Singur controversy. This is followed by two ethnographic cases from my own fieldwork in Singur, conducted on and off between 2007 and 2009.

Singur

In response to the land acquisition move in 2006, a section of the land owners who had had their agricultural land targeted for expropriation chose to organize a movement to protect their farmland. The movement of the 'unwilling farmers' was designed to be conspicuously inclusive and welcomed the support and participation of everybody sympathetic to its agenda of resisting the land acquisition—and, later, to have it undone—regardless of gender, caste, or political affiliation. Its activities were coordinated by the Singur Krishi Jomi Raksha Committee (SKJRC—the Committee to Save the Farmland of Singur) which had as its president the local member of the legislative assembly representing the opposition Trinamul Congress (TMC).

During the latter part of 2006, the Singur movement had taken out a number of processions and demonstrations locally demanding that the government withdraw its plans for Singur. They also conducted road and railway blockades on several occasions, and challenged the land acquisition both on the streets and in court (Nielsen 2009). The movement also succeeded in enlisting the support of a broad range of civil society groups, NGOs, and political parties (Nielsen 2010), most importantly the TMC, whose fiery leader Mamata Banerjee championed the unwilling farmers' cause in West Bengal and elsewhere in the country. While some scholars hold that the Singur movement was 'hugely successful' (Pal and Dutta 2013: 2) because it forced Tata Motors to withdraw, the on-the-ground situation remains, as this is written, effectively stalemated: the acquired land lies vacant and has not been returned to its erstwhile owners.

In 2007 I moved in with Prasanta Das and his extended family in Shantipara, a neighbourhood in one of the project-affected villages. Shantipara was dominated by the *mahishya* caste, a clean *sudra* numerous across large parts of southern Bengal. The mahishya, like the *sadgop*s and the *aguri*s, are considered and see themselves as *chasi*, that is, as respectable and thrifty agricultur-alists, and many of them had long since successfully established themselves as supervisory smallholders, who leased in labour to sustain their agricultural production. This ability to retreat to a supervisory role leaving the heavy physical agricultural work to others was, in turn, a marker of social distinction in a rural con-text where hierarchies prevail.

Prasanta, who was in his early thirties, had taken the lead in organizing the unwilling farmers of Shantipara—where upwards of 90 per cent of the households had resisted the land acquisition—under the banner of the SKJRC. He in addition played a role in the local TMC, heading the party's largely defunct or at least fairly inac-tive youth wing. Although he owned agricultural land, Prasanta did not consider himself a farmer. He was an independent businessman with a small office in Kolkata, and he made good money. Some of it he was now actively investing in land close to the Tata factory—ever since the coming of the factory was announced, land prices had soared as businesses and businessmen were expected to soon head for Singur in large numbers. They would need places to stay, and goods and services of many sorts. In other words, land that could be used for residential or commercial purposes was likely to be in great demand in the not too distant future. Yet these specula-tive investments notwithstanding, Prasanta spent a good deal of time campaigning against the land acquisition that had enabled the entry of Tata Motors to Singur in the first place.

'Peasant Community' and the Politics of Representation: Shantipara, Early 2008

Late one evening Prasanta told me that he had just received a call on his cell phone from Kolkata. It was Partha, a full-time activist of a Kolkata-based trade union that had worked actively with the SKJRC almost from the outset. Partha had informed Prasanta that a reporter from Reuters would be coming to Singur tomorrow, and that Prasanta should stay at home to welcome the reporter.

The reporter and his photographer arrive the next morning in the company of Partha. The reporter begins by interviewing

Anuradha, Prasanta's elder brother's wife, who provides detailed and concrete answers to his questions in a calm voice. She explains that she is part of a large joint family of 15 and that they used to own four or five *bighas*[1] which they lost—along with their mini-deep tubewell—when the land was acquired for the Tata factory. When asked about their present situation, she explains that they have so far been able to live off their stock of paddy from 2006; but when this runs out they will certainly begin to feel the pressure: 'We will suffer', she explains, 'but those families who suffer the most are those with no other sources of income outside of agriculture,' she adds for clarification. 'So your family has additional sources of income outside of agriculture,' the reporter immediately asks. Anuradha confirms this, explaining that one of her younger brothers-in-law works as a carpenter, while her husband works as a village primary school teacher. She makes no mention of Prasanta being a successful businessman.

We proceed upstairs where Prasanta is waiting to be interviewed. As we ascend the stairs, Partha tells me that he had planned for the reporter to meet Prasanta on this visit—that is why he had called him on the phone last night, asking him to be available throughout the day:

> Prasanta has a good overview and he speaks well. From the very first time I met him, I picked him—after hearing him speak at a public hearing we organized, I knew that he was good. That is why I want the reporter to meet him. He is very intelligent, has seen through the whole thing and can present all the arguments. He is also good because he thinks not so much about the short term effects [of the land acquisition], not just about himself; he thinks a lot about the long term effects and the larger issues. And he can present these thoughts clearly. That is why he [the reporter] should meet him.

Seated on a plastic chair in the upstairs bedroom, the reporter asks Prasanta to tell him about their movement. Prasanta explains that when the land acquisition was first announced, all of Singur was behind the movement. Later, when the government announced the compensation package, some people gradually began to give up their land. But the whole process has been flawed, he says, because the land records the government has used to calculate the compensation were old and outdated. Much of the land listed in the official land records as mono-crop was in fact multi-crop land. This error has occurred because a good deal of irrigation development has taken place over the past several decades, Prasanta explains. This has radically improved the quality and productivity of agricultural land in the area. But because the administration has failed to update its land records accordingly, many land losers would be under-compensated.

Prasanta is clearly accustomed to being interviewed. He speaks slowly in a calm voice, pausing at appropriate intervals to allow Partha to translate his words. He goes on to explain that accepting the compensation would not make economic sense. The government has claimed, he says, that the compensation was so handsome that all the farmers would have to do was deposit it in the bank and live off the interest for the rest of their lives. 'But don't they know that the rising inflation will eat away at both the interest and the savings?' he asks rhetorically. The land, in contrast, will always be there. And its value does not decrease, he adds.

The reporter points out that some locals have been offered skills training and upgrading by Tata Motors and various NGOs. Some have also been offered jobs inside the factory compound as guards or construction workers. 'So is it not possible to benefit from the factory after all?' he asks. Prasanta answers:

Listen! I am a businessman. I have been involved with rich business people, with people working for companies like Tata. I know how such people think and do their business. They always look for the best, so why should they choose a poor farmer with a minimum of professional training for a job, when they can hire the best people available? It is a hoax. People who have taken the training and joined Tata for work are fools. They will be cheated. They will be laid off when [the construction] work is done.

The reporter looks puzzled and asks Partha to verify that Prasanta had actually said that he was a businessman. Partha confirms this. The reporter then asks Prasanta whether he thinks the Tata Nano will eventually roll out from the factory in Singur. Prasanta looks stern, thinks for a while, and answers, 'No—the police will not be in a position to guard this factory forever. Sooner or later they will have to leave. Then the factory will have to leave, too.' He adds that their movement is not just about their own land and livelihoods—it is a matter of principle, and about what is just and unjust in society.

Having thus concluded the interview, the reporter thanks Prasanta for his time. Before the reporter has left the room, however, Prasanta hurries to add that he would not like to be referred to as a businessman when the article is in print. He would rather like to be described as 'the son of a farmer'. The reporter suggests a compromise, offering to refer to him as 'one of the local front figures of the movement'. That is accepted.

The reporter then heads for nearby Nadipara. I follow him on foot, taking a shortcut across the field to save time. As I walk along, I see Arun heading towards Nadipara on his bicycle. Arun is involved in the SKJRC and often takes part in coordinating its activities in Nadipara. He is also affiliated with the TMC, and sits on the local gram panchayat. Arun's position within the SKJRC is, however, somewhat complicated by the fact that while he publicly campaigns against the coming of the Tata factory under the banner of the SKJRC, his father had willingly decided to hand over his land to the project and claim the cash compensation.

By the time I reach Nadipara, Arun has already tracked down the reporter and is talking to him in an aggressive and almost rambling tone. The reporter tries to ask him a question, but he is constantly interrupted by Arun who, almost shouting, says that he refuses to share any information with anybody: 'I have told my story over and over again to so many different journalists! I have given information about Singur to so many people, but nothing has happened! Nothing of what I have said to all these people has made any difference.' The interpreter is struggling to keep up with Arun's tirade. The reporter raises his hand in an attempt to make Arun pause for a while, but to no avail. After a couple of minutes Arun falls silent, appears to calm down, and lets the reporter proceed into Nadipara. Surprised to see Arun behave like this, I ask him why he was so upset with the reporter who, I add, was probably only trying to do his job.

I know. It was just a show. A performance. You have to show them some emotion. If you just give them the cold facts about the movement they will not realize the kind of anger and suffering that is really there among people. It was Prasanta who called me on the phone just now, saying that this reporter was coming to Nadipara and that I should go and meet him and take him around. So I have met him.

Eventually Arun catches up with the reporter and guides him during his visit to Nadipara. In the past, Arun says, if you wanted to hire labourers from Nadipara you had to book them at least 10 days in advance, such was the demand for agricultural labour in the vicinity. But now, with much of the agricultural land having been converted into a factory, unemployment, poverty, and distress are rapidly increasing. The reporter speaks to both the widow and father of the late Shankar Maitri who recently died from starvation and mental agony. After that, the reporter proceeds to the house of the widow of Anjan Das who hanged himself recently, impoverished and depressed after the land he tilled as a sharecropper had been acquired for the factory.

Before the reporter heads back to Kolkata, he expresses an interest in talking to people who have willingly relinquished their land. Accompanied by Arun, he manages to meet two people near the central bazaar. Both appear reluctant to speak; but they both testify to having now regretted parting with their land and claiming the compensation. One of them explains that his father had had a heart attack just after the compensation had been paid to him, and that all the money had been spent on hospital bills. The other had spent the money on dowry for his daughter. Both are thus now broke and landless.

In the late afternoon I catch up with Prasanta. He is worried about the interview with Reuters, and about whether the article will be sympathetic to their cause. He is also slightly annoyed at having had to spend yet another day away from his office: 'My business suffers because of this movement,' he says.

*

I have narrated this first ethnographic case at length because it illustrates how taking control of representation through impression management formed an important part of the political work that local SKJRC activists such as Prasanta and Arun engaged in when confronted with journalists or other outside visitors. Impression management included explaining the logic and rationale of their protest in a language that the visiting journalist could comprehend, in this case a language that drew simultaneously on economic rationality, ideas about social justice, and emotional attachment to the land. As Partha's statement shows, Prasanta was considered particularly skilled at this since he came across as intelligent, calm, and far-sighted, and not as an 'irrational peasant' incapable of comprehending the complexities of industrial development. Impression management also included locating and introducing appropriate interview objects who had been particularly badly affected by the land acquisition, and who could tell emotional stories of great personal suffering and anguish that could rouse the sympathy of a larger national and international audience. And it included muting dissonant information by, for instance, effectively preventing the reporter from interviewing content, 'willing' farmers—of whom there were many—guiding him instead to two disgruntled 'willing-farmers-turned-unwilling'.

Importantly, it also included projecting an image of the affected villages in Singur as predominantly agricultural communities, deeply dependent on and emotionally attached to an overwhelmingly agrarian economy, the destruction of which threatened to lay the entire area to ruin. The many instances where this representation matched poorly with local realities—Prasanta being a businessman and not a farmer; his family having several sources of off-farm income; and Arun's family potentially playing both horses by simultaneously supporting *and* opposing the land acquisition—thus had to be glossed over to the best of their ability.

In this regard, local SKJRC activists like Prasanta and Arun were acutely aware of the larger politics of representation and debate that surrounded their resistance to the land acquisition. And they were highly sensitive to the sensibilities of the larger public, whose sympathy they hoped to win. This larger public debate and politics of representation which Prasanta and Arun thus explicitly related to, had almost from the outset become extremely polarized. To most parties to the debate, what was at stake in Singur was the very future of 'development' in contemporary India, and the relative role of agriculture and industry in it. In social activist circles, the Tata project, and the displacement and misery it appeared to cause, had acquired an almost iconic status as a symbol of the hegemony of a predatory neoliberal capitalism engaged in transforming the meaning of 'development' in a globalized Indian economy. Activist writings used phrases such as 'development fraud' (Anon. 2006) or 'feudal globalisation' (Shrivastava 2006) to describe what they saw happening around them in the Bengali countryside. The notion of 'the Singur paradigm'—coined by political analyst and activist Praful Bidwai (2007)—thus in many respects captures how social activists saw the Tata project as paradigmatic of these new forms of neoliberal 'development'. This framing is not unique to activist accounts, but is also echoed in part of the scholarly work on Singur, as well as on similar popular mobilizations against land acquisition elsewhere in India (for example, Basu and Das 2008; Jones 2009; Kapoor 2011; Mukharji 2009).

At the other side of the fence, the arrival of the Tata Nano on the Indian scene was widely praised in the media as proof of the country's new role as an assertive nation taking long economic strides to create a vast, prosperous middle class and attract unprec-edented levels of investment (Kaur 2012: 604). Among India's new middle class that is conventionally portrayed as the natural carrier of the country's intensified embrace of economic liberalization (Fernandes and Heller 2008), the Tata Nano almost immediately became a 'phantasmagoria of middle-class consumption', as Ananya Roy (2011) calls it. The protest against the Tata factory in Singur was accordingly seen as a threat to the realization of this middle-class dream because it obstructed or even derailed India's economic development.

The image of a traditional peasant community under threat from corporate capital and state brutality that Prasanta and Arun actively sought to produce and project is a potent and mobilizing one. It speaks, as Ananya Roy (2011: 271) succinctly points out, to the long urban tradition of idealizing 'the Bengali village' in the powerful pastoral motif of *Sonar Bangla*, a land of fields of gold. But, as indicated, it did not quite match local realities.

In Shantipara and elsewhere in Singur (Majumder 2012), Prasanta and many other unwilling farmers had long since retreated into supervisory roles and left the actual cultivation of their land to hired labourers. Economic pluri-activity was the norm as most households sought to straddle the agricultural and non-farm sectors—72 per cent of the households I surveyed in Shantipara in 2008 reported having off-farm incomes; and among the increasingly educated cohort of village youths, aspirations for 'something more' than a life in small-scale agriculture were widespread.

By pointing this out I do not mean to belittle the great suffering and true hardships the land acquisition had caused among the unwilling farmers. Poverty and distress did drive people to commit suicide, and the land acquisition had indeed had detrimental effects on the overall peasant economy and on individual household economies. But the peasant economy was not the only economy in town, nor was it an economy and a lifestyle that all, or even most, of the unwilling farmers aspired to. The potent image of being a peasant community under threat thus needed to be actively produced rather than automatically activated. That the SKJRC has been very successful in producing this image is borne out by how many activist accounts of Singur echo this style of representation. An illustrative example of this can be found in a fact-finding mission report written on behalf of the People's Coalition on Food Sovereignty. The report begins by posing the rhetorical question 'development for whom?' after which the authors proceed to argue that 'for the people of Singur, their land is their life and part of their culture. It is a place for learning and worship' (Lahiri and Ghosh 2006: 12). They add that 'for generations the local people cultivated the land and most of them cannot think of any other occupation beyond agriculture' (Lahiri and Ghosh 2006: 13):

> The survival and livelihoods of the peasants are closely related to the land and the agriculture that they practice. They come from generations of farmers and their skills and knowledge have been acquired through the decades of understanding, working and sustaining the land and the surrounding natural resources. These are what they know and do well. Their skills are not suitable for other occupations. (Lahiri and Ghosh 2006: 14)

The threat of eviction would therefore not only destroy local live-lihoods but also local histories (Lahiri and Ghosh 2006: 16) and identities rooted in a special relationship to the land.

Similar representations of the Singur movement as fundamen-tally rooted in pre-existing peasant community solidarity also, as I have argued elsewhere (Nielsen, forthcoming), pervade a consider-able part of the academic scholarship on Singur (for example, Jones 2009 and, more recently, Pal and Dutta 2013). In these accounts it is generally assumed that the unwilling farmers' collective orga-nization built on readily available forms of community solidarity. As I argue in what follows, by introducing a second ethnographic case, this form of 'solidarity' was in fact very fragile and had to be carefully stitched together and maintained over time.

The Politics of Caste and Class:
Nadipara, February 2008

It was approaching 9 p.m. on a cool February evening in Nadipara.[2] Unlike the chasi of Shantipara, the residents of Nadipara almost exclusively made their living as *khet majur*, that is, agricultural labourers without land to their name, who gain their livelihood primarily from working on other people's land (Thorner 1991: 265). With few exceptions the inhabitants of Nadipara all belonged to the SC *bauri* caste, and the stark social and material differences between Shantipara and Nadipara were evident to even the most casual observer. Sometimes, the mahishya of Shantipara would derogatorily refer to Nadipara as 'Kulipara'—the coolies' neigh-bourhood—to indicate the inferior social position of its inhabitants.

I had just left the village club which over the past hour or so had witnessed a heated debate between some of the khet majur villagers and the leadership of the SKJRC, which generally comprised men of the mahishya caste who resided in Shantipara and elsewhere. Ajay, an industrious and vocal khet majur man in his twenties, had complained that nobody in the movement's leadership cared about the plight of Nadipara's khet majur. The Singur movement, he alleged, was dominated and led by local land owners, and its agenda was shaped by *their* desire to retain their agricultural land in the face of expropriation. Although they owned hardly any land, Nadipara's khet majur had supported the land owners in this struggle because they wanted to fight for their right to make a living through tilling the land. But so far they had gotten nothing in return, and their concerns were hardly ever raised by the movement. What Ajay was in effect saying was that the concerns of the khet majur and the chasi differed significantly: should the movement ultimately fail in securing the return of the acquired land to its erstwhile owners, the land owners would still be legally entitled to financial compensation. But the khet majur would be left jobless and empty-handed.

By the time the meeting ended Ajay had repeatedly been assured by the movement's leaders, which included the SKJRC president, that this was a misconception on his part. The movement, the president explained, was genuinely concerned about the plight of the khet majur, and would continue to fight for their rights no matter what the outcome of the movement would be. But as most of us could hear from the quarrel he presently had with Prasanta, Ajay remained unconvinced. Prasanta explained that in a movement like this everybody should reconcile their differences and unite like brothers; but Ajay retorted that this was not so easy as long as the khet majur and their concerns were not given adequate attention. Prasanta replied that surely the khet majur had a stake in this movement too since, if the land was returned to its original chasi owners, the khet majur would once again have their old jobs back. Ajay said that Prasanta was of course right—but should this mean that all other concerns, 'our concerns', should never be raised at all? The president intervened to briefly explain that the matter would be resolved soon, and that this disagreement should not escalate any further. Prasanta abandoned his quarrel with Ajay and drove off into the night on his motorbike to attend another meeting while he mumbled 'khet majur *lok!!!*' (labouring folks) just loud enough for Ajay to hear.

When the meeting in Nadipara was held, I had lived and worked in Singur for some four months. By then I had witnessed and listened to the discontent of the khet majur with the local chasi movement leadership, of which Prasanta was a part, on several occasions. The controversy I had overheard that night in Nadipara was, in other words, not an isolated event. It surfaced with some regularity as the labouring bauri and the land-owning mahishya struggled to construct and manage a common political platform from which to challenge the land acquisition that had deprived the latter of their property and the former of their livelihood.

Since most of the local SKJRC leadership were drawn from among the land-owning chasi castes such as the mahishya, the bauri of Nadipara ended up mostly playing the role of movement foot soldiers within a local core–periphery structure (Nilsen 2010) that saw the mahishya lead and the bauri follow. In time, however, some khet majur, including Ajay, grew increasingly frustrated with the fact that they should suffer increasing deprivation fighting for a cause that first and foremost concerned the land owners. The articulation of this frustration, as expressed inter alia during the village meeting described earlier, came about in part through the intervention of party activists from the Majur Kranti Parishad (MKP—Workers' Revolutionary Council). As a revolutionary working-class party, the MKP showed a particular interest in addressing the situation of Singur's khet majur, whose plight they found to figure only sparingly in the Singur movement's politics, even though they too had been greatly affected by the land acquisition.

To mobilize the khet majur behind a more explicit khet majur agenda, the MKP activists adopted a two-pronged strategy that focused simultaneously on securing local livelihoods and sensitizing the khet majur to what Asit, an MKP activist, described as the class character of the Singur movement. Asit spent considerable time talking to the khet majur about *their* role in the movement and encouraged the khet majur to reflect on what would happen if the Singur movement decided to disband itself in the face of defeat. Asit had explained to them that whereas the land-owning chasi would accept the compensation that they were legally entitled to, the khet majur would get nothing, and there would be no movement left to raise their concerns. That was why, Asit argued, the khet majur *themselves* needed to take the lead in organizing and articulating their demands autonomously, rather than relying on the chasi to do it for them.

In many respects the intervention of MKP activists in Nadipara resembled what Nilsen (2012: 265) terms 'catalytic work'. Among

subaltern groups like the bauri, with limited experience of autonomous political mobilization, the intervention of urban and
educated activists may act as a catalyst that facilitates the emergence of a distinct subaltern voice. The MKP's message of the need
for a stronger khet majur voice within the SKJRC was appreciated and appropriated by many of the khet majur in Nadipara. In
early February 2008, a group of them agreed to set up the Singur
Akranta Bargadar Khet Majur Samiti (SABKMS—Association of
the Oppressed/Affected Sharecroppers and Landless Labourers of
Singur) with a base in Nadipara. The SABKMS would work as a
semi-autonomous association within the SKJRC where it would
seek to promote the voice of the khet majur. It would also, in the
event that the SKJRC disbanded, continue to struggle for workers'
rights and interests. The move, the SABKMS founder-members
agreed, would in fact strengthen rather than weaken the overall
movement as it would ensure a broader representation and potentially also broaden its mass base.

When I interviewed Asit at the time of the formation of the
SABKMS, he estimated that there were at least 1,000 affected khet
majur in Singur, and perhaps upwards of 5,000 if one also counted
seasonal migrant labour. As its first act, SABKMS activists would
therefore go from village to village and conduct a survey of its target constituency, that is, all those *bargadar* (sharecroppers) and
khet majur who had been negatively affected by the land acquisition. The task was entrusted to SABKMS supporters in Nadipara,
and Ajoy, who had raised his voice against the chasi leadership during the village meeting, took the lead in identifying people from
Nadipara to work on the survey alongside himself. Asit said at the
time that he and other MKP activists would organize a meeting
in Nadipara in a fortnight to take stock of the situation and to
formally establish the SABKMS. He indicated that the leadership
of the SKJRC would be present on the occasion to endorse the presence of the SABKMS, along with the media.

When I talked to Ajay about his survey work, he said that he
had generally received a positive response from the khet majur,
many of whom had told him that the SABKMS was precisely the
kind of organization they needed. But on one occasion he had
found that nobody had come to attend the meeting he had called to

collect their names. This had surprised Ajay since he had felt that the khet majur in this village had appeared enthusiastic when he had first introduced them to the SABKMS. He had then gone and knocked on the door of one of the khet majur families to remind them of the meeting, only to be told that nobody was going to attend because they had been 'warned' by some of the chasi leaders of the SKJRC that Ajay and his associates were Maoists, and that the police would come and pester them if they attended the SABKMS meeting. Evidently, the chasi SKJRC leadership had tried to obstruct the work of the SABKMS.

On the day of the scheduled stock-taking meeting, I arrived in Nadipara at 2 p.m. to find the dais that had been erected deserted. When I managed to locate Ajay, he explained that there had been 'problems'. Two days earlier Abhijit, an important local TMC leader from Shantipara, had gone from door to door in Nadipara around midnight, accompanied by other chasi SKJRC leaders from Shantipara, threatening the khet majur to stay away from the SABKMS meeting. They had done the same thing the previous morning, and had later called a meeting in the local club, where they had warned the khet majur that the MKP were in fact Maoists in disguise. If the police found out that Nadipara was hobnobbing with Maoists, Abhijit had ostensibly warned, the police would come and trash them and destroy their houses. Abhijit had also reminded the khet majur of how often the SKJRC-TMC leadership had stood up for Nadipara by bringing them rice and dal in times of distress. And he had insisted that there was no need for a divisive meeting like this.

Ajay concluded his story by saying that all these threats from the SKJRC leadership had made people hesitate to join the SABKMS meeting. In consultation with some MKP activists who had by then arrived in Nadipara, it was decided to postpone the meeting to 4 p.m. In the meantime Ajay went from door to door calling on people to attend. Eventually, some 40 to 50 villagers turned up alongside the 30 or so MKP activists who had travelled there from elsewhere in the state. With a local target constituency of at least 1,000 bargadar and khet majur, the turnout was disappointing. And because nobody from the local SKJRC leadership attended, the meeting lacked an official stamp of approval. The media did not turn up either.

The next day I interviewed Ajay about the low turnout. He explained that he had gone yesterday evening to a village from where as many as 70 khet majur had told him just a few days back that they would attend. Since none of them had turned up the previous day, he had gone back to ask them what had happened. They had explained that Swapan, a chasi movement organizer from a neighbouring village, had been present when Ajay had first visited them to talk about the SABKMS. Swapan had 'lurked in the background', they said, and speculated that he had reported what Ajay had said about the SABKMS to the rest of the SKJRC leadership. The SKJRC leaders had, in turn, come around and threatened them to stay away from the previous day's SABKMS meeting. After concluding his story Ajay explained that Swapan was like the 'Criminal Investigation Department' of the SKJRC, always spinning around on his motorbike, checking how things were, talking to the people, and keeping his finger on the pulse. Swapan reported to the rest of the SKJRC leadership, who took action if and when they found it necessary.

As is evident, the chasi SKJRC leadership was not enthusiastic about the autonomous mobilization of the khet majur on a separate platform and worked to contain its spread. When I interviewed Prasanta about the SABKMS some days later, he stressed that it was a misconception on the part of the khet majur that the Singur movement was a chasi movement: 'If that was the case', he asked rhetorically, 'could we then have been so successful in mobilizing so many people under the banner of the SKJRC?' The success of the movement had come about because, ultimately, it was about social justice. That was why everybody could unite and their movement grow so strong. Prasanta thus found it unreasonable that the SABKMS sought to establish a platform of its own:

> The problem is, the people of the MKP come to us and say that they want to make a list of all the khet majur for use in the movement's campaigns. So we say 'OK, no problem, make your list along with us as a collaborative effort—in that way our movement can remain united.' But when they go to the people of Nadipara, what they really do is say that our president and Abhijit and the other leaders, they never think about the plight of the khet majur. That is why we felt the need to reprimand Ajoy and Asit in quite a harsh language.

The SABKMS's mobilization would 'only create a rift between the majur and the chasi that will ultimately break the unity of the movement', Prasanta argued, adding that the real reason for the poor turnout at the SABKMS meeting was that people had seen through this divisive agenda and did not approve of it. Hence the meeting had been poorly attended and poorly organized, with no banners, no mikes, and only a minuscule dais.

When I spoke to Ajay about his experience of mobilizing Nadipara behind a khet majur agenda through the SABKMS, he said that it had been an entirely new experience to him. He appreciated the way the MKP spoke because they talked of the empowerment and rights of the poor people. And it had meant that 'his eyes were now opening'. He had started to notice and openly criticize how the movement leaders only came to Nadipara when they wanted the khet majur to participate in rallies or meetings—otherwise they never came:

> They come and call on us to go to the rallies and shout slogans like 'I will never give up my land!' But we khet majur never had any land in the first place. Now I raise this issue with the leadership and they do not like it. I also raise the issue of how they make our women line up in the scorching sun with bowls in their hands like beggars when they come to Nadipara with emergency relief. I ask them 'would you ever treat your own women that way?' They only answer that I don't understand the situation, and that they have their prestige and honour to think about. But what about us? Don't we have honour, too?

The support extended to the initial mobilization behind the SABKMS shows how the effort made to raise a distinct khet majur voice resonated more broadly with the lived experience of the khet majur. In the process, local social hierarchies rooted in class and caste were brought to the forefront and constantly made the SKJRC's common platform shaky—and at times threatened to submerge it completely.

Forging a 'moral community' out of common ties to a piece of land under threat was thus a cumbersome and generally incomplete task that, to paraphrase Baviskar (2008: 5), involved the difficult work of constructing political identities, forging alliances, and transcending differences. On the part of the chasi SKJRC leadership, this 'work' involved a mix of persuasion, coercion, and intimidation vis-à-vis the khet majur; but also, eventually, elements of co-optation, selective incorporation, and the distribution of patronage. Chasi SKJRC leaders, for example, began to speak increasingly of the need to fight for the rights of the bargadar and the khet majur during local rallies and meetings. This demand also appeared on several movement posters and thus made its way into the vocabulary and repertoire of movement claims. Moreover, chasi SKJRC leaders who had been elected on TMC tickets to the local gram panchayat in May 2008 sought to appease the discontent khet majur by channelling resources from the local state to Nadipara. Thus, by early 2009, upwards of 11 families in Nadipara had been awarded houses under the Indira Awaas Yojana from the new gram panchayat. In addition, the gram panchayat made some efforts to provide jobs to Nadipara under the National Rural Employment Guarantee Act on a greater scale than before.

Compared to the ways in which local SKJRC activists engaged in a strategic politics of representation vis-à-vis visiting outsiders, the mobilization of the khet majur behind the SABKMS brings to the fore precisely those contentious issues of caste and class hierarchies that the SKJRC's politics of representation was intended to gloss over. On the ground in Singur, opponents of the land acquisition were clearly differentially positioned within this 'peasant community', and, as I argue in the conclusion, it is debatable to what extent Chatterjee's notion of strategic community formation helps us to better make sense of these on-the-ground dynamics of contemporary subaltern politics.

* * *

Chatterjee is certainly right in suggesting that the original Subaltern Studies approach to peasant mobilization needs to be reconceptualized in light of the changing dynamics of the global political economy and the deepening of popular democracy in India. Chatterjee's recent work on the 'politics of the governed' is an important contribution in this respect. Not only does it appear, its critics notwithstanding, to offer new and powerful conceptual tools with which to look at the ways in which popular politics works (cf. Harrison 2012: 238), Chatterjee's reconceptualization is also embedded in what Gupta and Sivaramakrishnan (2011: 5) call 'an ambitious retheorization of the Indian state' after liberalization, and seeks to link changing forms of governance to discrete acts of popular mobilization in novel ways.

Chatterjee's attempt to redefine the notion of 'community' forms part of this general reconceptualization. In its new avatar, 'community' in effect comes closer to denoting the *process* of constructing a moral commitment to a commonality of purpose, rather than a kind of pre-existing solidarity that is readily activated during political struggles: 'moral communities' now have to be formed one way or the other. Chatterjee's observation that contemporary 'popular' or subaltern mobilizations thus involve considerable strategic work (and networking) is, as I have suggested, a much-needed corrective to the original Subaltern Studies framework, although it is perhaps not a particularly novel one.

Like a good deal of the scholarship labouring within the broad 'postcolonial' tradition, however, Chatterjee too ends up de-emphasizing local class divisions and precludes a closer investigation of how 'ordinary society is divided, for example between relatively prosperous people and the very poor', as Jeffrey (2010: 17) puts it. Thus, notwithstanding Chatterjee's reframing of communities as 'strategically created' rather than 'a priori given', the end result is, as Gudavarthy (2012) points out, to reinforce rather than deconstruct the impression that subaltern 'communities' are relatively undifferentiated collectivities within which aims, desires, aspirations, and interests are equally shared. I have devoted the better part of this chapter to presenting two ethnographic cases because they, empirically, shed light on both the analytical utility of the notion of 'community' in Chatterjee's reinvention of the subaltern project, as well as the limits to it.

As I have shown, the trope and image of 'the peasant community' under threat is a potent and mobilizing one, in West Bengal and elsewhere. Local SKJRC activist were acutely aware of this, and of the larger public debates that engulfed their anti-land-acquisition mobilization. Accordingly, a good deal of their political work consisted in producing publicly available representations of

Singur's unwilling farmers as part and parcel of a peasant community under threat. What was strategically created in the first ethnographic example, however, was not so much a moral community as a social fact, but rather a moral community as a public representation. Simultaneously, the local SKJRC organizers were faced with another set of challenges which, as the second case brought out, was directly related to the operations of local social hierarchies and patterns of social distinction rooted in caste and class. Navigating these hierarchies was a process marred by contradictions, tensions, contestations, and considerable ambivalence; and it entailed the use of threats, violence, repression, as well as attempts at co-optation and appeasement. Subsuming this process of holding together a rural anti-land-acquisition movement under the abstract and decontextualized rubric of 'strategic community formation' would therefore, I suspect, gloss over a good deal more than it would reveal. In this regard, the notion of 'community', even in its most recent avatar, may make a poor analytical substitute for a careful and empirically grounded engagement with the on-the-ground dynamics of contemporary subaltern politics, an engagement that must, as the Singur case has shown, have one eye on the particularities of place, identity, and inequality, and the other on the larger politics of representation.

Notes

1. One bigha is one third of an acre.
2. Sections of this ethnographic example are reproduced in modified form from Nielsen (forthcoming).

9

On the Edge of Civil Society
in Contemporary India

SUBIR SINHA

A persistent concern within Subaltern Studies approaches to Indian history—the delineation of the domains of 'elite' and 'subaltern', and the relations between them—is exemplified in the writings of Partha Chatterjee, including his writings on 'civil' and 'political' society that increasingly focus on contemporary Indian politics.[1] In his work, he suggests a long lineage of these two formations and their ultimate exteriority to each other. Based on the premise that differential exposure to 'the west' since the late fifteenth century caused a split in Indian politics between 'civil society' of western-ized nationalist and postcolonial elites, and 'political society' of the 'masses' (Chatterjee 1998), he has explored their engagements in different colonial and postcolonial contexts.

In this chapter, I review Chatterjee's rendering of the politics of civil and political society in contemporary India and his recent attempts to ground it in 'political economy'. This is an analytically interesting and important turn as, even though Marxian political economy was a common theme in the early years of the Subaltern Studies project, it progressively lost salience. For Chatterjee, 'global capitalism' and 'development' both now have implications for the constitution of these domains and the political forms that characterize them. For example, Chatterjee (2001: 179) states that 'in the context of the globalization of capital' we are 'witnessing an on-going opposition between modernity and democracy, i.e., between civil society and political society'. Training his lens made of quite particular readings of Gramsci and Foucault on welfare and development, Chatterjee (2004) refined his category of political society by arguing that 'governmentality' created a 'politics of the governed', that is, of the 'denizens of 'political society'. The most explicit of his attempts to ground political society in the political economy of development is his essay on 'Democracy and Economic Transformation in India' (Chatterjee 2008). Here, Chatterjee draws on Sanyal's (2006) work on primitive accumulation in postcolonial capitalist development, arguing that electoral compulsions force governmental development and welfare interventions to amelio-rate the conditions of the victims of primitive accumulation, in effect 'reversing' it.[2] Finally, these explorations are given a skein of unity in an essay in Chatterjee (2011), where he debates these categories in relation to western political philosophy.

These writings have provoked vigorous debate. Critics, in essence, argue, and I agree, that civil and political society do not have the attributes that Chatterjee ascribes to them, and that the denizens of political society—today's subaltern—act in ways that differ substantially from his description, taking recourse to, and helping to remake, 'modernity' *and* 'democracy'. But in this essay I ask a different set of questions: what kinds of civil and political society do primitive accumulation and contem-porary capitalism produce in India? What does the leadership/hegemony/domination of civil over political society entail? How are the boundaries between these two domains maintained, and what are some features of 'contacts' and 'battles' between them? In trailing these questions, I draw on the mobilization of solidar-ity for Binayak Sen, a medical doctor providing care in a tribal area, arrested for being a Maoist and jailed without bail for sedi-tion before being released in 2011, and the politics of Residents' Welfare Associations (RWAs) in Delhi in relation to domestic workers.

'Democracy and Economic Transformation in India' and Its Critics

In keeping with Subaltern Studies approaches that claimed as a major point of departure from 'canonical Marxism' their view that the European path to capitalism, in which primitive accumulation converted peasants into proletarians, is not replicable in countries 'such as India' (for example, Chakrabarty 2000; Guha 1989),[3] Chatterjee (1994) used Gramscian analytics to argue that unlike 'the west', India's postcolonial, modernizing bourgeoisie did not achieve hegemony, and had to form alliances with 'traditional' elites representing pre-capitalist forms. In this 'passive revolution', for capital accumulation to appear legitimate to the people, the state had to make it less painful by protecting and accommodating pre-capitalist forms via planning, leading to a 'gradualist' path of development. In his writings on political society, Chatterjee does not reactivate this argument, or take recourse to political economy in any substantive way. This makes it difficult to understand how political society was formed in the first place, its modes and repertoires of political action, and its relations with civil society at a time of especially rapid economic and political transitions (Sinha 2012, 2013).

With 'Democracy and Economic Transformation', Chatterjee addressed this major weakness. He needed an account of 'neoliberalism' and 'globalization' in India over the past three decades, which he found in Kalyan Sanyal's 2006 work, *Rethinking Capitalist Development*.[4] Sanyal shares with Subaltern Studies approaches the idea of the non-replicability of the 'classic' transition to capitalism, arguing that there will be no 'complete' transition in India at all, and a 'zone of non-capital'—economic forms that may be involved in petty commodity production but are not based on the capital–labour relation—will persist. He argues this is because, firstly, postcolonial capitalism *creates* non-capitalist forms as it dispossesses and impoverishes peasants but cannot accommodate them as wage workers. Inhabiting this zone are Shanin's (1986) 'plebeian survivors'—'the increasingly mobile, slum dwellers, part farmers, lumpen traders and pimps'—who constitute the majority of the population of India and the world.

Secondly, for Sanyal both accumulation and its legitimation happen on a global scale, and the politics of legitimation involves *international* programmes of poverty alleviation, human rights, and so on. Primitive accumulation creates the excluded, but since today they are also citizens with rights—and that is a key difference with the political context of classical primitive accumulation—they become targets of development interventions. Programmes of development and welfare that ameliorate their condition keep them in suspended animation in the zone of non-capital. Sanyal suggests that more resources flow from the zone of capital (in the form of development assistance) to that of non-capital than vice versa, what he considers to be another key difference with the classical trajectory. Pastoral government, necessitated by the power of the excluded, 'reverses' primitive accumulation and limits capitalist development.

Chatterjee follows Sanyal's zones of capital/non-capital distinction, designating those incorporated into the zone of capital as 'civil society' now recomposed by Deregulation and competition between states for foreign direct investment has made the capitalist class more diverse. The new urban middle classes, associating it with corruption and venality, withdrew support from the developmentalist state, now accepting the moral-ethical leadership of corporate capitalism. Neoliberalism has transformed the conditions of subalternity too. In villages, peasants no longer face an exploiting landlord class, whose power was eroded by the slow playing out of the reforms of the 1950s. Also, governmental technologies and electoral democracy have penetrated rural India, and the state is no longer external to the peasant community. As tax on land and agricultural produce is no longer a major source of government revenue, the relation between state and peasantry is no longer directly extractive. Large-scale migration to cities is not a result of pauperization—villagers are not compelled to migrate, they choose to. Political society comprises most of the rural population, and the urban poor. Though they are formally 'citizens' with rights to vote, they relate to state and government not through the juridical-constitutional framework of rights, but through 'temporary, contextual, and unstable arrangements arrived at via direct negotiation' (Chatterjee 2008: 57). They manipulate electoral democracy and governmental categories for local and unstable negotiation for benefits that are exceptional, rather than general rights. They use violence, the hallmark of the old subaltern, only to attract state attention to a particular problem and to elicit a particular response. Chatterjee concurs with Sanyal that 'managing' political society via development programmes and democracy is a *necessary* condition for continued primitive and proper capital accumulation. So civil society needs the consent of political society to pursue growth, and has to provide for its needs.

It is accurate that for the majority of the urban middle classes, and especially for the 'new middle classes', there is no alternative to 'corporate' capitalist development.[5] However, there is, within this class, also a counter-tendency; some segments of it are involved in politics supportive of the 'rights' of new subalterns and in development interventions aimed at the amelioration of their conditions, for example via the work of non-governmental organizations (NGOs) or solidarity work with subaltern politics. John and Deshpande (2008) correctly state that concerns with the poor are as old as capitalism itself. In my view this produces a pro-poor constituency within bourgeois civil society with an equally long history of 'solidarity' with the poor. They translate, connect, and mediate between different domains and planes of politics in India today. There *are* electoral imperatives necessitating welfare programmes for the poor, but the category of 'the excluded' which forms the basis of Chatterjee's political society is incomplete and inaccurate to describe those who lose out as processes of capitalist development unfold.

Responding to Chatterjee (2008), Baviskar and Sundar (2008), John and Deshpande (2008), and Mihir Shah (2008) argue against Chatterjee's categories and the attributes he assigns them. Baviskar and Sundar (2008: 87) point to the National Rural Employment Guarantee Scheme, the Right to Information Bill, and the Forest Rights Bill where subalterns forced state action for *stable rights*. Sinha (2012, 2013) shows that movements of the rural poor frame demands for rights using science, law, policy, and constitutional discourses of rights and citizenship, rather than local, unstable, particular benefits.[6] Chatterjee's periodization of the state's biopolitical penetration of the countryside and its internalization by the community, too, is problematic, as Agrawal (2005) and Sinha (2008) have shown. Negative—extractive and predatory—penetration of the state, too, is deep in the countryside, and it is strange that Chatterjee does not see the formation and the politics of political society in relation to the absence of, or the actual forms of, the penetration of the state and the development apparatus.

For Chatterjee, emerging politics in tribal areas—a 'third domain'—differ from political society because of insufficient penetration of democracy and the development machinery into tribal areas. Though his framework purports to be based on ongoing primitive accumulation, he omits from his analysis its primary sites—which the tribal areas are—or their relations with the other two domains.[7] As John and Deshpande (2008) point out, there is a need to think about whether and why 'tribal areas' are residual to political society, which is itself residual to civil society. Certainly, the flow of people from this zone to cities for domestic and other work, the mushrooming 'placement agencies' acting as labour contractors, and unions of domestic workers and NGOs dedicated to ameliorating their conditions show that this zone is not exceptional.

What is the 'primitive accumulation' which underpins Chatterjee's account of a bifurcated (even trifurcated) polity? For Marx, it is 'the historical process of divorcing the producer from the means of production' (Marx 1967: 714). Among the modes of primitive accumulation, Marx lists violence and force, law, cheating, and theft of common and state land (Marx 1967: chapters 26–9, passim). For Byres (1994), it involves transfer of land by non-market means from non-capitalist to potentially capitalist classes, done with state compliance or mediation, by force, theft, eviction, or purchase at a nominal price, and the use of state machinery to evict weaker owners of land by politically powerful claimants. State violence and force feature prominently in these definitions, but for Chatterjee the state disappears as an active agent of primitive accumulation, only dispensing welfare to the excluded and the dispossessed to legitimate accumulation. How are we to understand, with this framework, actually unfolding primitive accumulation in India today, when the Government of India (2008) itself notes heavy, even violent, state involvement in creating special economic zones and export processing zones, mining deals, land clearing for housing development, infrastructure construction, and appropriation of common and public lands, which displace and dispossess rural and tribal populations? To comprehend the politics of primitive accumulation today, we need to understand the role of the state and its relation to tribals, the *active consent* of dominant elements of civil society in this process, and the *forced displacement* and migration of the tribal and rural poor beyond the voluntarism that mars Chatterjee's frame.

Chatterjee's (originally Sanyal's) category of 'reversal' is inadequate in understanding claims-making by subalterns, or state programmes in response. Only a small percentage of development funds committed to amelioration programmes reaches target populations. State actors relentlessly loot programmes, turning them into sites of primitive accumulation. This loot, via investments in real estate, stocks and shares, and higher education, becomes 'wealth' and provides a key connection between the old and new middle class, and so between old and new civil society. The amassing of wealth in the processes of primitive accumulation *and* its mitigation do not follow 'bourgeois values' of respect for rule of law, property rights, toleration, and universalism. Corruption, illegality, fraud, favours, and impunity negotiated with political leaders, rather than such values, are the norm. This is unsurprising, as historically it is the winners of the primitive accumulation process who have constructed civil society to defend and legitimize their victory.[8] Also, since extreme poverty exists, 'reversal' is not working. Clearly, not only exclusion and its amelioration, but also dispossession and exploitation, animate the politics of the victims of primitive accumulation today.

In this context, Samaddar (2007) asks whether civil and political society are really distinct, if this distinction matters, and if so, why? I ask further: who makes and maintains this distinction, how, and why? Moving beyond Chatterjee's apolitical reading of civil and political society and the processes that constitute them, I see the constitution of domains, and the relation between them, as politically fraught. Civil society is constructed as a separate domain because such constructions are central to projects of hegemony,[9] and so taking such a separation as given is to take hegemony as a natural state of affairs. Hegemony functions though an ensemble of institutions, which also provide the material for counter-hegemonic politics (Mouffe 1988), and because the creation of consent and persuasion involves language, seeking hegemony offers a generalized 'language of contention' (Roseberry 1994). The relations between 'civil and political society' are thus volatile; how political society is 'exterior' to civil society, and how exteriority is managed and maintained, changes over time.

The citizens of civil society both enunciate a domain of civility and give themselves the power to make exceptions to their own violation of its principles. The 'civility' of civil society is a necessary fiction; in reality, consent, coercion, and corruption/fraud are all deployed to secure hegemony, especially as hegemony itself becomes increasingly unstable at a time of primitive accumulation.[10] Those speaking on behalf of civil society use violence selectively towards those they want excluded from it. Indeed, violence is a key relation between the domain of civil society and its outside. It is given a fig-leaf of 'sovereignty' through the partial consent of civil society: the middle classes approve the use of state violence on Maoists and on separatists, but not on the Shiv Sena or the Maharashtra Navnirman Sena, or on illegal moral policing, even though some strong voices within this domain rise against such incidents.

The constructed nature of civil and political society, and the constitutive role of fraud and force in securing the borders between them, raises questions about what borders and bordering processes are at play, and how relations across borders are conducted. Borders are 'contact zones' (Pratt 1992). As Balibar (2002: 85) argues, 'in order to meet at the border, one needs interpreters, mediators and translators', suggesting a 'contact zone' between civil society and its outside. But borders are also 'battle zones' (Mendoza 1994): consider Mezzadra and Neilson's (2008) suggestion that 'the material circumstances of borders are those of tension and conflict, partition and connection, traversing and barricading, life and death', and that 'the border as an institution and as a set of social relationships is constituted by multifarious battles and negotiations'. As Somerville and Perkins (2003) note, bordering needs work. It is at these sites of interpretation, mediation, translation, negotiation, *and* 'battles' that hegemonic elements of civil society seek consent from, exercise coercion against, or perpetrate fraud on—while its counter-hegemonic elements practise solidarity with—political society and the undefined third domain. How are civil and political society, and the third domain, being constructed in the current context of rapid economic change, what borders exist between them, and how do contact and conflict across these borders play out in given scenarios? I turn to these questions in the following sections.

Saving the Good Doctor

On 14 May 2007, Binayak Sen, a prominent member of the activist NGO movement in India, was arrested and charged (under the Chhattisgarh Special Public Safety Act and the Unlawful Activities Prevention Act) with association with the banned Communist Party of India (Maoist) and with sedition. A gold medallist from the premier Christian Medical College, Vellore (CMC), and with a further degree in social health from Jawaharlal Nehru University, Sen had volunteered in poor regions of rural Bihar before moving in 1981 to a Quaker-run health centre in Hoshangabad.[11] He next worked with the Chhattisgarh Mukti Morcha (CMM), an independent (non-party-affiliated) miners' union formed by Shankar Guha Niyogi, a mine worker. The CMM drew its ideology from Marxism, Gandhian praxis, and tribal history. Its members were overwhelmingly tribal workers who worked in the recently denationalized and deregulated 'informal' mines.[12] Public sector mines provided heath care to their workers. However, with deregulation, more mining was carried out by 'informal' mines operated semi-legally by politically connected contractors. For informal mine workers, wages were low and paid sporadically. Contractors enforced a brutal labour regime and did not offer compensation or medical treatment to miners injured at work. The CMM, apart from campaigning militantly for the economic rights of mine workers, opened the Shaheed Hospital to provide them health care. Binayak Sen was involved in setting up the hospital, and began working here in 1981. In 1990, with his wife Ilina Sen, he set up Rupantar, an NGO that trains rural health workers and runs mobile clinics in remote tribal areas. The population among whom Rupantar worked was displaced by dam construction, its forest resources were rapidly receding, and, apart from health care, they had no schools, electricity, or drinking water.[13] In addition, Sen helped the establishment of grain banks in drought-prone areas (MFC 2008).

For his work in the tribal areas of Madhya Pradesh and Chhattisgarh, Sen became recognized as a prominent civil liberties and democratic rights activist, a pioneer in community health in extremely poor areas. He won international awards, and was an interlocutor in the civil society groups involved in dialogue for de-escalating violence in the ongoing war between Maoists and the state in central India. He opposed the state strategy of creating an anti-Maoist vigilante group, the Salwa Judum, as it increased violence in the tribal areas. He was appointed a member on the State Advisory Committee on community health, epidemiology, and capacity building, and was noted for his contribution to the government-run Chhattisgarh State Drug Formulary (Jacob 2009: 35). Sen also worked with the Jan Swasth Sahyog, another activist NGO working on public health, staffed by graduates of some of the top medical colleges in the country. Sen was also active in the People's Union for Civil Liberties (PUCL), founded by the noted Gandhian socialist Jayaprakash Narayan, and was its national vice-president.

The dominant development programme in Chhattisgarh is of infrastructure construction, aggressive commercial extraction from forests and mines, rapid industrialization, and large-scale introduction of biofuels and genetically modified (GM) crops in agriculture, although mining remains the central economic activity. Chhattisgarh embraced neoliberalism with alacrity, signing hundreds of memorandums of understanding with Indian and transnational corporations. Srivastava (2008) notes that since the formation of the Chhattisgarh State Mineral Policy in 2001, the state government has signed mining deals worth Rs 3.26 trillion. This involved clearing tribal villages to facilitate mining, both by the state security forces and Salwa Judum, a state-sponsored paramilitary group. Emergency powers granted state forces immunity from prosecution for extra-legal executions.

Hindutva projects attempt to hold together the contradictions unleashed by this programme, whose supposed beneficiaries are its main victims. Organizations connected to the Rashtriya Swayamsevak Sangh (RSS), particularly the Vanvasi Kalyan Ashrams, have been active in the area since the 1950s (see Thachil 2011). Concerned with the same social development desiderata as state agencies and the NGO sector generally, they mimic the strategies of Christian missionaries, mixing patronage, paternalism, proselytization, and programmes of welfare.[14] They intend to make tribals into Hindutva political subjects whose rightful place within a Hindu polity stems from the role assigned to them in Hindu mythology. This project has provided a crucial politics of support to Hindutva strategies for taking control of the state in Chhattisgarh, which has been ruled by the Bharatiya Janata Party (BJP) for more than a decade. Against them are Maoists, who purport to defend tribal rights to resources, and aim to instigate a 'people's war' against the state to install an alternative model of the polity and economy.

The competition over control of the same population groups and territories between incommensurate political projects has resulted in bloody conflict. Hindutva activists accuse Maoists of assassinating Swami Lakshmananand, who had established Vanvasi Kendras in tribal areas of neighbouring Odisha state, and also of being connected to Christian missionaries.[15]

Activist NGOs also intervened in the question of tribal rights. Local campaigns against mining were supported by the Indian People's Tribunal on Environment and Human Rights, a body of metropolitan academics, jurists, and other 'civil society' activists. As a civil liberties activist, Sen campaigned for local journalists and other opponents of this programme incarcerated for 'connections with Maoists', the category into which state security agencies put all opponents of this programme. He provided legal help to Kamaar tribals accused of 'encroaching' on state forests and fought for their land rights. He interceded successfully on their behalf with the Reserve Bank of India, to resolve cases of rampant corruption in state sector banks in which officers approved loans to tribals and siphoned off the major chunk (MFC 2008). Sen's activism aimed at making tribals aware of their rights, and securing such rights militated against the creation of a tabula rasa that state managers of primitive accumulation wanted to present to investors as a reason for preferring Chhattisgarh rather than another resource-rich area in India or worldwide. Sen was a 'translational agent' (see Sinha 2012) who mediated between the domains of everyday tribal life in the remote areas, different state agencies, the larger human rights, civil liberties, and public health activism networks, the National Alliance of People's Movements, and emerging associational forms in the region.

On 14 May 2007, Sen was arrested for allegedly acting as a courier for Maoists. Sen was often invited by the local police to provide health care to jailed inmates including Maoists, but now he was accused of passing secret communications between Narayan Sanyal, an incarcerated Maoist ideologue, and Pijush Guha, who was alleged to have given money to Sen to be passed on to the local Maoists. Sen had indeed met Sanyal several times, in his capacities as doctor and as a human rights and civil liberties activist. Indeed, he had requested these meetings on letterheaded PUCL stationary and was officially granted permission for them by the administration.

As Ilina Sen et al. (2010) note, the investigative process was shoddy and full of illegalities in planting, collecting, and presenting evidence. The court dismissed many witnesses for lacking credibility, and also evidence, such as the presence of the collected works of Marx and Engels and Lenin, and magazines published by left and far-left-wing organizations among Sen's belongings as indication of his guilt, as flimsy. At the same time, the courts repeatedly denied bail to Sen. After a controversial trial, he was incarcerated with no bail provision.

Solidarity with Binayak Sen came from a range of quarters that traverse the trifurcated model of society and politics in Chatterjee's 'Democracy and Economic Transformation'. The Campaign to Release Binayak Sen was transnational. At a local level, this involved the tribal poor who benefited from the health facilities provided by the Sens' initiatives. Justice for Sen, and strategies to achieve it, were discussed on Chhattisgarh-net, a Yahoo group of pro-poor development and rights activists. The CMC, Vellore, had awarded Sen its 2004 Paul Harrison Prize in recognition of his contributions to health provision in some of the poorest areas of India, and this helped galvanize CMC's well-networked and influential body of Old Boys' Associations. Indeed, in the UK and elsewhere, CMC Old Boys took the lead in organizing meetings, campaigns, and demonstrating in front of the Indian High Commission. In meetings in London, while there was open discussion on strategy, the Old Boys' Association pushed for profiling Sen as a doctor with a humanist social consciousness, who was for fundamental social change, but did not support Maoist violence. They highlighted his statements where he specifically was critical of Maoism.

Associations of medical and public health counter-experts (I use this term in the sense adapted by Nilsen 2013) formed another link in the emerging chain of solidarity. The Medico Friends Circle (MFC), an all-India coalition of 'socially conscious medical, public health and social science professionals and researchers, as well as community health and women's health rights activists' (MFC 2008), who share concerns and ideas about health care for the poor, and of which Sen had been a member for 30-odd years, also generated a powerful campaign for his release. The Jan Swasth Abhiyan, and the global People's Health Movement of which it was a part, campaigned for justice for Binayak. The Global Health Council awarded him their Jonathan Mann Prize in 2009, and the citation emphatically rejected the state's contention that he was a threat to security. In 2009, the globally influential medical journal *Lancet* also publicized Binayak's case. A signature campaign of prominent doctors and public health figures worldwide resulted in thousands signing a petition to the prime minister and the president of India. Pointing to the injustice of the arrest of an eminent public health campaigner, Sanjay Chaturvedi (2008) opined, 'Something must be very wrong somewhere.'

A third circle of solidarity was from outside the medical community, in the larger networks of activist NGOs and social movements. Sen was a key member of the National Alliance for People's Movements, a coalition of more than 100 entities, each with strong bases of support within and outside India. The New Trade Union Initiative, a confederation of non-party trade unions active primarily among informal workers (of which the CMM was a precursor), also campaigned via its affiliates. These movements called to implement constitutional protections for tribal homelands against memorandums of understanding signed without their consultation and knowledge.

A fourth circle comprised 'liberal' civil society in India and elsewhere. Important voices in corporate-owned media, both print and electronic in India, condemned the miscarriage of justice, wondered how this could happen in a modernizing country, and what message this would send to the world at large. Amnesty International labelled Sen a 'prisoner of conscience' and mounted a campaign for his release. The British House of Commons published an 'early day motion' with cross-party support.

Finally, support for Sen was mobilized within the academy and among intellectuals in and outside India. In 2007, the Indian Academy of Social Science awarded him its Kheitan Medal, but the courts refused him bail to travel to receive it. Campaigns on major Indian campuses including Jawaharlal Nehru University, Delhi University, and the Tata Institute of Social Sciences, Mumbai, involved seminars and demonstrations. Outside India, the Justice for Binayak campaign found natural allies in the campus left generally, and the left Indian diaspora specifically, with campaigns at Berkeley, Cambridge, the London School of Economics, and the School of African and Oriental Studies. Noam Chomsky was among those who signed a petition for his release in 2007, while Amartya Sen condemned his incarceration in an essay in 2010. As a result of sustained pressure by this multi-actor and multi-level campaign, Binayak Sen was granted bail in 2011.

The solidarity networks campaigned, variously, on behalf of Binayak Sen the human rights crusader, the good doctor who had abnegated self-interest in favour of responding to his calling, on wider issues concerning immunity for security forces, the legality of extra-judicial actions by the state, and the propriety of the judicial processes themselves. One issue debated within solidarity groups was whether to present Sen as a wronged non-violent public health and civil liberties campaigner, in other words, someone who opposed the state process while having loyalty both to the state form and the state idea, or whether to include others incarcerated in the wars unleashed by primitive accumulation, for example Soni Sori, a tribal activist also accused of being a Maoist, and similar others. State complicity and impunity, and 'special powers acts' in operation all over India, also were debated within the Justice for Binayak campaign. The consensus that emerged was that while the second type of tactic was important, that would complicate the specific case of Sen. The PUCL delegation that met the chief minister of Chhattisgarh in 2007 specifically made it a point to tell him that it was unjust to link Sen with Maoism. In this way, a boundary was drawn *within* the solidarity networks.

In Chatterjee's trifurcated political model, there is no possibility of solidarity of this sort. I will take up the question of those segments of the middle classes, such as Sen and a myriad others, who act against their 'class interests' in the conclusion to this chapter. For now, I will note that the primitive accumulation process creates split domains of politics, but not always along the fault lines Chatterjee suggests. It also creates splits within the domains: tribals split between supporting Hindutva forces, vigilante groups, paternalistic politicians, Maoists, and independent political initiatives such as Sen's; or the middle classes, some of whom provide active consent for the political programme of the state, including its violence, while others support the desiderata of these programmes but not the violation of civility it involves, and those who come from its counter-hegemonic sectors, with a history of solidarity with the poor. Even 'corporate capital' is not a uniform domain, simultaneously forming joint ventures in mining and industry that unleash the wars in which Sen was a casualty, and producing new media platforms, including television news shows, on which solidarity for Sen was mobilized.

After having discussed the politics of civil and political society at a primary site of primitive accumulation, I turn to a site in which the politics of primitive accumulation is displaced: the new bubbles of real estate in cities such as Delhi where two flows generated by primitive accumulation elsewhere—of capital and of labour—encounter each other.

RWAs as Neoliberal Civil Society

A random notice slipped under a friend's door contained the agenda of the meeting of the RWA of his gated community in a prominent

Delhi Development Authority 'colony' in south Delhi, including an item entitled 'Use of swings and playing areas by children of domestic servants, shopkeepers and dhobis'. The RWA wanted to ban this, keeping them for the exclusive use of the children of those who lived in the flats. They also requested residents to complete identification of 'servants' and tenants, and maintain vigilance on 'unauthorized' service providers—vegetable sellers, washermen, and such—entering the 'pocket'.[16] Residents in this 'middle-income group' area were a mix of professionals and retirees, from different regional backgrounds, though with north Indians present in greater numbers than others. Domestic workers and other service providers tended to be from rural Bihar, Bengal, and Bangladesh, the tribal areas of Odisha, Jharkhand, and Chhattisgarh, and from the hill regions. Apart from the 'live-ins', they reside mostly in *bastis* (officially unrecognized informal slums) built on vacant public lands between clusters of gated communities. The RWAs routinely pass orders disallowing the children of domestic workers the use of the parks in their areas, and use the threat of cancellation of their permissions of entry to enforce these orders. They also use similar threats to force vendors of goods and services to keep the prices for their services low.

Indian cities like Delhi have seen a housing boom since the late 1980s. New areas in the national capital region such as Vasant Kunj, Dwarka, the 'trans-Yamuna' areas, Gurgaon, and NOIDA, boast a large population, and are prized real estate. In many colonies, apartments were initially allocated though lottery, though in Gurgaon and NOIDA they were purchased directly from 'builders' (private developers). Substantial numbers of property owners have come from the provinces. The RWAs operate in most areas, and in large housing developments they are also federated. The RWAs charge contributions from residents to hire security guards, who monitor who comes into these areas. They also use part of the residents' contributions towards the upkeep of parks in their areas. Apart from residents' contributions, they sell advertising space to newspapers, private sector health care providers, local businesses, and so on. The RWAs entered the Delhi government's Bhagidari (Partnership) Scheme, which encourages their participation to assist municipal government in delivering a range of services: domestic water supply, recovery of municipal charges, maintenance of water pipelines, and so on.[17] Non-governmental organizations mediate between RWAs and government agencies. The RWAs run voter registration campaigns, and political parties try to use RWAs in their election campaigns.

While they are not the primary sites of primitive accumulation, these newly built housing colonies are constituted by flows emanating from such sites. Delhi's spread, and the creation of the 'National Capital Region', was made possible by the takeover of agricultural land by the Delhi government in previous decades for anticipated housing and commercial use. Likewise, in adjoining Haryana and Uttar Pradesh, private players speculated in land and made spectacular profit, facilitated by close links with politicians and administrators, and became real-estate magnates rapidly.[18] Parallel to housing, export production zones, technology parks, automobile manufacturing units, and other 'new economy' areas were developed. To connect these new spaces, transport infrastructure including roads, flyovers, and the Delhi metro were constructed. All this was part of the 'global city' fantasy of the emerging ruling classes. Today, prominent among residents of the gated communities are those working in the new economy, with advanced degrees and experience of education, work, and travel abroad.

Construction booms need not only capital and buyers and renters: they need labour. While this labour is heavily from Uttar Pradesh and Bihar, places of continued intense rural conflicts, recent flows have been from areas of near-classic primitive accumulation, where large-scale land transfers, including land grabs, have taken place for mining and industry, or from areas where the state has undertaken dam construction, which has dispossessed rural populations. The domestic worker category draws heavily from these groups, in addition to Bangladeshis, Nepalis, and middle-Himalayan migrants. The everyday contacts and battles in gated communities involve these actors. The RWAs attempt, but ultimately fail, to 'control' these contacts and win the battles.

Domestic work involves daily visitations into intimate middle-class spaces—their 'homes'—by social actors with whom they would otherwise have little interaction because they would consider themselves superior in social and cultural hierarchies of caste and class. Domestic care workers—'ayahs'—often stay with the families that employ them. Additionally, 'maid servants' who are employed by multiple residents to clean, cook, and wash come and go a few times daily.[19] Domestic workers and the new middle classes depend on each other in order to make a living (Schindler 2014).

The RWAs are the quintessential form of neoliberal civil society in India, expressing the power of the new middle classes. They consider 'participation' in governance to be a virtue, are supported by local authorities taking on new governance models, and reflect the socio-political profile of residents who come from the same class and caste backgrounds as bureaucrats and the media (Mooij and Tawa Lama-Rewal 2009). As an associational form, they bring together owners of property in the defence of property, in the enhancement and maintenance of its value and of the value of life in the gated community. Officers of the RWAs are elected, but leadership within RWAs is not secure.[20]

Gated communities complicate Chatterjee's civil/political society divide, firstly because they are not the bastions of civility—respect for law, property, and 'other-regarding behaviour'—that he assumes.[21] The very act of acquiring property in these localities often involves multiple acts of illegality. The advertised sale price is seldom the amount that is paid: the 'black/white ratio' is adjusted as per the needs and capacities of the transacting parties. Buyers hide the price they pay, as it would indicate that they had more incomes than they had declared to the state. Sellers under-report the price they receive to minimize tax payments. Sales done via 'power of attorney' avoid the cumbersome process of register-ing the sale with the notoriously corrupt Municipal Corporation of Delhi (MCD), which requires a combination of kickbacks and personal connections.

As for respect for property, residents routinely extend their flats illegally on to public land. A common element in RWA agendas across such colonies is the problem caused by this for the park-ing of cars. When these colonies were constructed, planners had assumed one car per residential unit, but now the numbers and sizes of cars far exceed their plan. Parking is an issue in which

New Subaltern Politics

there is no 'other-regarding behaviour', and its politics resembles a Hobbesian state of nature, with stories about physical violence resulting from disputes not uncommon. This has forced many RWAs to 'informally' convert public lands or to tolerate their conversion by residents, into parking lots.[22]

As a collective, RWAs are fearful of and exclusionary towards domestic workers and the providers of petty services. Their actions to these ends revolve centrally around 'security'. Crimes taking place inside homes against residents were reported to be on an upswing from the 1990s, when exponential urban growth took place, and new private media took a lead in creating not so much an awareness of security as panic. The RWAs have undertaken an extensive campaign of 'finger-printing' domestic workers and getting them registered with the Delhi police, as well as instituting 'verification' processes in domestic workers' 'native villages'. This is based on the assumption that most crime in Delhi is carried out by domestic workers. The RWAs exert considerable pressure on residents to conform to this, arguing that unregistered domestic workers pose a threat to the community generally, and not only to the households in which they work. But this has been beset with problems from the outset. R. S. Yadav, secretary general of the Federation of Vasant Kunj RWAs, noted early in the process of RWA formation in 1996 that security and other-regarding behaviour were intrinsically connected: 'Unfortunately, most residents are very insular and self-centred. A sense of community is lacking and many consider it infra dig to associate with neighbours, even refusing to respond to distress cries. While the present fear psychosis will pass, in the long run people need to cooperate' (A. Prakash 1996). Nearly 20 years later, cooperation was still lacking.[23] The NOIDA Sector 15A RWA reported enforcement problems: even after termination of employment, domestics were not surrendering passes issued to them to enter the gated communities.[24]

The RWAs' authority over their own members on this matter remains shaky. Though residents themselves raised the spectre of ghoulish domestics, they are reluctant to register domestic workers, as hiring child labour in contravention of child labour laws is common (*Times of India*, 8 June 2011).[25] Providing this information is risky for residents: they would have to pay tax on rent, comply with labour laws, and reveal whatever 'costs of entry' RWA officials, especially guards, charge petty shopkeepers and service providers. Residents of trans-Yamuna colonies reported other problems preventing them from participating in the servant verification drive: that the turnover of domestic servants was very high and it was onerous for them to fill out form after form; and that servants were cagey about the verification process (*Dainik Jagaran* 2013). As Kailash Katyal, president of the Mayur Vihar Phase 1 RWA federation, noted: 'Maids also feel scared while filling the forms and sometimes they throw a fit' (*Dainik Jagaran* 2013). Some would leave employment, and the reputational damage among the pool of workers caused by vigorously pursuing verification would make it difficult for residents to find replacements.

Domestic workers had good reason to resist verification, as it meant getting photos attested, providing proof of residence, confirmation of identity from their village or place of origin, and finally a visit from a constable to confirm address. All of these are sites of predation on them, or at least of uncomfortable interactions with elements of an apparatus of power. For the considerable numbers of domestic workers who come from Bangladesh, their situations are doubly precarious. Given widespread anti-Muslim sentiment among the middle classes, Bangladeshi domestic workers often take on 'neutral' or Hindu names and 'pass' as Indian Bengali, so for them verification holds real peril.[26]

The RWAs charge fees from children of domestic workers to use colony parks, though these are often developed with MLAs' or MPs' constituency funds and should be open to them for free. Bhagidari requires RWAs to extend education, health care, and vocational training to the poor, but often the opposite is the case (Chakrabarti 2008). The RWA of B-1 Block in Vasant Kunj stopped a resident and her NGO from running literacy classes for children of domestic workers on the grounds that 'the RWA must maintain decorum' in the colony (Dasgupta 2012). In other cases, NOIDA RWAs collaborate with municipal authorities to undertake programmes of 'improving' the poor, for example, of 'rehabilitation and resettlement' of beggars, provision of mental health and skills training to them, and even issuing them 'permits' and 'identity cards'. The RWAs have not endorsed these measures only as a benevolent gesture, but, given the automatic connection made by residents between the poor and criminality, they expect this to reduce crime.[27]

Many RWAs in Delhi are locked in legal conflict with basti residents and hawkers who have long used public spaces in and around their colonies, some even before the latter were built. Harassed now for the mess they create, sections of roads that they use are metamorphosing into parking lots (Dasgupta 2012). Schindler (2014) shows that in parts of Delhi, RWAs do not exclude hawkers but regulate their access. Either way, the RWAs' influence spills out into ordering not only space within the gated compounds, but urban space more generally. As Ghertner (2008) persuasively shows, RWAs often use discourses of 'nuisance', and moral and aesthetic arguments to lock out the poor from the spaces and amenities within the gated community but also, importantly, in areas contiguous to it.

The modes of new middle-class exercise of power over informal service sector workers and the urban poor influence their associational form and their idioms of political mobilization. The National Domestic Workers' Movement was launched in 1985 by Sr Jeanne Devos, a Belgian nun with considerable social movement experience.[28] Sympathetic NGOs and counter-experts had set up the Delhi Domestic Workers' Forum, winning court battles in 1995 to combat harassment, non-payment of wages, abuse, and sexual exploitation. New legislation and the expanding interest of NGOs in the welfare of domestic workers further limit the worst oppressions. The Domestic Worker Welfare and Social Security Act of 2010 provides a number of rights to workers similar to workers in other sectors, while at the same time keeping the specificity of domestic work, for example, its gendered nature.[29] To counter RWA challenges to their use of urban space, two associations of the urban poor, Sanjha Manch and the Delhi Janwadi Adhikar Manch, report encroachments on public lands by middle-class property owners.[30]

Domestic workers recently launched a second-generation union movement, the Delhi Domestic Workers' Union (DDWU), an organization that is predicated on the *class* identity of workers. A constituent of the National Domestic Workers' Movement, the

DDWU is connected with the Construction Workers' Union and the Car Cleaners' Union, quite possibly because these are two sectors in which husbands of women domestic workers find employment. Just as RWAs had finger-printed domestic workers, the DDWU asks for registration of employers and placement agencies. Funds collected in the registration process and from workers themselves would fund programmes to provide identity cards, bank accounts, regular medical check-ups, shelters, dispute regulation, regulation of placement agency, and prevent child labour in domestic work, including trafficking of children for such work. Delhi Domestic Workers' Forum and Union members regularly carry out 'rescue operations' to free child workers, and to report abuse of domestic workers. Its 2013 campaigns were for higher wages, adequate food from employers, non-payment of wages to workers and depositing them with placement agencies, denial of education and health care, and the absence of social security such as provident fund, gratuity, crèche facilities, maternity benefits, and pensions.[31] The campaign has drawn in a prominent social work institute, the Nirmala Niketan, and the National Commission for Women. The DDWU is connected to the international movement of domestic workers, the International Labour Organization's campaign for decent work, and to international development agencies via the National Domestic Workers' Movement and the feminist NGO Jagori.[32]

Lately, political parties such as the Bahujan Samaj Party, the Samajwadi Party, the Lok Janshakti Party, the Janata Dal (United), and the Rashtriya Janata Dal have tried to establish themselves among migrant workers from their zones of influence in Uttar Pradesh and Bihar, providing them with another avenue to redress grievances and demands reforms and rights.[33] Domestic workers formed a core constituency for the new Aam Aadmi Party which won 67 of 70 seats in the latest Delhi assembly elections. The National Platform for Domestic Workers, in addition to associations specifically of and for domestic workers, features speakers from many political parties, which provides them with an important avenue for pushing through favourable legislation.

The very act of migration to the metropolis, and the peculiarities of domestic work, destabilizes the boundary between civil and political society. The confrontations set up this way explain partly the emergence of such workers' political subjectivity. The other part of the explanation, however, is located in experiences of solidarity between workers and political parties, movement networks, NGOs, and trade unions. What this says about civil and political society, and the border between them, is a question I address in the next section.

Rethinking Subalternity in Neoliberal Contexts

In his subversion of the subalternist approach, Ranabir Samaddar (2007: 113) asks: 'can we think of a political society as distinct from civil society in terms of norms, functions, mores and structure, in the definition of which the difference with the civil is critical, and the task of building on this difference is . . . rewarding?' To end this chapter, let me recall Chatterjee's definition of political society as 'the vast domain outside the designated spheres of modern politics, where *the untutored masses* made claims on the state and formed their own associations and organizations, *unmindful of the formal grammar of rights and citizenship*' (1998; emphasis mine). While this formulation describes some contexts, it ignores a central feature of the politics of postcolonial primitive accumulation that marks it as different from the 'western' trajectory: the presence not only of formal political and legal equality, but also of multi-level solidarity networks—NGOs, social movements, trade unions, political parties—that provide mediation and translation between the new victims of primitive accumulation, and the language of universal rights: civil liberties, right to health, workers' rights, decent work, and so on.

In contrast to Chatterjee (2004: 137) for whom the habitation and livelihoods of the poor are 'often premised on the violation of the law', I have shown in Binayak Sen's case that dominant sections of actually existing civil society feel they have impunity from the law, and in denying access to it to the poor and those in solidarity with them, *they deny the law's universalism*: this is a key condition for primitive accumulation today. While officials clear slums on legal, aesthetic, moral, and public health grounds, claiming that they cannot authorize the permanent regularization of the poor's illegal occupation of private or public lands as that would threaten 'the entirety of property relations' (Chatterjee 2004: 136), they tolerate *encroachment of public lands by the middle classes*. Middle-class solidarity thus cuts across 'civil society' to 'state' domains, evident in new forms of governmentality, such as the bhagidari between RWAs and the state. Servant verification schemes exemplify the will of civil society to dominate political society. In Chhattisgarh, it is not the poor who are capable of 'controlled organization of violence', but those pursuing other projects—Hindutva, Maoism, and rapid growth through state-led primitive accumulation. Chatterjee talks of 'the security of the peaceful legality of civil society' (Chatterjee 2004: 136), but security in the time of primitive accumulation involves *violence and illegality* in the pursuit of state power and rapid economic growth. The suspension of the norms of civil society in order to protect civil society and the use of chicanery and violence against the enemies of rapid growth shows the limits of the liberalism of bourgeois civil society. Claiming universalism while policing its borders and actively excluding the poor is the central feature of the politics of civil society. When the poor and those in solidarity with them claim the universalism of the values of *ideal* civil society, they threaten the borders that *actual* civil society creates around itself.

To explain how contemporary capitalist dynamics in India influences emerging subaltern political subjectivity, one must reject Chatterjee's strategy of stating a normative civil society that perhaps did not even exist in 'the west', and then measuring deviations from it to derive his concepts of civil and political society in India. Instead, I suggest we see the assumption of a position of 'civility', and the processes of giving meaning to that term, themselves as political acts, as claims to power. This will enable conceptualizing differently how the domains of civil society and its outsides are being drawn today, as well as the relations between them.

To posit an a priori heuristic separation between domains is problematic because their evolution is interlinked, which establishes between them 'a contingent, non-predetermined relation' (Laclau 1984: 32). Still, there are two reasons why those who claim to belong to civil society enunciate these distinctions. Champions of rapid capitalist development operate in a setting in which there is not the 'amnesia' Marx refers to, but rather the stark conditions of 'compressed capitalism' (Bagchi and D'Costa 2012).[34] So enunciating the distinctiveness of civil society and nominating themselves as the privileged voices of such civil society is part of their strategy to secure hegemony as the 'natural leaders' of society. For progressive elements of the bourgeoisie who act in solidarity with the victims of primitive accumulation, the invocation of civil society is both to put limits on the rapacity of the process, and the primary justification for the needs and rights of its victims. The *relational* evolution of subjectivity is evident in domestic workers' associationalism. As recent migrants, they were initially organized in loose networks of region, caste, kin, and, for Christian tribals, churches. While these forms remain, faced with abuse and non-payment of salaries from their employers and suspicions of criminality, domestic workers formed unions and linked with NGOs and political parties. The politics of those coming from the undefined third domain now uses the language of law in framing their interactions with their employers, pursuing rights and reforms from the state, and linking up with national and international campaigns for them.

What is common to sites of primitive accumulation today is the presence of solidarity networks that cut across Chatterjee's civil and political society, and the undefined third domain, and which have multiple histories: feminism, environmentalism, human rights, socialism, and movements for human dignity have for decades connected and constituted 'the local' and 'the global'. There is, therefore, an already existing set of discourses of rights and practices of solidarity that are not generated *by* the victims of primitive accumulation, but *on their behalf*. Discourses of solidarity and political projects aiming to encompass them have a profound impact on the constitution of new subaltern subjectivity, even as the fields of the political and the economic limit both the formation of new political collectivities and the terms on which they enter and create networks of solidarity.

For Chatterjee (2001: 178), the recent globalization of capital unleashes opposition between the *modernity* of civil society and the *democracy* of political society. For him the paradox is that the democracy practised by the denizens of political society goes counter to the tenets of modern civility that constitute civil society. What I have shown is that the relation between modernity, civil society, democracy, and political society are quite different because key aspects of modernity are denied to political society by the citizens of civil society, who often violate these tenets and use democracy and claims to civility as instruments of class power. The paradox of capitalist modernity in India is a different one: that in order for it to succeed, it has to deny to its victims access to the language and apparatus of modernity and universalism. Perhaps the opposition that is emerging in the context of contemporary compressed capitalism is a different one: between capitalism and its votaries of rapid development on one side, and civility, citizenship, and social rights on the other.

Notes

1. Other noteworthy attempts are Spivak's (2000a, 2000b) concept of 'the new subaltern' and Chakrabarty's attempt (2005) to distinguish between 'proper' and 'improper' politics.

2. Sanyal also suggests that international development programmes now legitimate capital accumulation on a world scale, a productive line of inquiry that Chatterjee does not yet include in his framework.

3. It is another matter that 'canonical Marxism' too has long recognized this, including Marx himself. See for example Anderson (2010), and Bernstein's (2007) notion of 'classes of labour'.

4. Chatterjee's engagement with these themes was limited to reflections on the 'war on terror' and its aftermath, and on the 'global city' imaginary of India's middle classes.

5. It is noteworthy that this class today forms the core of the support for the prime ministerial campaign of the business-friendly Narendra Modi.

6. Similarly, Mannathukkaren (2010) reads the politics around the People's Plan Campaign in Kerala to argue that they necessitate going beyond the civil/political society binary altogether.

7. Tribals are the chief victims of the new primitive accumulation, accounting for 9 per cent of the population, but 40 per cent of the displaced, according to the Government of India (2008).

8. Speaking of the colonization of Ireland, Wood (2003: 71) notes that the dispossession of the Irish peasantry by the 'plantation' of English and Scottish colonists was aimed at making the land more productive,

by exporting wholesale the property relations of south-east England. The incorporation of Ireland into the English economy went hand in hand with attempts to 'civilize' the Irish. The whole exercise was to move the Irish from barbarism to civility. Irish laws were not laws but merely 'lewd' and 'unreasonable custom'.

9. Thomas (2009) thinks of claims to distinction of civil society as a 'class hegemonic project'.

10. This is in line with Gramsci's suggestion in his 'Notes on Machiavelli' that 'the "normal" exercise of hegemony on the now classical terrain of the parliamentary regime is characterized by the combination of force and consent, which balance each other reciprocally, without force predominating excessively over consent. Indeed, the attempt is always made to ensure that force will appear to be based on the consent of the majority, expressed by the so-called organs of public opinion—newspapers and associations—which, therefore, in certain situations, are artificially multiplied. Between consent and force stands corruption/fraud' (Gramsci 1971: 247n49).

11. Hoshangabad then was a centre of innovative and progressive NGO initiatives aimed at the advancement of the tribal poor.

12. Amar Kanwar's installation 'The Sovereign Forest' offers an excellent account of Guha and his assassination.

13. Describing life in what corresponds to Chatterjee's third domain, Jacob (2009) writes of the deprivations of water, sanitation, food security, education, and employment, leading to a cynicism regarding the democratic process. This makes for 'fertile ground' for supporting the Maoists' project of violent armed revolution.

14. The current RSS-affililated BJP chief minister of the state, Raman Singh, has assiduously cultivated the image of 'chawal wale baba', or 'the saint who distributes free rice'.

15. After Niyogi's killing in 1991, the CMM's potential for social transformation was dispersed into tribal identity politics, in social development projects, and opposition to GM agriculture being introduced in the state.

16. The colonies are segmented into 'sectors', which are further segmented into 'pockets'.

17. For details of Bhagidari, see http://delhigovt.nic.in/bhagi.asp (accessed 15 February 2014). The RWAs have taken on extensive roles in urban governance.

18. Some of these magnates used their newfound wealth to become politicians themselves.

19. Waldrop (2004) sensitively shows the ways that residents restrict the access within the home to domestic workers, and constantly use language to affirm their class and caste superiority.

20. On occasion, residents have suspected RWA office bearers of colluding with the Municipal Corporation of Delhi to start mixed use or commercial use of land in residential areas, for which they received sizeable kickbacks (*Hindu* 2006). Schindler (2014: 563–4) recounts disputes around elections of RWA office bearers.

21. For example, Greater Kailash Phase II RWAs erected gates on main arterial roads leading to other south Delhi colonies such as Chittaranjan Park and Alaknanda. As one urban planner resident of Chittaranjan Park said, 'This is Talibanization of city planning. Everybody thinks that they can do what they want to *without caring about their neighbours*' (*Times of India* 2012; emphasis mine.)

22. This is most starkly the case with the so-called 'farmhouses' on the outskirts of the city. The original allocation of land required that these allotments show some evidence of farming or food processing, but over time these plots housed palatial constructions, many housing fancy restaurants, or event venues. The Delhi Development Authority and the MCD both undertake periodic campaigns of demolishing such 'encroachments'. However, the standard procedure is for RWAs to petition the governments for a blanket amnesty for such construction, and their 'regularization', while arranging an informal collection to keep municipal authorities from actually going through with demolitions.

23. Gurgaon police commissioner Alok Mittal, who had directed officers of RWAs and other housing societies to keep a record of all the tenants, domestic helps, fruit and vegetable vendors, and washermen in their respective areas, reported poor cooperation (*Hindustan Times* 2013).

24. 'Surrender & cancellation of RWA (Sector 15A Noida) passes issued to servants, domestic helps and drivers at the time of their removal', http://n15a.communitysamvada.com/index.php?option=com_insti tutions&view=detail&type=announcements&task=detail&id=2&tid=10 (accessed 7 February 2015).

25. 'Throughout the day, several people enter and exit from our society on the pretext that they are employed as maids in different flats. There is no one to keep a track on them' (*Dainik Jagaran* 2013).

26. At the time of writing, the BJP has made the eviction of illegal Bangladeshi Muslim migrants a key issue in its election campaign.

27. Sunil Sethi of the NOIDA Sector 15 RWA noted the security problems posed by 'hundreds of beggars [who] are seen on the roads near the red lights, junctions and even in the locality where people are residing' (*Dainik Jagaran, City Plus*, 31 January 2014).

28. The need for such a movement is explained on the National Domestic Workers' Movement website, http://majesticwork.com/ndwm/

post-1985/ (accessed 12 March 2015): 'Bishops of the tribal areas expressed their concern for girls, women and children who were leaving villages to go to towns. They felt that something must be done to help them.'

29. Concern for domestic workers has not been absent in the Indian legislative and judicial process, even though comprehensive 'policy' and 'law' have been a long time coming. Neeta and Palriwal (2011: 99) note that the first bill for domestic workers' rights was introduced in the Rajya Sabha in 1957.

30. The Manch was a forum of about 20 unions and associations that included migrant solidarity groups.

31. The July 2013 campaign of the National Domestic Workers' Union featured speeches by prominent politicians from the Communist Party of India, the Janata Dal (United), Sanjay Paswan of the BJP, Mohini Giri, former head of the National Commission for Women, Vijayalakshmi Reddy from the All India Trade Union Congress, and Annie Raja of the National Federation of Indian Women (UCAN India 2013).

32. The relations between NGOs and leaders among slum dwellers is often tense, as Webb (2013) shows.

33. This is in line with Harriss's (2006) suggestion that political parties are important avenues for grievance redressal for the urban poor.

34. As the process of primitive accumulation in England was a long-drawn-out one, by the nineteenth century people forgot the brutality and illegality it had necessarily involved. As Marx puts it, 'In the 19th century, the very memory of the connexion between the agricultural labourer and the communal property, had, *of course*, vanished' (Marx 1990: 889; emphasis mine).

Postscript

Subaltern Studies

Then and Now

DAVID ARNOLD*

It is now more than 30 years since the Subaltern Studies project first announced itself in print (Ranajit Guha 1983b). In that time it has become a truly international project—partly through the publication of the original *Subaltern Studies* volumes and the work of the scholars closely associated with the project, but also through the many other academics who have helped to develop the idea of Subaltern Studies or to critique it. Over the course of those three decades the geographical parameters of Subaltern Studies have been pushed outwards from its original home in South Asia to other regions like Latin America and the Middle East (Atabaki 2007; Ismail 2013; Mallon 1994a), though there has been significantly less impact on studies of Africa, Southeast Asia, and East Asia. Even so, as the essays in this volume further suggest, South Asia (and, within

*. I am indebted to Alf Nilsen, Srila Roy, and other participants in the Bergen conference for their comments on an earlier draft of this note, and to Alpa Shah for her constructive engagement. The essay remains, though, the author's personal view.

it, India) remains the main regional focus for Subaltern Studies and its principal proving ground. From its initial concentration in the history of nineteenth- and early twentieth-century India, the temporal locus of Subaltern Studies has shifted forward in time, into contemporary society and politics: a reverse move, backwards from the colonial era into pre-colonial history, has barely happened at all. If the place of Subaltern Studies in the writing and conceptualization of history remains relatively assured (if still contested), then much of its recent growth and critical energy has been concentrated in politics, anthropology, sociology, cultural geography, and postcolonial studies. These are developments that those of us involved in the original Subaltern Studies group in the late 1970s and early 1980s could hardly have hoped for or expected.

This postscript will not attempt to offer some definitive statement of what Subaltern Studies is, was, or aspires to, or of its intellectual shortcomings and achievements. Other scholars have already undertaken that task (for example, Ludden 2002a). Instead I want to reprise the radicalism (or otherwise) of the early Subaltern Studies project, as this seems to be a critical point of departure and site of contention for many recent authors (including several in this volume), who see more of analytical value and political worth in the earlier manifestations of Subaltern Studies than in some of its later incarnations.

Subaltern Studies was always meant to be relevant. Indeed, in a rather naive sense, it was intended to be a kind of political activism and not merely the kind of academically ensconced exercise some critics would now accuse it of being. The historical scholarship from which Subaltern Studies drew inspiration in the 1970s and 1980s, including that of E. P. Thompson and Eric Hobsbawm, was characterized by a similar expectation that the academy should not be aloof from political commitment and social activism. That collective ambition has long since disappeared, especially with the literary turn in Subaltern Studies in the mid-1980s and the shift from a specific focus on the subaltern classes as generally understood to what has variously been characterized as *bhadralok* studies or, apparently still more depressingly, postcolonial theory (Chibber 2013; Ramachandra Guha 1995). But any current reconceptualization of Subaltern Studies has to address the still pertinent question of what such a field of study is for and whether it can ever be for anything more than the massed ranks of the academy. One reason for the revival of interest in the early Subaltern Studies project, and the desire to reactivate its latent radicalism or to critique it (as in Luisa Steur's essay in this volume) by locating it alongside other radical academic traditions like that of Marxian anthropology and sociology, lies precisely in the desire to bring the understanding of the subaltern into more contemporary focus, to make it a more active tool of analysis and engagement.

One of the premises of Subaltern Studies at the outset—and perhaps one of its fundamental difficulties and conceptual constraints—was that while drawing inspiration from the present, Subaltern Studies spoke through the language of the past—in part in the belief that the past could meaningfully be used to explain, interrogate, and structure the present. That may now seem a less pertinent way of approaching the central problematic of subalternity, but it is not so different from Gramsci's discussion of Italian history in the *Prison Notebooks* to ground and dissect contemporary politics, or Thompson seeking the origins of contemporary class formations in eighteenth- and nineteenth-century England. When the Subaltern Studies group first came into existence under Ranajit Guha's leadership in the late 1970s, it was obvious enough what 'the present' was that needed to be investigated and analysed. It was evident in the crisis of Indian democracy created by Indira Gandhi's increasing authoritarianism and the Emergency of 1975–7, the violent suppression of the Naxalite movement and the railway strike of 1974, and the underlying economic and social malaise of a society still not far from outright famine. In such compelling circumstances it was unsurprising that Guha wrote of India's democracy as being 'long dead, now buried' (1976), and, in the first volume of *Subaltern Studies*, lamented the 'failure of the Indian bourgeoisie to speak for the nation' (1982b: 5). Perhaps one can, in retrospect, see the Emergency years as an aberration or challenge that ultimately served to reinforce the power of India's democratic instincts and processes (Ramachandra Guha 2007: 493–521). And, 60 years on from India's independence, and with more than 20 years of economic liberalization and globalization to boot, it is possible to argue that the long-gone colonial era of state repression and popular resistance has less political relevance and analytical traction now (though that is debateable), and that the nature of subalternity has changed and requires fresh modes of analysis (Chatterjee 2012). But the colonial past and its historical legacies did not seem so distant in the 1970s and 1980s.

The triple combination in Guha's opening manifesto—in which 'failure', 'bourgeoisie', and 'nation' are inextricably linked—seemed to be a particularly resonant combination, and it is understandably one that Vivek Chibber makes much critical play with in his scornful account of Subaltern Studies (Chibber 2013). 'Failure' aptly captures the deep sense of anger and frustration many Indian left-wing intellectuals and activists felt in the 1970s. It particularly associates Subaltern Studies, in its original manifestation, with stories of loss rather than tales of empowerment, which is what some subaltern narratives are more concerned with today. Guha's manifesto identified Subaltern Studies with the 'failure' of India after 1947 to fulfil the high expectations created by the nationalist movement, through Gandhi and Nehru in particular, but also by the revolutionary Marxism of the time. This was especially so at a time when Mao's China was held up on the left as an exemplar of what a revolutionary society in Asia could achieve. We now read Mao's China, like Nehru's India, rather differently, but it is striking how the India–China comparison persists and is still often used to India's detriment.

Perhaps one could argue that that galling sense of 'failure'—part Marxist, part liberal democratic, part bourgeois patriotic—that India hasn't lived up to expectations is less acute now than it was in the 1970s, given India's economic growth and social transformation since the 1990s, but it still lingers—in discussion about persistent poverty, about violence and discrimination against *dalits*, or in the treatment of women as exemplified by the recent Delhi rape case—and is surely one factor in the enduring appeal of Subaltern Studies.

In his ultimately unhelpful critique (which appears to offer little other than a return to an orthodox, even doctrinaire, Marxism), Chibber makes the claim that Subaltern Studies is only of interest insofar as it represents a 'theoretical project'. He remarks that 'if the phenomenon [of Subaltern Studies] merely consisted in a revamped call for history from below ... or a jeremiad against the depredations of colonialism, or the celebration of Third World agency, then whatever else it achieved, it could hardly merit attention as a theoretical project' (Chibber 2013: 9). I don't accept that. The value of Subaltern Studies has always been as a template rather than a prescription, a guide as to how things might be done rather than a dogmatic set of rules. Subaltern Studies began with a political polemic grounded in a close reading of India's modern history and historical sociology: only subsequently did it go in serious search of theory. Even though Gramsci's work became a central theoretical guide, and, thanks to Guha, gave the project its 'subaltern' designation, it was, at the outset, more an approach or orientation than a theory—a 'perspective' as Veena Das described it (1989). One of the reasons for the failure of the early Subaltern Studies writers to engage more fully and critically with questions of hegemony (a failure alluded to in these essays and elsewhere) was precisely because the entirety of Gramsci's thought appeared less salient at the time than his specific observations on the subaltern classes. That said, hegemony did subsequently begin to figure in the work of Guha (1989) and Chatterjee (1993), though the scholarly understanding of Gramsci's hegemony, like his subalternity, has undoubtedly advanced—and become more nuanced—since then (for example, Green 2002, 2011b; Roseberry 1994). Without wishing to advocate any kind of narrow empiricism (on which history can easily overdose), I would suggest that any reconceptualization of subaltern politics has to take into account the need for a close reading of material life, of social being and cultural text, and not just the theory needed to analyse and interpret it—which in part is what the essays in this volume set out to do.

Subaltern Studies in its initial phase was committed to the idea of recovery—despite sceptics like Gayatri Spivak, who suggested that subaltern consciousness and experience was governed by an almost irretrievable alterity, a standpoint which Rashmi Varma duly takes issue with in her essay. There existed the possibility (even the responsibility) of *trying* to recover the lives, the thought-processes, the activities of subordinated groups and classes. In this task of recuperation the historical method (exemplified by Guha's dissection of the 'prose of counter-insurgency' [1983b])—searching out sources and reading them, where necessary, 'against the grain', questioning their surface meaning and partisan provenance but still accepting them as sources nonetheless, finding empirical material or oral testimony to substantiate, instantiate, and contest wider sociological and political claims—was a matter of more than casual importance or untutored wish-fulfilment. It was crucial, conceptually and methodologically, to Subaltern Studies as originally conceived that, for the all the multiple difficulties involved in recuperation, the subaltern did speak and was not just to be spoken for. This was itself part of Subaltern Studies' 'theoretical' purpose and radical intent. Moving away from the grounding of historical methodology into the discursive methodology of literary studies and social theory was always bound to be problematic for Subaltern Studies, especially in overlaying and critiquing the voice of the subaltern with so many layers of interpretation and expostulation.

The original Subaltern Studies project did its historical grounding in three ways. The first was to see primary significance in the colonial period in India. Subaltern Studies never had much to say about pre-colonial India, and historiographically that has surely been one of its most serious lacunae, if only because it has further distanced Subaltern Studies from the recent growth of academic interest in the medieval and early modern period. But the colonial focus, conversely, strengthened the argument about how modern India was made in and through colonialism (imposed, in part, on a 'feudal' base) and how colonially driven processes of hegemony and coercion, of class formation and national integration, were critical in creating India's lopsided and heterogeneous colonial modernity, but also in fashioning India's postcolonial condition. Making sense of the postcolonial was not something the early volumes of *Subaltern Studies* had much truck with, but it has become one of the ways in which the subaltern idea has been critically redeployed and re-valorized (Chaturvedi 2000a).

One could argue hypothetically that the colonial presence really was not that fundamental to India (which is what some non-subaltern historians have always argued), and/or that India has long since, or largely, moved out of the orbit of colonialism and its legacies. It might then follow that grounding Subaltern

Studies in the colonial, temporally and thematically, was, in the long term, unhelpful and a tactical mistake. One response to this would be to stress the similarities between colonialism and globalization, and to reason that just as there are elite perspectives on India under colonialism, so are there elite understandings of India under globalization, perspectives that equally omit or marginalize the local and subaltern dimension. Situating subalternity primarily in the historical and social specificity of the colonial era also arguably made the idea of there being two separate and autonomous domains of politics—elite and subaltern—all too easy to construct, and critics then and now have understandably seen in this an extreme over-simplification and an excessive commitment to ideas of bifurcation. Guha's approach has always been to seek out aggregation—creating the largest possible combination of subalterns rather than dividing them up and separating them out by class, gender, and ethnicity. This has had the virtue of making the understanding of the subaltern invitingly wide and socially inclusive in opposition to those views of Indian society that are constantly intent on fragmentation and compartmentalization, even among the lower classes. For Guha, the binary principle and the dynamism of the dialectic were fundamental—to history, politics, and philosophy—and needed to be present in everything: after Hegel and Marx, the universality of the dialectic was incontestable. We might think otherwise now, but its adoption and its exemplification through historical example and social instantiation helped give Subaltern Studies its critical edge and polemical advantage within an academic domain in which (as perhaps now too) the blurring of boundaries, the multiplying of categories and the contestation of grand narratives seemed the prevalent orthodoxy.

The emphasis upon the colonial period in the early volumes of *Subaltern Studies* also gave prominence to issues of racial identity, conflict, and differentiation—highlighted by Chatterjee's (1993: 20) statement that race was 'perhaps the most obvious mark of colonial difference'. In retrospect, one might argue that this explicit identification of colonialism with race failed to recognize the complex and changing nature of each of these components and that recent scholarship has gone much further in critically examining race, its coercive forms, and hegemonic effects (Kolsky 2010). But the other issue with regard to race is that if it was so crucial in defining a colonial regime of power, how does race then figure in the postcolonial politics of dominance and subordination? One could argue that since 1947, the race factor has become externalized—in the rather superior way in which the West continues to regard India or in the attitudes encountered in the South Asian diaspora in Europe and North America. But one might also argue that race was never just race alone—in the oppositional sense of Europeans versus Indians—but always a part of a much more complicated British and Indian understanding of social differentiation in which Enlightenment thought, scholarly Orientalism, colonial ethnography, and Hindu revivalism all played a part in the making or reformulation of such seemingly primordial categories as Aryans and Dravidians, *adivasi*s and *dalit*s, categories and concepts which still play a major part (as Ajantha Subramanian's essay indicates) in ideas of hegemony and experiences of subalternity today. In his recent book, Gyanendra Pandey (2013) has explored some of these issues of race, caste, and difference through the study of *dalit*s in India and African-Americans in the United States.

Secondly, the historical grounding of Subaltern Studies was in the Indian peasantry and in *adivasi* societies with peasant-like attributes. It is not hard to understanding why peasants were at the core of this analysis. The 1960s and 1970s were the golden age of peasant studies. In the Marxian discourse of the time, the success or failure of the peasant literally or metaphorically armed were matters of paramount concern. The historical role of the peasantry in academic debates about feudalism and capitalism was subject to close critical scrutiny as was the attempt to differentiate between different 'classes' of the peasantry. In the 1970s peasants were the archetypal subalterns, and as Guha's *Elementary Aspects* suggested in 1983, peasant consciousness and peasant resistance provided the paradigmatic statement of Indian subalternity (cf. Arnold 1984). This had important implications for the way in which the 'subaltern' was defined—as essentially rural—and with that uncertainty about class identity and solidarity that had informed so much writing about peasants from Marx onwards. The peasant also tended to be seen as male: apart from gender blindness, the role of peasant and *adivasi* women was more difficult to recuperate from such sources and forms of insurgent social action as Subaltern Studies initially addressed. Much important work, in both historical and contemporary studies, has since been done in relation to gender and sexuality by using and extending the subaltern category, as Srila Roy does in her essay. But, at the least, Subaltern Studies helped create a language of description and analysis that had the potential to cover a wide diversity of subordinate or marginalized groups in ways that complemented or complicated the language of class.

Some of that intense peasant-gazing might today appear rather arcane and, in an increasingly urbanized and industrialized India, of diminished relevance, though Chatterjee (2012) has made a serious effort to revisit questions of peasant identity, subalternity, and civil society in contemporary India, and the issue of contemporary society and state is discussed in the essays here by Alf Gunvald Nilsen, Kenneth Bo Nielsen, Luisa Steur, and Subir Sinha. Current discussion of this nature helps to inform and enrich the ways in which we view peasant subalternity today; but it also in retrospect raises questions about the way in which peasant society was represented in early subaltern scholarship. Part of the radicalism of contemporary Subaltern Studies lies in the potentiality it creates for re-reading subaltern pasts and revisiting histories.

A focus on peasants and rural society also distracted the early subaltern scholars from a more searching examination of urban industrial society. That is regrettable especially since it made the original subaltern project apparently less relevant to discussion of a growing and vitally important section of Indian subalterns. When industrial workers were addressed, as in Dipesh Chakrabarty's (1983) essay on Calcutta jute workers, it was often in such a way as to emphasize 'feudal' legacies rather than proletariat possibilities. That overall neglect has allowed critics the opportunity to assert that Subaltern Studies was un-Marxist and even wilfully ignorant of class. As a partial corrective to that lacuna, important historical and sociological work on industrial labour has since been done (S. Basu 2004; Chandavarkar 1994; Joshi 2008), whether outside the Subaltern Studies fold or in explicit opposition to it. There are now very different and more nuanced ways of viewing urban subalternity and hegemony (as in Manali Desai's discussion here of Ahmedabad).

Subaltern Studies lost sight of the problem of the poor, which should have been central to its concerns and which, given the persistence of endemic poverty, remains one of the greatest challenges to any reconceptualization of subaltern politics today. I regret, too, that Subaltern Studies had little to say about the materiality of subaltern lives (both urban and rural) and the profound technological changes that (in contrast to a rather static view of the peasantry) helped transform them. I have tried to address some of these issues as they affect peasants, artisans, and urban workers in my book on 'everyday technology' (Arnold 2013). Apart from the intrinsic importance of the subject (to which I may or may not have done justice), I regard this as a demonstration of the continuing challenge and vitality of Subaltern Studies. We need to engage with a new set of technological as well as social factors—the role of radio, television, and cinema, the changing technologies of state repression and popular resistance, the technologies of reproductive health and sexual hygiene. I would add to this the politics of subaltern intimacy. Intimacy has often been understood (at least in colonial historiography) as a history of transgression, as in sexual liaisons or coercive intimacies between European elites and Indian subalterns, but there is much more that could be done with other forms of intimacy, not just those that are explicitly sexual. There are also the intimacies of the interventionist state (not least in relation to public health and population policies) and of the material objects that structure and inform everyday life. Alpa Shah provides insight into these possibilities in her 2013 article by showing intimacy in relation to everyday behaviour (food, drink, gestures) and the role of intimacy in building support for Maoist movements in eastern India (but also, since intimacy is two-edged, as a site of betrayal).

Thirdly, the historical grounding of subalternity was in resistance. Resistance served several functions. It offered a site of analysis for, and a putative demonstration of, an otherwise elusive or inaccessible consciousness. It was a frank celebration of action over passivity and compliance (so often historically seen as the mark of the Indian subaltern); it favoured the focus on the agency of peasants and *adivasis* and gave India a quasi-revolutionary tradition and stature to measure alongside Western Europe, Russia,

New Subaltern Politics

China, and Vietnam. It provided an explanation as to why such flawed resistance was not in itself enough to effect revolutionary change. This foregrounding of resistance has met with various degrees of criticism—about the atypicality and exceptionality of overt revolt, about the greater prevalence and intelligibility of everyday resistance, about the citing of revolt as mere romanticism in the face of more varied and interactive relations with states and elites (cf. P. Williams et al. 2011). But the highlighting of resistance seemed particularly paradoxical in a project that lauded Gramsci as its intellectual progenitor. *Subaltern Studies* soon ran out of peasant uprisings to study and resistance to document. A slide away from physical revolt to degrees of intellectual and cultural resistance was then perhaps inevitable. But even if resistance was overplayed, it has surely remained one of the critical markers by which we continue to assess what subaltern politics is and does, even if we now recognize the greater power that coercion and hegemony exercise.

There are three further areas of discussion I want briefly to touch upon here as having a bearing on the essays in this volume. The first relates to the state, and especially from a historical perspective, the colonial state. It is now evident that this issue received rather one-dimensional treatment in the early phase of Subaltern Studies though rather more extended treatment in Chatterjee's *The Nation and Its Fragments* (1993) and Guha's *Dominance without Hegemony* (1998). It is easy enough to see the colonial state as a monolith or as the principal embodiment of colonial power, especially when it serves as the repressive antithesis to subaltern protest and popular resistance. But the state had, and has, a more complex existence and there has been a great deal of more recent writing that has helped to illuminate the diverse nature and hegemonic role of the state both for the colonial era and since. Highly significant, too, has been the work of Akhil Gupta (1995) and others in writing about the 'everyday state', analysing the ways in which a state actually operates at a local, everyday level and the compromises and negotiations needed to work alongside it. This further brings to light the politics of corruption, exploitation, subordination, and violence within the lower echelons of the state machine and its daily interaction with subaltern groups.

The colonial state may have been less pervasive but its action and effects were not altogether dissimilar.

A second issue, not unrelated to this first, is the question of hegemony or, as Guha (1998) termed it, 'dominance without hegemony'. I struggle with this concept and the way it is presented on several levels—not least for its highly formulaic representation of dominance and subordination and its curious sanskritization of subalternity. It is difficult to talk about dominance *without* hegemony since for Gramsci coercion (physical dominance) and hegemony (consent) were in essence part of the same package. William Roseberry's (1994) discussion of the fragility of hegemony and his argument for hegemony as a process rather than a fixed entity, appears far more persuasive and in accord with Indian actuality. Coercion and consent are extremes situated on the same continuum, part of the same centaur-like body, and our skill, whatever our disciplinary field, surely lies in discerning how far a given regime of power, at a particular moment in time or a given locality, favours one over the other. Any understanding of colonial hegemony needs to be complicated by the fact that that regime was itself hegemonic—and within this hegemonic endeavour should be included the role of missionaries and others agencies outside the formal state structure. The state played a substantial role in reshaping attitudes and reordering social behaviour across a wide range of issues—including the status and representation of women, the position of *dalits*, attitudes to *adivasis*, the dissemination of education, and public health provision. In none of these was it entirely successful—in part because it was colonial and so, to varying degrees, alien and remote—but it also remained heavily reliant on the army and other means of coercive control (as in 1857, 1919, and 1942) when it felt its interests to be fundamentally threatened or believed force was necessary to achieve a 'moral effect'. At the same time, sections of the Indian population, and not just a narrow cast of elites, took up, shared in, and employed in their own hegemonic or counter-hegemonic struggles, many of those colonially inspired claims and ambitions. 'Dominance without hegemony' fails to capture this level of complexity and the processes of historical change that underpinned it.

Finally, there is the question of religion and 'religiosity', raised in particular by Aparna Sundar's essay in this volume. My (*Chambers*) dictionary gives the meaning of 'religiosity' as 'spurious or sentimental religion'. The initial Subaltern Studies view was instrumentalist in the sense that religion was seen as a means of gaining access to, and locating evidence for, subaltern consciousness and collectivity. Through religious beliefs and practices the world was made legible for the subalterns and for those who sought to understand their thoughts and actions. But the underlying view was also that excessive attention had been given to religion (as to caste) in the dominant western and neocolonial understanding of Indian society. It stood for an Orientalist misreading of subalternity as being, in essence, mere superstition and magical miscomprehension. Perhaps, as a result, Subaltern Studies failed, at the outset, to take religion seriously enough. The problem of religion was also, again, one linked to recovery. As Gramsci's work suggests, recovering the voice of the subaltern is not the same as endorsing and valorizing it. Rather the task is to comprehend it and to locate it within a wider cacophony of hegemonic and resistant voices. In the final analysis Subaltern Studies as a project surely deserves credit for trying to recover and comprehend those voices and not just reducing social experience and cultural expression to a crude and deterministic class analysis in which consciousness and conduct are relegated, once more, to the margins.

Bibliography

Abrams, Philip (1982). *Historical Sociology*, Ithaca: Cornell University Press.

Agarwala, Rina (2013). *Informal Labor, Formal Politics, and Dignified Discontent in India*, Cambridge: Cambridge University Press.

Agrawal, Arun (2005). *Environmentality: Technologies of Government and the Making of Subjects*, Durham: Duke University Press.

Ahmad, Irfan (2012). 'Theorizing Islamism and Democracy: Jamaat-e-Islami in India', *Citizenship Studies*, 16(7): 887–903.

Akanksha (2009). 'The Politics of Lesbian Visibility in Indian Socio-Cultural Context', *Swakanthey* [In her own voice], January, Kolkata: Sappho.

Akanksha and Malobika (2007). 'Sappho: A Journey through Fire', in Brinda Bose and Subhabrata Bhattacharyya (eds), *The Phobic and the Erotic: The Politics of Sexualities in Contemporary India*, pp. 363–8, Kolkata: Seagull Books.

Amin, Shahid (1989). 'Gandhi as Mahatma: Gorakhpur District, Eastern UP, 1921–2', in Ranajit Guha (ed.), *Subaltern Studies III: Writings on South Asian History and Society*, pp. 1–62, New Delhi: Oxford University Press.

Anandhi, S. (1995). 'Collective Identity and Secularism: Discourse of the Dravidian Movement in Tamil Nadu', in Rudolph C. Heredia and Edward Mathias (eds), *Secularism and Liberation: Perspectives and Strategies for India Today*, pp. 176–98, New Delhi: Indian Social Institute.

———— (2000). 'Land to the Dalits: Panchami Land Struggle in Tamil Nadu', Bengaluru: Indian Social Institute.

Anderson, Kevin (2010). *Marx at the Margins*, Chicago: University of Chicago Press.

Anon. (2006). 'Land Grab and "Development" Fraud in India', *Analytical Monthly Review*, September, http://mrzine.monthlyreview. org/2006/amr210906.html (accessed 27 August 2012).

Arnold, David (1984). 'Gramsci and Peasant Subalternity in India', *Journal of Peasant Studies*, 11(4): 155–84.

———— (2013). *Everyday Technology: Machines and the Making of India's Modernity*, Chicago: University of Chicago Press.

Arrighi, Giovanni (1994). *The Long Twentieth Century: Money, Power and the Origins of Our Times*, London: Verso.

Atabaki, Touraj (2007). *The State and the Subaltern: Modernization, Society and the State in Turkey and Iran*, London: Tauris.

Azhagi, Mulai (2012). 'Iyer Iyengar Technology', *Viduthalai*, 26 July (Tamil).

Bagchi, Amiya Kumar, and Anthony D'Costa (2012). 'Transformation and Development: A Critical Introduction to India and China', in A. K. Bagchi and Anthony D'Costa (eds), *The Political Economy of Transition in India and China*, pp. 1–28, New Delhi: Oxford University Press.

Bagchi, Amiya Kumar, Panchanan Das, and Sadhan Kumar Chattopadhyay (2005). 'Growth and Structural Change in the Economy of Gujarat, 1970–2000', *Economic and Political Weekly*, 40(28): 3039–47.

Balibar, Etienne (2002). *Politics and the Other Scene*, London: Verso.

Banaji, Jairus (2010). *Theory as History: Essays on Modes of Production and Exploitation*, Leiden: Brill Academic Publishers.

Baruah, Sanjibh (1999). *India against Itself: Assam and the Politics of Nationality*, New Delhi: Oxford University Press.

Basu, Dipankar, and Debarshi Das (2008). 'Accumulation by Dispossession under the Aegis of a "Communist Party"—David Harvey on Bengal', *Sanhati*, 10 December, http://sanhati.com/excerpted/1162/ (accessed 14 August 2012).

Basu, Subho (2004). *Does Class Matter? Colonial Capital and Workers' Resistance in Bengal, 1890–1937*, New Delhi: Oxford University Press.

Baviskar, Amita (2008). 'Introduction', in Amita Baviskar (ed.), *Contested Grounds: Essays on Nature, Culture, and Power*, pp. 1–12, New Delhi: Oxford University Press.

Baviskar, Amita, and Nandini Sundar (2008). 'Democracy versus Economic Transformation?', *Economic and Political Weekly*, 43(46): 83–9.

Bayly, Susan (1989). *Saints, Goddesses and Kings: Muslims and Christians in South Indian Society 1700–1900*, Cambridge: Cambridge University Press.

——— (1999). *Caste, Society and Politics in India: From the Eighteenth Century to the Modern Age*, Cambridge: Cambridge University Press.

Bene, Christophe (2003). 'When Fishery Rhymes with Poverty: A First Step beyond the Old Paradigm on Poverty in Small-Scale Fisheries', *World Development*, 31(6): 949–75.

Berktay, Halil (1991). 'Three Empires and the Societies They Governed: Iran, India and the Ottoman Empire', *Journal of Peasant Studies*, 18(3–4): 242–63.

Bernstein, Henry (2007). 'Capital and Labour from Centre to Margins', keynote address presented at the conference on 'Living on the Margins: Vulnerability, Exclusion and the State in the Informal Economy', Cape Town, March.

Bhagwati, Jagdish, and Arvind Panagariya (2013). *Why Growth Matters: How Economic Growth in India Reduced Poverty and the Lessons for Other Developing Countries*, New York: Public Affairs Books.

Bhargava, Rajeev (2007). 'The Distinctiveness of Indian Secularism', in T. N. Srinivasan (ed.), *The Future of Secularism*, pp. 20–53, New Delhi: Oxford University Press.

Bhatia, Mohita (2013). 'Secularism and Secularisation: A Bibliographical Essay', *Economic and Political Weekly*, 48(50): 103–10.

Bhatt, Chetan (2001). *Hindu Nationalism: Origins, Ideologies and Modern Myths*, Oxford: Berg.

Bidwai, Praful (2007). 'West Bengal on the Wrong Track? The Singur Syndrome', in Dola Sen and Debashis Bhattacharya (eds), *Singur and Nandigram and …—The Untold Story of Capitalised Marxism*, pp. 36–7, Kolkata: Kanoria Jute and Industries Limited Sangrami Shramik Union.

Biswas, Ranjita (2007). 'The Lesbian Standpoint', in Brinda Bose and Subhabrata Bhattacharyya (eds), *The Phobic and the Erotic: The Politics of Sexualities in Contemporary India*, pp. 263–90, Kolkata: Seagull Books.

Blackburn, Robin (1988). *The Overthrow of Colonial Slavery: 1776–1848*, London: Verso.

Bose, Brinda, and Subhabrata Bhattacharyya (eds) (2007). *The Phobic and the Erotic: The Politics of Sexualities in Contemporary India*, Kolkata: Seagull Books.

Breman, Jan (2001). 'An Informalized Labour System: End of Labour Market Dualism', *Economic and Political Weekly*, 36(52): 4804–51.

—— (2003). *The Labouring Poor in India: Patterns of Exploitation, Subordination, and Exclusion*, New Delhi: Oxford University Press

—— (2004). *The Making and Unmaking of an Industrial Working Class*, Chicago: University of Chicago Press.

Buttigieg, Joseph (1995). 'Gramsci on Civil Society', *Boundary*, 2(22–3): 1–32.

Byres, T. J. (1994). 'The State and Development Planning in India', in T. J. Byres (ed.), *The State, Development Planning and Liberalisation in India*, New Delhi: Oxford University Press.

Chadha, Ashish. 2006. 'Battle for Brand IIT', *Hindu*, 25 June.

Chakrabarti, Poloumi (2008). 'Inclusion or Exclusion? Emerging Effects of Middle-Class Citizen Participation on Delhi's Urban Poor', *IDS Bulletin*, 38(6): 96–104.

Chakrabarty, Dipesh (1983). 'Conditions for the Knowledge of Working-Class Conditions: Employers, Government and the Jute Workers of Calcutta, 1890–1940', in Ranajit Guha (ed.), *Subaltern Studies II: Writings on South Asian History and Society*, pp. 259–310, New Delhi: Oxford University Press.

—— (2000). *Provincializing Europe: Postcolonial Thought and Historical Difference*, Princeton: Princeton University Press.

—— (2002). *Habitations of Modernity: Essays in the Wake of Subaltern Studies*, Chicago: University of Chicago Press.

—— (2005). 'In the Name of Politics: Sovereignty, Democracy and the Multitude in India', *Economic and Political Weekly*, 40(30): 3293–301.

—— (2013). 'Subaltern Studies in Retrospect and Reminiscence', *Economic and Political Weekly*, 47(12): 23–7.

Chandavarkar, Rajnarayan (1994). *The Origins of Industrial Capitalism in India: Business Strategies and the Working Classes in Bombay, 1900–1940*, Cambridge: Cambridge University Press.

Chandhoke, Neera (2010). 'Secularism', in Niraja Gopal Jayal and Pratap Bhanu Mehta (eds), *The Oxford Companion to Politics in India*, pp. 333–46, New Delhi: Oxford University Press.

Chandra, Uday (2013a). 'Negotiating Leviathan: Statemaking and Resistance in the Margins of Modern India', PhD dissertation, Yale University.

—— (2013b). 'Beyond Subalternity: Land, Community, and the State in Contemporary Jharkhand', *Contemporary South Asia*, 21(1): 52–61.

Chatterjee, Partha (1982). 'Agrarian Relations and Communalism in Bengal, 1926–1935', in Ranajit Guha (ed.), *Subaltern Studies I: Writings on South Asian History and Society*, pp. 9–39, New Delhi: Oxford University Press.

Chatterjee, Partha (1983). 'More on Modes of Power and the Peasantry', in Ranajit Guha (ed.), *Subaltern Studies II: Writings on South Asian History and Society*, pp. 311–50, New Delhi: Oxford University Press.

——— (1986). *Nationalist Thought and the Colonial World*, Princeton: Princeton University Press.

——— (1988). 'For an Indian History of Peasant Struggle', *Social Scientist*, 16(11): 3–17.

——— (1993). *The Nation and Its Fragments*, Princeton: Princeton University Press.

——— (1994). 'Development Planning and the Indian State', in Terence J. Byres (ed.), *The State, Development Planning and Liberalisation in India*, pp. 82–103, New Delhi: Oxford University Press.

——— (1998). 'Five Hundred Years of Fear and Love' *Economic and Political Weekly*, 33(22): 1330–6.

——— (2001). 'On Civil and Political Society in Postcolonial Democracies', in Sudipta Kaviraj and Sunil Khilnani (eds), *Civil Society: History and Possibilities*, pp. 165–78, Cambridge: Cambridge University Press.

——— (2004). *Politics of the Governed: Reflections on Popular Politics in Most of the World*, New York: Columbia University Press.

——— (2008). 'Democracy and Economic Transformation in India', *Economic and Political Weekly*, 43(16): 53–62.

——— (2011). *Lineages of Political Society*, New York: Columbia University Press.

——— (2012). 'After Subaltern Studies', *Economic and Political Weekly*, 47(35): 44–9.

——— (2013). 'Subaltern Studies and *Capital*', *Economic and Political Weekly*, 48(37): 69–75.

Chatterjee, Upamanyu (1988). *English, August: An Indian Story*, New Delhi: Penguin.

Chaturvedi, Sanjay (2008). 'Detention of Dr Binayak Sen: Something Must Be Seriously Wrong Somewhere', *Indian Journal of Community Medicine*, 33(4): 212–13.

Chaturvedi, Vinayak (ed.) (2000a). *Mapping Subaltern Studies and the Postcolonial*, London: Verso.

——— (2000b). 'Introduction', in V. Chaturvedi (ed.), *Mapping Subaltern Studies and the Postcolonial*, pp. vii–xix, London: Verso.

Chibber, Vivek (2013). *Postcolonial Theory and the Specter of Capital*, London: Verso.

Chiriyankandath, James (1993). 'Communities at the Polls: Electoral Politics and the Mobilization of Communal groups in Travancore', *Modern Asian Studies*, 27(3): 643–65.

Chopra, Deepta Philippa Williams, and Bhaskar Vira (2011). 'Politics of Citizenship: Experiencing State–Society Relations from the Margins', *Contemporary South Asia*, 19(3): 243–7.

Clarke, Simon, Paul Hogget, and Simon Thompson (2006). *Emotions, Politics and Society*, London: Palgrave Macmillan.

Corbridge, Stuart, and Alpa Shah (2013). 'Introduction: The Underbelly of the Indian Boom', *Economy and Society*, 42(3): 335–47.

Corbridge, Stuart, and John Harriss (2000). *Reinventing India: Liberalization, Hindu Nationalism, and Popular Democracy*, Cambridge: Polity.

Corbridge, Stuart, John Harriss, and Craig Jeffrey (2013). *India Today: Economy, Politics and Society*, Cambridge: Polity Press

Corbridge, Stuart, Glyn Williams, Manoj Srivastava, and Réne Véron (2005). *Seeing the State: Governance and Governmentality in India*, Cambridge: Cambridge University Press.

Corrigan, Philip, and Derek Sayer (1985). *The Great Arch: English State Formation as Cultural Revolution*, Oxford: Basil Blackwell.

Cossman, Brenda (2012). 'Continental Drift: Queer, Feminism, Postcolonial', *Jindal Global Law Review*, 4(1): 17–35.

Countercurrents (2011). 'Tale of a village's struggle for survival', 14 July 2011, http://www.countercurrents.org/thervoy140711.htm (accessed 29 December 2014).

Cvetkovich, Anne (2003). *An Archive of Feelings: Trauma, Sexuality, and Lesbian Public Cultures*, Durham: Duke University Press.

da Costa, Dia (2007). 'Tensions of Neoliberal Development: State Discourse and Dramatic Oppositions in West Bengal', *Contributions to Indian Sociology*, 41(3): 287–320.

da Costa, Emilia Viotti (1994). *Crowns of Glory, Tears of Blood: The Demerara Slave Rebellion of 1823*, Oxford: Oxford University Press.

Dainik Jagaran (2013). 'Residents ignore servant verification, police helpless', *City Plus*, 2 March.

Das, Bikram K. (1997). 'Translator's Note', in *Paraja* by Gopinath Mohanty, New Delhi: Oxford University Press.

Das, Veena (1989). 'Subaltern as Perspective', in Ranajit Guha (ed.), *Subaltern Studies VI: Writings on South Asian History and Society*, pp. 310–24, New Delhi: Oxford University Press.

Dasgupta, Debarshi (2012). 'Wielders of terror: Drunk on power, RWAs are exceeding their brief', *Outlook Magazine*, 14 May, http://www.out-lookindia.com/article.aspx?280789 (accessed 20 December 2013).

Dave, Naisargi (2012). *Queer Activism in India: A Story in the Anthropology of Ethics*, Durham and London: Duke University Press.

Davidson, Alistair (1984). 'Gramsci, the Peasantry and Popular Culture', *Journal of Peasant Studies*, 11(4): 139–53.

Dean, Mitchell (2009). *Governmentality: Power and Rule in Modern Society*, London: Sage Publications.

Della Cava, Ralph (1992). 'Vatican Policy, 1978–90: An Updated Overview', *Social Research*, 59(1): 169–99.

Desai, Meghnad (2011). *The Rediscovery of India*, London: Bloomsbury Press.

Devi, Mahasweta (1995). 'Pterodactyl', in *Imaginary Maps: Three Stories* by Mahasweta Devi (translated and introduced by Gayatri Chakravorty Spivak), pp. 95–196, New York and London: Routledge.

Devy, Ganesh (2002). 'Introduction', in *Painted Words: An Anthology of Tribal Literature*, pp. ix–xvii, New Delhi: Penguin Books.

Diocese of Kottar, http://www.kottardiocese.org/Vision.aspx (accessed 10 February 2015).

Dirks, Nicholas B. (2001). *Castes of Mind: Colonialism and the Making of Modern India*, Princeton: Princeton University Press.

Down to Earth. 'Koodankulam meltdown', 1–15 April.

Dube, Saurabh (1992). 'Myths, Symbols and Community: Satnampath of Chattisgarh', in Partha Chatterjee and Gyanendra Pandey (eds), *Subaltern Studies VII: Writings on South Asian History and Society*, pp. 121–58, New Delhi: Oxford University Press.

Duggan, Lisa, and Jose Esteban Munoz (2009). 'Hope and Hopelessness: A Dialogue', *Women & Performance: A Journal of Feminist Theory*, 19(2): 275–83.

Dugger, Celia W. (2000). 'Return passage to India: Emigres pay back', *New York Times*, 29 February.

Duschinski, Haley (2009). 'Destiny Effects: Militarization, State Power, and Punitive Containment in Kashmir Valley', *Anthropological Quarterly*, 82(3): 691–717.

Dutta, Aniruddha (2012). 'Claiming Citizenship, Contesting Civility: The Institutional LGBT Movement and the Regulation of Gender/Sexual Dissidence in West Bengal, India', *Jindal Global Law Review*, 4(1): 110–41.

Ferguson, James (1990). *The Anti-Politics Machine: 'Development,' Depoliticization, and Bureaucratic Power in Lesotho*, Minneapolis: University of Minnesota Press.

Ferguson, James, and Akhil Gupta (2002). 'Spatializing States: Towards an Ethnography of Neoliberal Governmentality', *American Ethnologist*, 29(4): 981–1002.

Fernandes, Leela, and Patrick Heller (2008). 'Hegemonic Aspirations: New Middle Class Politics and India's Democracy in Comparative

Perspective', in Ronald J. Herring and Rina Agarwala (eds), *Whatever Happened to Class? Reflections from South Asia*, pp. 146–65, New Delhi: Daanish Books.

Fernando, S. Verantius (1984). 'The Portugese Patronage (Padroado) and the Evangelisation of the Pearl Fishery Coast', *Indian Church History Review*, 18(2).

Foucault, Michel (1990). *The History of Sexuality: An Introduction*, vol. 1, New York: Vintage Books.

——— (2007). *Security, Territory, Population: Lectures at the College de France, 1977–1978*, London: Palgrave.

——— (2008). *The Birth of Biopolitics: Lectures at the College de France, 1978–1979*, London: Palgrave.

Frankel, Francine (2005). *India's Political Economy: The Gradual Revolution 1947–2004*, New Delhi: Oxford University Press.

Friedman, Jonathan (2013). 'Capitalist Markets and the Kafkaesque World of Moralization', in Edward Fischer (ed.), *Cash on the Table: Markets, Values and Moral Economies*, pp. 51–66, Santa Fe: SAR Press.

Fuller, Chris J., and Haripriya Narasimhan (2008). 'From Landlords to Software Engineers: Migration and Urbanization among Tamil Brahmins', *Comparative Studies in Society and History*, 50 (1): 170–96.

——— (2010). 'Traditional Vocations and Modern Professions among Tamil Brahmans in Colonial and Post-colonial South India', *Indian Economic and Social History Review*, 47(4): 473–96.

Fuller, Chris J., and John Harriss (2001). 'For an Anthropology of the Modern Indian State', in C. J. Fuller and V. Bénéï (eds), *The Everyday State and Society in Modern India*, pp. 1–30, London: Hurst and Company.

Gagdekar, Roxy (2012). 'Dalits live in fear of cops in Gandhi's Gujarat', 9 October, http://www.dnaindia.com/ahmedabad/report-dalits-live-in-fear-of-cops-in-gandhi-s-gujarat-1750642 (accessed 20 December 2014).

Geetha, V. (2011a). 'Reconstructing Social Reform as Secularism: The Example of the Tamil Self-Respecters', in V. Geetha and Nalini Rajan, *Religious Faith, Ideology, Citizenship: The View from Below*, pp. 31–55, New Delhi: Routledge.

——— (2011b). '"Applying Law to their Advantage": Muslim Women Debate Faith, Gender and Citizenship', in V. Geetha and Nalini Rajan, *Religious Faith, Ideology, Citizenship: The View from Below*, pp. 166–90, New Delhi: Routledge.

Ghertner, D. Asher (2008). 'Analysis of New Legal Discourse behind Delhi's Slum Demolitions', *Economic and Political Weekly*, 43(20): 57–66.

Ghosh, Kaushik (2006). 'Between Global Flows and Local Dams: Indigenousness, Locality, and the Transnational Sphere in Jharkhand, India', *Cultural Anthropology*, 21(4): 501–34.

Gidwani, Vinay (2009). 'Subalternity', in N. Thrift and R. Kitchen (eds), *International Encyclopedia of Human Geography*, pp. 65–71, Amsterdam: Elsevier Science.

Gilbert, Michael Joseph, and Daniel Nugent (eds) (1994). *Everyday Forms of State Formation: Revolution and the Negotiation of Rule in Modern Mexico*, Durham: Duke University Press.

Gilmartin, David (2006). 'Imperial Rivers: Irrigation and British Visions of Empire', in Durba Ghosh and Dane Kennedy (eds), *Decentering Empire: Britain, India, and the Transcolonial World*, pp. 76–103, Hyderabad: Orient BlackSwan.

Gorski, Philip S., and Ates Altinordu (2008). 'After Secularization?', *Annual Review of Sociology*, 34: 55–85.

Gould, Deborah (2002). 'Life during Wartime: Emotions and the Development of ACT UP', *Mobilization: An International Journal* (special issue on Emotions and Social Movements edited by Doug McAdam and Ron Aminzade), 7(2): 177–200.

———— (2009). *Moving Politics: Emotion and ACT UP's Fight against AIDS*, Chicago: University of Chicago Press.

Government of India (2008). *Development Challenges in Extremist Affected Areas: Report of and Expert Group to the Planning Commission*, New Delhi: Government of India.

Gramsci, Antonio (1971). *Selections from the Prison Notebooks*, London: Lawrence and Wishart.

Green, Marcus (2002). 'Gramsci Cannot Speak: Presentations and Interpretations of Gramsci's Concept of the Subaltern', *Rethinking Marxism*, 14(3): 1–24.

———— (2011a). 'Rethinking the Subaltern and the Question of Censorship in Gramsci's *Prison Notebooks*', *Postcolonial Studies*, 14(4): 387–404.

———— (2011b). 'Subaltern Politics', in George Thomas Kurian, James E. Alt, Simone Chambers, Geoffrey Garrett, Margaret Levi, and Paula D. McLain (eds), *The Encyclopedia of Political Science*, pp. 1628–9, Washington, D.C.: CQ Press.

Gudavarthy, Ajay (ed.) (2012). *Re-framing Democracy and Agency in India: Interrogating Political Society*, London: Anthem Press.

Guha, Ramachandra (1985). 'Forestry and Social Protest in British Kumaun, c. 1893–1921', in Ranajit Guha (ed.), *Subaltern Studies IV: Writings on Indian History and Society*, pp. 54–100, New Delhi: Oxford University Press.

Guha, Ramachandra (1995). 'Review: Subaltern and Bhadralok Studies', *Economic and Political Weekly*, 30(33): 2056–8.

———(1999). *Ecological Change and Peasant Resistance in the Himalaya*, Berkeley: University of California Press.

——— (2007). *India after Gandhi: The History of the World's Largest Democracy*, London: Picador.

Guha, Ranajit (1976). 'Indian Democracy: Long Dead, Now Buried', *Journal of Contemporary Asia*, 6(1): 39–53.

——— (1982a). 'Preface', in Ranajit Guha (ed.), *Subaltern Studies I: Writings on South Asian History and Society*, pp. vii–viii, New Delhi: Oxford University Press.

——— (1982b). 'On Some Aspects of the Historiography of Colonial India', in Ranajit Guha (ed.), *Subaltern Studies I: Writings on Indian History and Society*, pp. 1–8, New Delhi: Oxford University Press.

——— (1983a). *Elementary Aspects of Peasant Insurgency in Colonial India*, New Delhi: Oxford University Press.

——— (1983b). 'The Prose of Counter-Insurgency', in Ranajit Guha (ed.), *Subaltern Studies II: Writings on South Asian History and Society*, pp. 43–59, New Delhi: Oxford University Press.

——— (1988). 'On Some Aspects of the Historiography of Colonial India', in Ranajit Guha and Gayatri Chakravorty Spivak (eds), *Selected Subaltern Studies*, pp. 37–44, Oxford: Oxford University Press.

——— (1989). 'Dominance without Hegemony and Its Historiography', in Ranajit Guha (ed.), *Subaltern Studies VI: Writings on Indian History and Society*, pp. 210–309, New Delhi: Oxford University Press.

——— (1998). *Dominance without Hegemony: History and Power in Colonial India*, Cambridge: Harvard University Press.

——— (2002). *History at the Limit of World-History*, New York: Columbia University Press.

Gupta, Akhil (1995). 'Blurred Boundaries: The Discourse of Corruption, the Culture of Politics, and the Imagined State', *American Ethnologist*, 22(2): 375–402.

——— (1998). *Postcolonial Developments: Agriculture in the Making of Modern India*, Durham: Duke University Press.

——— (2001). 'Governing Population: The Integrated Child Development Services Program in India', in Thomas Blom Hansen and Finn Stepputat (eds), *States of Imagination: Ethnographic Explorations of the Postcolonial State*, pp. 65–96, Durham: Duke University Press.

——— (2012). *Red Tape: Bureaucracy, Structural Violence and Poverty in India*, Durham: Duke University Press.

Gupta, Akhil, and Aradhana Sharma (2006a). 'Globalization and Postcolonial States', *Current Anthropology*, 47(2): 277–307.

———— (2006b). 'Introduction: Rethinking Theories of the State in an Age of Globalization', in Aradhana Sharma and Akhil Gupta (eds), *Anthropology of the State: A Reader*, pp. 1–41, Oxford: Wiley-Blackwell.

Gupta, Akhil, and K. Sivaramakrishnan (2011). 'Introduction: The State in India after Liberalization', in Akhil Gupta and K. Sivaramakrishnan (eds), *The State in India after Liberalization: Interdisciplinary Perspectives*, pp. 1–27, London: Routledge.

Gupta, Alok (2005). '"*Englishpur ki* Kothi": Class Dynamics in the Queer Movement in India', in Arvind Narrain and Gautam Bhan (eds), *Because I Have a Voice: Queer Politics in India*, pp. 123–42, New Delhi: Yoda Press.

Gupta, Dipankar (2010). *Caged Phoenix: Can India Fly?*, New Delhi: Penguin Books.

———— (2013). *Revolution from Above: India's Future and the Citizen Elite*, New Delhi: Rupa Books.

Haldon, John (1993). *The State and the Tributary Mode of Production*, London: Verso.

Hall, Stuart (1996). 'New Ethnicities', in D. Morley and K.-H. Chen (eds), *Stuart Hall: Critical Dialogues in Cultural Studies*, pp. 442–51, London: Routledge.

Hall, Stuart, and Alan O'Shea (2013). 'Common-Sense Neoliberalism', in Stuart Hall, Doreen Masey, and Michael Rustin (eds), *After Neoliberalism? The Kilburn Manifesto*, pp. 1–18, London: Lawrence and Wishart.

Halperin, Sandra (2004). *War and Social Change in Modern Europe:* The Great Transformation *Revisited*, Cambridge: Cambridge University Press.

Hardiman, David (1984). 'Adivasi Assertion in South Gujarat: The Devi Movement of 1922–3', in Ranajit Guha (ed.), *Subaltern Studies III: Writings on South Asian History and Society*, pp. 196–230, New Delhi: Oxford University Press.

Harrison, Tom (2012). 'Clubbing Together: Village Clubs, Local NGOs and the Mediations of Political Society', in Ajay Gudavarthy (ed.), *Re-framing Democracy and Agency in India: Interrogating Political Society*, pp. 235–52, London: Anthem Press.

Harriss, John (2006). 'Middle Class Activism and the Politics of the Informal Working Class: A Perspective on Class Relations and Civil Society', *Critical Asian Studies*, 38(4): 445–66.

Harriss, John (2011a). 'What Is Going On in India's "Red Corridor"? Questions about India's Maoist Insurgency', *Pacific Affairs*, 84(2): 309–27.

——— (2011b). 'How Far Have India's Economic Reforms Been "Guided by Compassion and Justice"? Social Policy in the Neoliberal Era', in Sanjay Ruparelia, Sanjay Reddy, John Harriss, and Stuart Corbridge (eds), *Understanding India's New Political Economy: A Great Transformation?*, pp. 127–40, London: Routledge.

Harriss, John, and Craig Jeffrey (2013). 'Depoliticizing Injustice', *Economy and Society*, 42(3): 507–20.

Harriss-White, Barbara (2003). *India Working: Essays on Society and Economy*, Cambridge: Cambridge University Press.

Harvey, David (2003). *The New Imperialism*, Oxford: Oxford University Press.

Haynes, Douglas, and Gyan Prakash (1992). 'Introduction: The Entanglement of Power and Resistance' in Douglas Haynes and Gyan Prakash (eds), *Contesting Power: Resistance and Everyday Social Relations in South Asia*, pp. 1–22, Berkeley: University of California Press.

Hehir, Bryan J. (1993). 'Catholicism and Democracy: Conflict, Change and Collaboration', in John Witte (ed.), *Christianity and Democracy in Global Context*, pp. 15–30, Boulder, CO: Westview Press.

Hershatter, Gail (1993). 'The Subaltern Talks Back: Reflections on Subaltern Theory and Chinese History', *Positions* 1: 103–30.

Hindu (2006). 'We want to live decently', 13 September.

——— (2011). 'Cases against priests for encouraging protests', 17 November.

Hindustan Times (2013). 'Residents, police not on the same page on servant verification', 19 June.

Holmes, Mary (2004). 'Feeling beyond Rules: Politicizing the Sociology of Emotion and Anger in Feminist Politics', *European Journal of Social Theory*, 7(2): 209–27.

Houtart, Francois (1984). 'Religion and Anti-Communism: The Case of the Catholic Church', *Socialist Register*, 21: 349–63.

Ilaiah, Kancha (2005). *Why I am Not A Hindu: A Sudra Critique of Hindutva Philosophy, Culture and Political Economy*, 2nd revised edn, New Delhi: Bhatkal and Sen.

Iqtidar, Humeira, and David Lehmann (2012). 'Introduction: Secularism and Citizenship beyond the North Atlantic World', *Citizenship Studies*, 16(8): 953–9.

Iqtidar, Humeira, and Tanika Sarkar (2013). 'Reassessing Secularism and Secularisation in South Asia', *Economic and Political Weekly*, 48(50): 38–42.

Ismail, Salwa (2013). 'Urban Subalterns in the Arab Revolutions: Cairo and Damascus in Comparative Perspective', *Comparative Studies in Society and History*, 55(4): 865–94.

Jacob, K. S. (2009). 'Health, Health Workers and Human Rights: Dr Binayak Sen and the Silence of the Medical Fraternity in India', *National Medical Journal of India*, 22(1): 35–7.

Jaffrelot, Christophe (1996). *The Hindu Nationalist Movement and Indian Politics*, New Delhi: Viking.

——— (2003). *India's Silent Revolution: The Rise of the Lower Castes in North India*, London: C. Hurst & Co.

——— (2013). 'A class of his own', *Indian Express*, 17 April.

Jayadev, Arjun, Sripad Motiram, and Vamsi Vakulabharanam (2011). 'Patterns of Wealth Disparities in India since the 1990s', in Sanjay Ruparelia, Sanjay Reddy, John Harriss, and Stuart Corbridge (eds), *Understanding India's New Political Economy: A Great Transformation?*, pp. 81–100, London: Routledge.

Jeffrey, Craig (2001). '"A Fist Is Stronger Than Five Fingers": Caste and Dominance in Rural North India', *Transactions of the Institute of British Geographers*, 26(2): 217–36.

——— (2010). *Timepass: Youth, Class, and the Politics of Waiting in India*, Stanford: Stanford University Press.

Jeffrey, Craig, and Jens Lerche (2001). 'Dimensions of Dominance: Class and State in Uttar Pradesh', in Chris J. Fuller and Veronique Bénéï (eds), *The Everyday State and Society in Modern India*, pp. 91–114, London: Hurst and Company.

Jeffrey, Craig, Patricia Jeffery, and Roger Jeffery (2008). 'Dalit Revolution? New Politicians in Uttar Pradesh', *Journal of Asian Studies*, 67(4): 1365–96.

Jeremias, George (1989). 'Pastoral Ministry among Fishermen in the Diocese of Kottar with Special Reference to Poverty', PhD dissertation, Pontificia Universitas Lateranensis, Rome.

Jessop, Bob (1982). *The Capitalist State: Marxist Theories and Methods*, Oxford: Martin Robertson.

——— (1990). *State Theory: Putting the Capitalist State in Its Place*, Cambridge: Polity Press.

——— (2008). *State Power*, Cambridge: Polity Press.

John, Mari, and Satish Deshpande (2008). 'Theorizing the Present? Problems and Possibilities', *Economic and Political Weekly*, 43(46): 83–6.

Jones, Jonathan David (2009). *Negotiating Development: A Study of the Grassroots Resistance to India's 2005 Special Economic Zones Act*, PhD dissertation, University of Florida.

Joseph, Gilbert Michael, and Daniel Nugent (1994). 'Popular Culture and State Formation in Revolutionary Mexico', in Gilbert M. Joseph and Daniel Nugent (eds), *Everyday Forms of State Formation: Revolution and the Negotiation of Rule in Modern Mexico*, pp. 3–23, Durham: Duke University Press.

Joshi, Chitra (2008). *Lost Worlds: Indian Labour and Its Forgotten Histories*, London: Anthem Press.

Kalb, Don (2011). *Headlines of Nation, Subtexts of Class*, New York and London: Berghahn Books.

Kalyvas, Andreas (2002). 'The Stateless Theory: Poulantzas' Challenge to Postmodernism', in S. Aronowitz and P. Bratsis (eds), *Paradigm Lost: State Theory Reconsidered*, pp. 105–41, Minneapolis: University of Minnesota Press.

Kapoor, Dip (2011). 'Subaltern Social Movement (SSM) Post-Mortems of Development in India: Locating Trans-Local Activism and Radicalism', *Journal of Asian and African Studies*, 46(2): 130–48.

Kapoor, Ilan (2008). *The Postcolonial Politics of Development*, London: Routledge.

Kappen, Sebastian (1986). 'Towards an Indian Theology of Liberation', in Paul Puthanangady (ed.), *Towards an Indian Theology of Liberation*, pp. 301–18, Bengaluru: Indian Theological Association and National Biblical, Catechetical and Liturgical Centre.

Kapur, Ratna (2000). 'Law and the Sexual Subaltern: A Comparative Perspective', *Cleveland State Law Review*, 48(1): 15–23, http://engagedscholarship.csuohio.edu/clevstlrev/vol48/iss1/4 (accessed 3 January 2015).

——— (2005). *Erotic Justice: Law and the New Politics of Postcolonialism*, London: Routledge.

——— (2009). 'Out of the Colonial Closet, but Still Thinking "Inside the Box": Regulating "Perversion" and the Role of Tolerance in De-radicalising the Rights Claims of Sexual Subalterns', *NUJS Law Review*, 21; 2(3): 381–96.

——— (2012). 'Multi-tasking Queer: Reflections on the Possibilities of Homosexual Dissidence in Law', *Jindal Global Law Review*, 4(1): 36–59.

Kaur, Ravinder (2012). 'Nation's Two Bodies: Rethinking the Idea of "New" India and Its Other', *Third World Quarterly*, 33(4): 603–21.

Kaviraj, Sudipta (1994). 'Crisis of the Nation-State in India', *Political Studies*, 42: 115–29.

——— (2010a). 'On State, Society, and Discourse in India', in *The Imaginary Institution of India*, Ranikhet: Permanent Black.

Kaviraj, Sudipta (2010b). 'On the Construction of Colonial Power: Structure, Discourse, Hegemony', in *The Imaginary Institution of India*, Ranikhet: Permanent Black.

——— (2013). 'Languages of Secularity', *Economic and Political Weekly*, 48(50): 93–102.

Khair, Tabish (2001). *Babu Fictions: Alienation in Contemporary Indian English Novels*, New Delhi: Oxford University Press.

Khanna, Akshay (2005). 'Beyond "Sexuality"(?)', in Arvind Narrain and Gautam Bhan (eds), *Because I Have a Voice: Queer Politics in India*, pp. 89–103, New Delhi: Yoda Press.

——— (2007). 'Us "Sexuality" Types: A Critical Engagement with the Postcoloniality of Sexuality', in Brinda Bose and Subhabrata Bhattacharyya (eds), *The Phobic and the Erotic: The Politics of Sexualities in Contemporary India*, pp. 159–200, Kolkata: Seagull Books.

Kohli, Atul (2006a). 'Politics of Economic Growth in India, 1980–2005: Part 1: The 1980s', *Economic and Political Weekly*, 41(13): 1251–9.

——— (2006b). 'Politics of Economic Growth in India, 1980–2005: Part 2: The 1990s and Beyond', *Economic and Political Weekly*, 41(14): 1363–71.

——— (2012). *Poverty amid Plenty in the New India*, Cambridge: Cambridge University Press.

Kolsky, Elisabeth (2010). *Colonial Justice in British India*, Cambridge: Cambridge University Press.

Krause, Kristine, and Katharina Schramm (2011). 'Thinking Through Political Subjectivity', *African Diaspora*, 4: 115–34.

Kumar, Ashwani (2008). *Community Warriors: State, Peasants and Caste Armies in Bihar*, London: Anthem Press.

Kumar, D. Suresh (2008). 'JEE fails to get the best: IIT dons', *Times of India*, 31 July, http://timesofindia.indiatimes.com/india/JEE-fails-to-get-the-best-IIT-dons/articleshow/3307741.cms (accessed 22 December 2014).

Kumar, Vinoj (2007). 'Dalits not welcome in IIT Madras', *Tehelka Magazine*, 16 June.

Kurien, John (2000). 'The Kerala Model: The Central Tendency and the "Outlier"', in Govindan Parayil (ed.), *Kerala: The Development Model: Reflections on Sustainability and Replicability*, pp. 178–97, London and New York: Zed Books.

Laclau, Ernesto (1984). 'New Social Movements and the Plurality of the Social', in D. Slater (ed.), *New Social Movements and the State in Latin America*, pp. 27–42, Amsterdam: CEDLA.

Laclau, Ernesto, and Chantal Mouffe (1985). *Hegemony and Socialist Strategy: Towards a Radical Democratic Politics*, London: Verso.

Lahiri, D. P., and Arpita Ghosh (2006). 'Our Land, Their Development', in IMSE (ed.), *Battle of Singur: A Sordid Story of Violation of Human Rights*, pp. 9–30, Kolkata: IMSE and PCFS.

Lazarus, Neil (2011). *The Postcolonial Unconscious*, Cambridge: Cambridge University Press.

Legg, Stephen, and Srila Roy (2013). 'Neo-Liberalism, Post-Colonialism and Hetero-Sovereignties: Emergent Sexual Formations in Contemporary India', *Interventions: International Journal of Postcolonial Studies*, 15(4): 461–73.

Lehmann, David (1990). *Democracy and Development in Latin America: Economics, Politics and Religion in the Post-War Period*, Philadelphia: Temple University Press.

——— (1996). *Struggle for the Spirit: Religious Transformation and Political Culture in Brazil and Latin America*, Cambridge: Polity Press.

Leslie, Stuart, and Robert Kargon (2006). 'Exporting MIT: Science, Technology, and Nation-Building in India and Iran', *Osiris* 21(1): 110–30.

Levien, Michael (2012). 'The Land Question: Special Economic Zones and the Political Economy of Dispossession in India', *Journal of Peasant Studies*, 39(3–4): 933–69.

——— (2013). 'The Politics of Dispossession: Theorizing India's "Land Wars"', *Politics & Society*, 41(3): 351–94.

Levine, Daniel H., and Scott Mainwaring (1989). 'Religion and Popular Protest in Latin America: Contrasting Experiences', in Susan Eckstein (ed.), *Power and Popular Protest: Latin American Protest Movements*, pp. 203–40, Berkeley: University of California Press.

Lipsitz, George (1998). *The Possessive Investment in Whiteness: How White People Profit from Identity Politics*, Philadelphia: Temple University Press.

Littwin, Lawrence (1989). 'Religions and Revolution: A Brief for the Theology of Liberation', *Socialist Register*, 25: 264–77.

Ludden, David (1985). *Peasant History in South India*, Princeton: Princeton University Press.

——— (2002a). 'A Brief History of Subalternity', in David Ludden (ed.), *Reading Subaltern Studies: Critical History, Contested Meaning and the Globalization of South Asia*, pp. 1–39, London: Anthem Press.

——— (ed.) (2002b). *Reading Subaltern Studies: Critical History, Contested Meaning and the Globalisation of South Asia*, New Delhi: Permanent Black.

Madan, T. N. (1998). 'Secularism in Its Place', in Rajeev Bhargava (ed.), *Secularism and its Critics*, pp. 297–320, New Delhi: Oxford University Press.

Madhok, Sumi (2013). *Rethinking Agency: Developmentalism, Gender and Rights*, New Delhi: Routledge.

Majumder, Sarasij (2012). '"Who Wants to Marry a Farmer?" Neoliberal Industrialization and the Politics of Land and Work in Rural West Bengal', *Focaal: Journal of Global and Historical Anthropology*, 64: 84–98.

Mallon, Florencia E. (1994a). 'Reflections on the Ruins: Everyday Forms of State Formation in Nineteenth Century Mexico', in J. Gilbert and D. Nugent (eds), *Everyday Forms of State Formation: Revolution and the Negotiation of Rule in Modern Mexico*, pp. 69–106, Durham: Duke University Press.

———— (1994b). 'The Promise and Dilemma of Subaltern Studies: Perspectives from Latin American History', *American Historical Review*, 99(5): 1491–515.

———— (1995). *Peasant and Nation: The Making of Postcolonial Mexico and Peru*, Berkeley: University of California Press.

Mann, Michael (1984). 'The Autonomous Power of the State: Its Origins, Mechanisms and Results', *European Journal of Sociology*, 25(2): 185–213.

Mannathukkaren, N. (2010). 'The "Poverty" of Political Society: Partha Chatterjee and the People's Plan Campaign in Kerala, India', *Third World Quarterly*, 31(2): 295–314.

Marx, Karl (1967 [1867]). *Capital: A Critique of Political Economy*, vol. 1, New York: International Publishers.

———— (1990). *Capital: A Critique of Political Economy*, vol. 1, London: Penguin Books.

Mathew, George (1983). 'Hindu–Christian Communalism: An Analysis of the Kanyakumari Riots', *Social Action*, 33: 407–19.

Mendoza, Louis (1994). 'The Border between Us: Contact Zone or Battle Zone?', *Modern Fiction Studies*, 40(1): 119–39.

Menon, Dilip (2007). 'Why Communalism in India Is about Caste', in T. N. Srinivasan (ed.), *The Future of Secularism*, pp. 60–82, New Delhi: Oxford University Press.

Menon, Nivedita (2004). *Recovering Subversion: Feminist Politics beyond the Law*, New Delhi: Permanent Black.

———— (2007). 'Outing Heteronormativity: Nation, Citizen, Feminist Disruptions', in Nivedita Menon (ed.), *Sexualities*, pp. 3–51, New Delhi: Women Unlimited.

Menon, Nivedita, and Aditya Nigam (2007). *Power and Contestation in India since 1989*, London: Zed Books.

Mezzadra, Sandro, and Brett Neilson (2008). 'Border as Method, or the Multiplication of Labour', *EIPCP Web Journal*, http://eipcp.net/transversal/0608/mezzadraneilson/en (accessed 26 January 2015).

MFC (Medico Friends Circle) (2008). 'Release Dr Binayak Sen', http://binayaksen.net/wp-content/uploads/MSF-Binayak-Booklet.pdf (accessed 12 December 2013).

Michelutti, Lucia (2008). *The Vernacularisation of Democracy: Politics, Caste and Religion in India*, New Delhi: Routledge.

Mindry, Deborah (2001). 'Nongovernmental Organisations, "Grassroots", and the Politics of Virtue', *Signs*, 26(1): 1187–211.

Mitchell, Timothy (2002). *Rule of Experts: Egypt, Techno-Politics, Modernity*, Berkeley: University of California Press.

Moe, Nelson (2010). 'Production and Its Others: Gramsci's "Sexual Question"', in Marcus Green (ed.), *Rethinking Gramsci*, pp. 131–46, London: Routledge.

Mohanty, Gopinath (1997). *Paraja* (translated by Bikram K. Das), New Delhi: Oxford University Press.

Mooij, Jos, and Stephanie Tawa Lama-Rewal (2009). 'Class in Metropolitan India: The Rise of the Middle Classes', in J. Ruet and Stephanie Tawa Lama-Rewal (eds), *Governing India's Metropolises*, pp. 81–104, New Delhi: Routledge.

Moore, Donald S. (1998). 'Subaltern Struggles and the Politics of Place: Remapping Resistance in Zimbabwe's Eastern Highlands', *Cultural Anthropology*, 13(3): 344–81.

Morris, Rosalind C. (2010). 'Introduction', in R. C. Morris (ed.), *Can the Subaltern Speak: Reflections on the History of an Idea*, pp. 1–20, Columbia: Columbia University Press.

Morton, Adam D. (2007). *Unravelling Gramsci: Hegemony and Passive Revolution in the Global Political Economy*, London: Pluto Press.

Mosse, David (1994). 'The Politics of Religious Synthesis: Roman Catholicism and Hindu Village Society in Tamil Nadu, India', in Charles Stewart and Rosalind Shaw (eds), *Syncretism/Anti-Syncretism: The Politics of Religious Synthesis*, pp. 85–107, London and New York: Routledge.

——— (2013). *The Saint in the Banyan Tree: Christianity and Caste Society in India*, Berkeley: University of California Press.

Mouffe, Chantal (1988). 'Hegemony and New Political Subjects: Towards a New Concept of Democracy', in C. Nelson and L. Grossberg (eds),

Marxism and the Interpretation of Culture, pp. 89–101, Chicago: University of Illinois Press.

Mukharji, Projit Bihari (2009). '"Communist" Dispossession Meets "Reactionary" Resistance: The Ironies of the Parliamentary Left in West Bengal', *Focaal: European Journal of Anthropology*, 54: 89–96.

Mukherjee, Anahita (2009). 'Two Dalit youths attempt suicide at Powai IIT', *Times of India*, Mumbai, 15 July.

Mukherji, Nirmalangshu (2012). *The Maoists in India: Tribals under Siege*, London: Pluto Press.

Murray, Martin J. (1981). 'The Rubber Plantations of Colonial Indochina: The Colonial State and the Class Struggle between Wage-Labor and Capital', in *The Development of Capitalism in Colonial Indochina (1870–1940)*, Berkeley: University of California Press.

Nagappan, Sundara Babu (2012). 'Assertion for Resources and Dignity: Dalit Civil Society Activism in Tamil Nadu', Caste Out of Development? Civil Society Activism and Transnational Advocacy on Dalit Rights and Development, https://casteout.files.wordpress.com/2013/06/babu.pdf (accessed 9 March 2015).

Nandy, Ashis (1998). 'The Politics of Secularism and the Recovery of Religious Toleration', in Rajeev Bhargava (ed.), *Secularism and Its Critics*, pp. 321–44, New Delhi: Oxford University Press.

Narchison, J. R., E. Francis, V. Paul Leon, and Felix Wilfred (1983). *Called to Serve: A Profile of the Diocese of Kottar*, Nagercoil: Bishop's House.

Narrain, Arvind, and Gautam Bhan (2005). 'Introduction', in Arvind Narrain and Gautam Bhan (eds), *Because I Have a Voice: Queer Politics in India*, pp. 1–29, New Delhi: Yoda Press.

Nayyar, Deepak (2006). 'India's Unfinished Journey: Transforming Growth into Development', *Modern Asian Studies*, 40(3): 797–832.

Needham, Anuradha Dingwaney, and Rajeswari Sunder Rajan (eds) (2007). *The Crisis of Secularism in India*, Durham and London: Duke University Press.

Neeta, N., and Rajni Palriwal (2011). 'The Absence of State Law: Domestic Workers in India', *Canadian Journal of Women and the Law*, 23: 97–119.

Neveling, Patrick (2014). 'Structural Contingencies and Untimely Coincidences in the Making of Neoliberal India: The Kandla Free Trade Zone, 1965–91', *Contributions to Indian Sociology*, 48(17): 17–43.

Nielsen, Kenneth Bo (2009). 'Farmers' Use of the Courts in an Anti-Land Acquisition Movement in India's West Bengal', *Journal of Legal Pluralism and Unofficial Law*, 59: 121–44.

Nielsen, Kenneth Bo (2010). 'Contesting India's Development? Industrialisation, Land Acquisition and Protest in West Bengal', *Forum for Development Studies*, 37(2): 145–70.

—— (forthcoming). 'Managing "Communities" of Resistance: Negotiating Caste and Class in an Anti-Land Acquisition Movement in West Bengal', in Uday Chandra and Daniel Taghioff (eds), *Staking Claims: The Politics of Social Movements in Contemporary Rural India*, Oxford: Oxford University Press.

Nilsen, Alf Gunvald (2009). 'The Authors and the Actors of Their Own Drama: Towards a Marxist Theory of Social Movements', *Capital and Class*, 33(3): 109–39.

—— (2010). *Dispossession and Resistance in India: The River and the Rage*, London: Routledge.

—— (2011). '"Not Suspended in Mid-air": Critical Reflections on Subaltern Encounters with the Indian State', in Sara M. Motta and Alf Gunvald Nilsen (eds), *Social Movements in the Global South: Dispossession, Development and Resistance*, pp. 104–29, Basingstoke: Palgrave Macmillan.

—— (2012). 'Adivasis In and Against the State: Subaltern Politics and State Power in Contemporary India', *Critical Asian Studies*, 44(2): 251–82.

—— (2013). 'Against the Current, from Below: Resisting Dispossession in the Narmada Valley, India', *Journal of Poverty*, 17(4): 460–92.

—— (2015). 'Democratic Struggles in the Bhil Heartland: Historical Trajectories and Contemporary Scenarios', in Uday Chandra and Daniel Taghioff (eds), *Staking Claims: The Politics of Social Movements in Contemporary Rural India*, New Delhi: Oxford University Press (forthcoming).

Nilsen, Alf Gunvald, and Laurence Cox (2013). 'What Would a Marxist Theory of Social Movements Look Like?', in Colin Barker, Laurence Cox, John Krinsky, and Alf Gunvald Nilsen (eds), *Marxism and Social Movements*, pp. 63–81, Leiden: Brill.

Nugent, Daniel, and Ana Maria Alonso (1994). 'Multiple Selective Traditions in Agrarian Reform and Agrarian Struggle: Popular Culture and State Formation in the *Ejido* of Namiquipa, Chihuahua', in Gilbert Michael Joseph and Daniel Nugent (eds), *Everyday Forms of State Formation: Revolution and the Negotiation of Rule in Modern Mexico*, pp. 209–46, Durham: Duke University Press.

O'Hanlon, Rosalind (1988). 'Recovering the Subject: Subaltern Studies and Histories of Resistance in Colonial South Asia', *Modern Asian Studies*, 22: 189–224.

O'Hanlon, Rosalind, and David Washbrook (1992). 'After Orientalism: Culture, Criticism, and Politics in the Third World', *Comparative Studies in Society and History*, 34(1): 134–67.

Omvedt, Gail (1993). *Reinventing Revolution: New Social Movements and the Socialist Tradition in India*, New York: East Gate.

Ong, Aiwha (2006). *Neoliberalism as Exception: Mutations in Citizenship and Sovereignty*, Durham: Duke University Press.

——— (2007). 'Neoliberalism as a Mobile Technology', *Transactions of the Institute of British Geographers*, 32(1): 3-8.

Ortner, Sherry (2005). 'Subjectivity and Cultural Critique', *Anthropological Theory*, 5(1): 31–52.

Pal, Mahuya and Mohan J. Dutta (2013). '"Land Is Our Mother": Alternative Meanings of Development in Subaltern Organizing', *Journal of International and Intercultural Communication*, 6(3): 203–20.

Pandey, Gyanendra (1983). 'Rallying round the Cow: Sectarian Strife in the Bhojpuri Region, c. 1888–1917', in Ranjait Guha (ed.), *Subaltern Studies II: Writings on South Asian History and Society*, pp. 60–129, New Delhi: Oxford University Press.

——— (2013). *A History of Prejudice: Race, Caste, and Difference in India and the United States*, Cambridge: Cambridge University Press.

Parry, Benita (1987). 'Problems in Current Theories of Colonial Discourse', *Oxford Literary Review*, 9 (1–2): 27–58.

Pati, Biswamoy (2006). 'Tata and the Orissa Model of Capitalist Development', *Social Scientist*, 34(3–4): 37–42.

Pedwell, Carolyn, and Anne Whitehead (2012). 'Affecting Feminism: Questions of Feeling in Feminist Theory', *Feminist Theory*, 13(2): 115–29.

Ponni (2013). 'Justice will prevail', *Kafila*, 11 December 2013, http://kafila.org/2013/12/11/justice-will-prevail/ (accessed 3 January 2015).

Poulantzas, Nicos (1978). *State, Power, Socialism*, London: Verso Books.

Prakash, Amit (1996). 'Suburban terror: Spiralling crime creates fear psychosis in Vasant Kunj', *Outlook Magazine*, 14 February, http://www.outlookindia.com/article.aspx?200788 (accessed 1 February 2014).

Prakash, Gyan (1990). 'Writing Post-Orientalist Histories of the Third World: Perspectives from Indian Historiography', *Comparative Studies in Society and History*, 32(2): 383–408.

——— (1992). 'Can the "Subaltern" Ride? A Reply to O'Hanlon and Washbrook', *Comparative Studies in Society and History*, 34(1): 168–84.

——— (1994) 'Subaltern Studies as Postcolonial Criticism', *American Historical Review*, 99(5): 1475–90.

Prashad, Vijay (2012). *The Poorer Nations: A Possible History of the Global South*, London: Verso.

Pratap, Surendra, Sanjiv Pandita, and Fahmi Panimbang (2012). 'Liberalisation of the Economy and the Politics of Corporate Social Responsibility in India', in *The Reality of Corporate Social Responsibility: Case Studies on the Impact of CSR on Workers in China, South Korea, India and Indonesia*, pp. 104–34, Hong Kong: Asia Monitor Resource Center.

Pratt, Mary Louise (1992). *Imperial Eyes: Travel Writing and Transculturation*, London: Routledge.

Rajagopalan, C., and Jaspal Singh (1968). 'The Indian Institutes of Technology: Do They Contribute to Social Mobility?', *Economic and Political Weekly*, 3(14): 565–70.

Ram, Kalpana (1992). *Mukkuvar Women: Gender, Hegemony and Capitalist Transformation in a South Indian Fishing Community*, New Delhi: Kali.

——— (1995). 'Rationalism, Cultural Nationalism and the Reform of Body Politics: Minority Intellectuals of the Tamil Catholic Community', *Contributions to Indian Sociology*, 29 (1–2): 291–318.

——— (2008) '"A New Consciousness Must Come": Affectivity and Movement in Tamil Dalit Women's Activist Engagement with Cosmopolitan Modernity', in P. Werbner (ed.), *Anthropology and Cosmopolitanism: Rooted, Feminist and Vernacular Perspectives*, pp. 135–57, Oxford: Berg.

Rao, Anupama (2009). *The Caste Question: Dalits and the Politics of Modern India*, Berkeley: University of California Press.

Ray, Raka, and Mary Katzenstein (2005). 'In the Beginning There Was the Nehruvian State', in Raka Ray and Mary Katzenstein (eds), *Social Movements in India: Poverty, Power, and Politics*, pp. 1–31, Lanham, MD: Rowman and Littlefeld.

Roche, Patrick A. (1984). *Fishermen of the Coromandel*, New Delhi: Manohar.

Roosa, John (2006). 'When the Subaltern Took the Postcolonial Turn', *Journal of the Canadian Historical Association*, 17(2): 130–47.

Rose, Nikolas (1999). *Powers of Freedom: Reframing Political Thought*, Cambridge: Cambridge University Press.

Roseberry, William (1989). *Anthropologies and Histories: Essays in Culture, History, and Political Economy*, New Brunswick, NJ: Rutgers University Press.

——— (1994). 'Hegemony and the Language of Contention', in Michael Joseph Gilbert and Daniel Nugent (eds), *Everyday Forms of State*

Formation: Revolution and the Negotiation of Rule in Modern Mexico, pp. 355–66, Durham: Duke University Press.

Roy, Ananya (2011). 'Slumdog Cities: Rethinking Subaltern Urbanism', *International Journal of Urban and Regional Research*, 35(2): 223–38.

Roy, Srila (2011). 'Politics, Passion and Professionalization in Contemporary Indian Feminism', *Sociology*, 45(4): 587–602.

——— (2014). 'New Activist Subjects: The Changing Feminist Field of Kolkata, India', *Feminist Studies*, 40(3): 628–56.

Ruparelia, Sanjay (2013). 'India's New Rights Agenda: Genesis, Promises, Risks', *Pacific Affairs*, 86(3): 569–90.

Salih, Sara (ed.) with Judith Butler (2004). *The Judith Butler Reader*, Oxford: Blackwell Publishing.

Samaddar, Ranabir (2007). *The Emergence of the Political Subject*, New Delhi: Sage Publications.

Sanyal, Kalyan (2006). *Rethinking Capitalist Development: Primitive Accumulation, Governmentality and Postcolonial Capitalism*, New Delhi: Routledge.

Sarkar, Sumit (1994). 'Orientalism Revisited: Saidian Frameworks in the Writing of Modern Indian History', *Oxford Literary Review*, 16: 205–24.

——— (1997). *Writing Social History*, New Delhi: Oxford University Press.

Sayer, Derek (1994). 'Everyday Forms of State Formation: Some Dissident Remarks on "Hegemony"', in Michael Joseph Gilbert and Daniel Nugent (eds), *Everyday Forms of State Formation: Revolution and the Negotiation of Rule in Modern Mexico*, pp. 367–77, Durham: Duke University Press.

Schindler, Seth (2014). 'The Making of "World-Class" Delhi: Relations between Street Hawkers and the New Middle Class', *Antipode*, 46(2): 557–73.

Schurhammer, Georg (1973–82). *Francis Xavier, His Life, His Times*, Rome: Jesuit Historical Institute.

Scott, James C. (2010). *The Art of Not Being Governed: An Anarchist History of Upland Southeast Asia*, Hyderabad: Orient BlackSwan.

Sen, Amartya, and Jean Drèze (2013). *An Uncertain Glory: India and Its Contradictions*, New Delhi: Penguin Books.

Sen, Ilina, Sudha Bhardwaj, and Kavita Srivastava (2010). 'Note on the Binayak Sen Judgement', mimeo, Raipur, 26 December.

Sewell, William H. (1992). 'A Theory of Structure: Duality, Agency, and Transformation', *American Journal of Sociology*, 98(1): 1–29.

Shah, Alpa (2010). *In the Shadows of the State: Indigenous Politics, Enviromentalism, and Insurgency in Jharkhand, India*, Durham: Duke University Press.

——— (2013). 'The Intimacy of Insurgency: Beyond Coercion, Greed or Grievance in Maoist India', *Economy and Society*, 42(3): 480–506.

Shah, Chayanika (2005). 'The Roads that E/merged: Feminist Activism and Queer Understanding', in Arvind Narrain and Gautam Bhan (eds), *Because I Have a Voice: Queer Politics in India*, pp. 143–54, New Delhi: Yoda Press.

Shah, Ghanshyam (1988). 'Grass-roots Mobilization in Indian Politics', in Atul Kohli (ed.), *India's Democracy: An Analysis of Changing State–Society Relations*, pp. 262–304, Princeton: Princeton University Press.

——— (1994). 'The BJP and Backward Castes in Gujarat', *South Asia Bulletin*, 14(1): 57–65.

Shah, Mihir (2008). 'Structures of Power in Indian Society: A Response', *Economic and Political Weekly*, 43(46): 78–83.

Shani, Ornit (2005). 'The Rise of Hindu Nationalism in India: The Case Study of Ahmedabad in the 1980s', *Modern Asian Studies*, 39(4): 861–96.

Shanin, Teodor (1986). 'Chayanov's Message: Illuminations, Miscomprehensions and the Contemporary "Development Theory"', in Daniel Thorner, Basile Kerblay, and R. E. F. Smith (eds), *A.V. Chayanov: The Theory of Peasant Economy*, pp. 1–24, Madison: University of Wisconsin Press.

Sharma, Aradhana (2006). 'Crossbreeding Institutions, Breeding Struggle: Women's Empowerment, Neoliberal Governmentality, and State (Re)Formation in India', *Cultural Anthropology*, 21(1): 60–95.

——— (2008). *The Logics of Empowerment: Development, Gender and Governance in Neoliberal India*, Minneapolis: University of Minnesota Press.

Sharma, Maya (2006). *Loving Women: Being Lesbian in Unprivileged India*, New Delhi: Yoda Press.

Sharpe, Jenny, and Gayatri Chakravorty Spivak (2002). 'A Conversation with Gayatri Chakravorty Spivak: Politics and the Imagination', *Signs*, 28(2): 609–24.

Shrivastava, Aseem (2006). '(Not) OK TaTa!' Znet, 8 December, http://www.zcommunications.org/not-ok-tata-by-aseem-shrivastava (accessed 27 August 2012).

Shuler, Jack (2009). *Calling Out Liberty: The Stono Slave Rebellion and the Universal Struggle for Human Rights*, Jackson: University Press of Mississippi.

Sidbury, James (1997). *Ploughshares into Swords: Race, Rebellion, and Identity in Gabriel's Virginia, 1730–1810,* Cambridge: Cambridge University Press.

Silver, Beverly (2003). *Forces of Labour: Workers' Movements and Globalization since 1870,* Cambridge: Cambridge University Press.

Sinha, Subir (2008). 'Lineages of the Developmentalist State: Transnationality and Village India, 1900–1965', *Comparative Studies in Society and History,* 50(1): 57–90.

——— (2012). 'The Long March from the Margins: Subaltern Politics, Justice and Nature in Postcolonial India', in Etienne Balibar, Sandro Mezzadra, and Ranabir Sammadar (eds), *The Borders of Justice,* pp. 79–98, Philadelphia: Temple University Press.

——— (2013). 'Workers and Working Classes in Contemporary India: A Note on Analytic Frames and Political Formations', in Marcel van der Linden and Karl-Heinz Roth (eds), *Beyond Marx: Confronting Labour History and the Concept of Labour with the Global Labour Relations of the Twenty-First Century,* pp. 145–72, Leiden: Brill.

Sivaramakrishnan, Kalyanakrishnan (2002). 'Situating the Subaltern: History and Anthropology in the *Subaltern Studies* Project', in David Ludden (ed.), *Reading Subaltern Studies: Critical History, Contested Meaning, and the Globalisation of South Asia,* pp. 212–55, New Delhi: Permanent Black.

Sivasubramanian, A. (1996). 'Fin-Levy (*Thuvik Kuthagai*) Agitation in Idinthakarai, Tamil Nadu 1964–67', *South Indian Studies,* 2: 260–71.

Smith, Gavin (2011). 'The Residual Population: Non-labourers or Non-citizens?', paper presented at the American Anthropology Association Annual Meeting, Montreal, 16–20 November.

——— (2014). *Intellectuals and (Counter-) Politics.* New York and London: Berghahn Books.

Somerville, Margaret, and Tony Perkins (2003). 'Border Work in the Contact Zone: Thinking Indigenous/Non-indigenous Collaboration Spatially', *Journal of Intercultural Studies,* 24(3): 253–66.

Spivak, Gayatri Chakravarty (1988a). 'Can the Subaltern Speak?', in C. Nelson and L. Grossberg (eds), *Marxism and the Interpretation of Culture,* pp. 271–317, Urbana: University of Illinois Press.

——— (1988b). 'Subaltern Studies: Deconstructing Historiography', in Ranajit Guha (ed.), *Subaltern Studies IV: Writings on South Asian History and Society,* pp. 3–32, New Delhi: Oxford University Press.

——— (1990). *The Postcolonial Critic: Interviews, Strategies, Dialogues* (edited by S. Harasym), New York: Routledge.

Spivak, Gayatri Chakravarty (1994). 'How to Read a "Culturally Different" Book', in Francis Baker, Peter Hulme, and Margaret Iverson (eds), *Colonial Discourse/Postcolonial Theory*, pp. 126–50, Manchester: Manchester University Press.

———— (1995). 'The Author in Conversation', 'Translator's Preface', and 'Afterword', in *Imaginary Maps: Three Stories* by Mahasweta Devi, New York and London: Routledge.

———— (2000a). 'The New Subaltern: A Silent Interview', in V. Chaturvedi (ed.), *Mapping Subaltern Studies and the Postcolonial*, pp. 324–40, New York: Verso.

———— (2000b). 'Discussion: An Afterword on the New Subaltern', in Partha Chatterjee and Pradeep Jeganathan (eds), *Subaltern Studies XI: Community, Gender and Violence*, pp. 305–44, London: Hurst and Company.

———— (2005). 'Scattered Speculations on the Subaltern and the Popular', *Postcolonial Studies*, 8(4): 475–86.

———— (2012). *An Aesthetic Education in the Era of Globalization*, Cambridge: Harvard University Press.

Spivak, Gayatri Chakravorty, Donna Landry, and Gerald M. McLean (1996). 'Subaltern Talk: Interviews with the Editors (1993–94)', in Gayatri Chakravorty Spivak, Donna Landry, and Gerald M. McLean (eds), *The Spivak Reader: Selected Works of Gayatri Chakravorty Spivak*, pp. 287–308, New York and London: Routledge.

Spodek, Howard (2011). *Ahmedabad: Shock City of the Twentieth Century*, Bloomington: Indiana University Press.

Srivastava, Devyani (2008). 'Mining War in Chhattisgarh', Institute for Peace and Conflict Studies, http://www.ipcs.org/article/naxalite-violence/mining-war-in-chhattisgarh-2577.html (accessed 8 February 2014).

Subramanian, Ajantha (2003). 'Modernity from Below: Local Citizenship on the South Indian Coast', *International Social Science Journal*, 175 (March): 135–44.

———— (2009). *Shorelines: Space and Rights in South India*, Stanford: Stanford University Press.

———— (2011). Comments on 'New Subalterns' panel, Annual Conference of the Association of Asian Studies, Honolulu, 31 March–3 April.

Sundar, Aparna, and Nandini Sundar (2012). '"The Habits of the Political Heart": Recovering Politics from Governmentality', in Ajay Gudavarthy (ed.), *Re-framing Democracy and Agency: Interrogating Political Society*, pp. 269–88, London: Anthem Press.

Sundar, Nandini (2006). 'Bastar, Maoism and Salwa Judum', *Economic and Political Weekly*, 41(29): 3187–92.

———— (2007). *Subalterns and Sovereigns: An Anthropological History of Bastar (1854–2005)*, 2nd edn, New Delhi: Oxford University Press.

———— (2010). 'Vigilantism, Culpability and Moral Dilemmas', *Critique of Anthropology*, 30(1): 113–21.

———— (2011). 'The Rule of Law and Citizenship in India: Post-Colonial Dilemmas', *Citizenship Studies*, 15(3–4): 419–32.

———— (2012). 'Insurgency, Counter-insurgency, and Democracy in Central India', in Robin Jeffrey, Ronojoy Sen, and Prathima Singh (eds), *More Than Maoism: Politics, Policies, and Insurgencies in South Asia*, pp. 149–68, New Delhi: Manohar Publishers.

Swarr, Amanda Lock, and Richa Nagar (2003). 'Dismantling Assumptions: Interrogating "Lesbian" Struggles for Identity and Survival in India and South Africa', *Signs: Journal of Women in Culture and Society*, 29(21): 491–516.

Tejani, Shabnum (2008). *Indian Secularism: A Social and Intellectual History*, Bloomington: Indiana University Press.

Thachil, Tariq (2011). 'Embedded Mobilization: Nonstate Service Provision as Electoral Strategy in India', *World Politics*, 63 (July): 434–69.

Tharoor, Shashi (2006). 'Looking to the future with Brand IIT', *Times of India*, 30 December, http://timesofindia.indiatimes.com/home/shashi-tharoor//Looking-to-the-future-with-Brand-IIT/articleshow/1568438.cms?curpg=2 (accessed 22 December 2014).

Thomas, Peter (2009). *The Gramscian Moment: Philosophy, Hegemony, and Marxism*, Leiden and Boston: Brill.

Thompson, Edward P. (1978). 'Eighteenth Century English Society: Class Struggle without Class', *Social History*, 3(2): 133–65.

Thompson, Simon, and Paul Hoggett (2012). *Politics and the Emotions: The Affective Turn in Contemporary Political Studies*, London: Bloomsbury.

Thorner, Daniel (1991). 'Agrarian Structure', in Dipankar Gupta (ed.), *Social Stratification*, pp. 261–70, New Delhi: Oxford University Press.

Tilly, Charles (1984). *Big Structures, Large Processes, Huge Comparisons*, New York: Russell Sage Foundation.

Times of India (2012). 'Colony conflict: Greater Kailash-II resident welfare association wants to shut gate on others', 26 September.

Tombeur, James (1990). *Led by God's Hand: Reflections on My Faith Experience and Pastoral Ministry*, Thiruvananthapuram: Nalini Nayak.

UCAN India (2013). 'Domestic workers demand comprehensive law for their rights', 1 August, http://www.ucanindia.in/news/domestic-workers-demand-comprehensive-law-for-their-rights/21583/daily (accessed 24 January 2014).

UNDP (United Nations Development Programme) (2013). *Human Development Report 2013—The Rise of the South: Human Progress in a Diverse World*, New York: UNDP.

Vanaik, Achin (1990). *The Painful Transition: Bourgeois Democracy in India*, London: Verso.

——— (2001). 'The New Indian Right', *New Left Review*, 9: 43–67.

Varadharajan, Asha (1995). *Exotic Parodies: Subjectivity in Adorno, Said, and Spivak*, Minneapolis: University of Minnesota Press.

Varma, Rashmi (2002). 'Developing Fictions: The "Tribal" in the New Indian Writing in English', in Amitava Kumar (ed.), *World Bank Literature*, pp. 216–33, Minneapolis: University of Minnesota Press.

Villavarayan, J. (1956). *The Diocese of Kottar: A Review of Its Growth*, Nagercoil: Assisi Press.

Waghmore, Suryakant (2013). *Civility against Caste: Dalit Politics and Citizenship in Western India*, New Delhi: Sage Publications.

Waldrop Anne (2004). 'Gating and Class Relations: The Case of a New Delhi "Colony"', *City and Society*, 16(2): 93–116.

Walker, Kathy Le Mons (2008). 'Neoliberalism on the Ground in Rural India: Predatory Growth, Agrarian Crisis, Internal Colonization, and the Intensification of Class Struggle', *Journal of Peasant Studies*, 35(4): 557–620.

Warner, Michael (1993). 'Introduction', in Michael Warner (ed.), *Fear of a Queer Planet: Queer Politics and Social Theory*, pp. vii–xxxi, Minneapolis: University of Minnesota Press.

Webb, Martin (2013). 'Meeting at the Edges: Spaces, Places and Grassroots Governance Activism in Delhi', *South Asia Multidisciplinary Academic Journal (SAMAJ)*, http://samaj.revues.org/3677 (accessed 3 January 2015).

Werbner, Richard P. (ed.) (2002). *Postcolonial Subjectivities in Africa*, London and New York: Zed Books.

Wilfred, Felix (1981). 'The Social Orientation of the CBCI (1944–1980)', in D. S. Amalorpavadass (ed.), *The Indian Church in the Struggle for a New Society*, pp. 827–62, Bengaluru: National Biblical, Catechetical and Liturgical Centre.

Williams, Philippa (2012). 'India's Muslims, Lived Secularism and Realising Citizenship', *Citizenship Studies*, 16(8): 979–95.

Williams, Philippa, Bhaskar Vira, and Deepta Chopra (2011). 'Marginality, Agency and Power: Experiencing the State in Contemporary India', *Pacific Affairs*, 84(1): 7–23.

Williams, Raymond (1977). *Marxism and Literature*, New York: Oxford University Press.

——— (2011). *The Country and the City*, London: Spokesman Books.

Wolf, Eric (1982). *Europe and the People without History*, Berkeley: University of California Press.

——— (2001). *Pathways of Power: Building an Anthropology of the Modern World*, Berkeley: University of California Press.

Ellen Meiksins *Wood* (2003). *The Empire of Capital*, London: Verso.

Index

62, 79; *see also* economic
liberalization
Neveling, Patrick 177
New middle class, new middle
classes 213, 229, 231, 242, 245
New subalterns (Gayatri
Chakravorty Spivak) 10–11, 229
New Trade Union Initiative 227
Nielsen, Kenneth Bo 24–6, 200,
202, 206, 215, 224, 265
Nilsen, Alf Gunvald 1, 21, 24, 31,
38, 49, 52–3, 78, 126, 149, 204,
217, 237, 257, 265
Nirmala Niketan 246
NOIDA 240, 243–4, 252
Non-agricultural occupations 182
Non-brahmin 79, 86–7, 91
Non-capitalist forms 227
Non-Governmental Organizations
(NGOs) 16, 42, 120, 145, 160,
162, 171, 184, 189, 191, 194–5,
205–6, 209, 229–30, 233–5, 237,
241, 244–7, 249, 251, 253
NGO staff 138
Non-hegemonic sexual identities
153
Non-state spaces (James Scott) 33
North America 264

Odisha, Orissa 112, 235, 240
OECD Guidelines for
Multinational Companies 196
Omvedt, Gail 3
Ong, Aiwha 54, 62
Organic intellectuals 138, 140–1
Organization for Economic
Cooperation and Development
(OECD) 195–6
Orientalist 126, 264, 269
Orissa *see* Odisha
Ortner, Sherry 82

Other Backward Classes 22, 55,
62–4, 66–9, 73, 75, 82, 131; *see
also* Backward castes

Panchami lands 184, 200
Panchayat 183–4, 190, 198, 210,
222
Pandey, Gyanendra 127, 264
Paraiyar 179
Paraja 105, 112, 114–6, 118, 123–4
Paravar 131–3, 139, 145
Parish associations 129
Parliamentary democracy 2, 20,
61, 78; *see also* democracy,
electoral democracy
Parochial governance 132
Parry, Benita 10
Passive revolution 34, 57, 60, 73–4,
192, 227
Pathological sexuality 152
Patronage 63, 128, 222, 235
Paul Harrison Prize 236
Peasantry, peasant 6–7, 18, 33–4,
36, 73, 116–8, 124, 138, 178–9,
181–3, 187–9, 198, 200, 203–4,
207, 212–5, 222–4, 227–8, 240,
264–6
Peasant consciousness, peasant
identity 33–4, 181, 203,
264–5
Peasant insurgency, peasant
rebellion 47, 181–2, 187,
203–4, 267
Peasant politics 33, 178, 203
Peasant protest, peasant
resistance 36, 193, 203–4,
222, 264
Peasant society 33, 178, 181,
184, 187, 192–3, 198–9, 265
Peasant-communal politics
(Partha Chatterjee) 13, 33

People's Coalition on Food
Sovereignty 214
People's Health Movement 237
People's Union for Civil Liberties
(PUCL) 234, 236, 239
Periyar, E. V. R. 127
Persuasion 17, 35, 222; see also
consent
Petitions 36, 143, 180, 237–8, 252
Phule, Jyotirao 127
Placement agencies 230, 246
Political activism 40, 138, 161,
238; see also activism
Political agency 1, 3, 9, 11, 13–5,
21, 23, 99, 111, 150
Political authenticity 55
Political economy 13, 23, 36, 77–8,
129, 148, 189, 197, 212, 225,
227; see also Marxist political
economy
Political horizon 172
Political life 156, 162
Political participation 18, 130
Political possibility 158–9, 164,
172, 179–80, 199
Political project 4, 18, 45–7, 51,
172, 235
Political silencing 150
Political society (Gramsci) 48, 60
Political society (Partha
Chatterjee) 16, 21, 24–6, 38, 74,
179, 181, 189, 191–3, 199, 204,
225–7, 228–33, 239, 242, 246–50
Political subjectivity 54–6, 59, 62,
71, 73
Pope John XXIII 134
Population groups 204–5, 235
Population policies 266
Populism 7, 38
Portuguese priests 133
Postcolonial capitalism 226–7, 247

Postcolonial India 5, 31–2, 111,
124, 151; see also postcolonial
state, post-independence India
Postcolonialism, postcolonial
studies, postcolonial theory
21–3, 26, 103–8, 111, 113–4,
119, 123–4, 223, 258; see also
postcolonial literary theory
Postcolonial literary theory 103,
105; see also postcolonial
theory
Postcolonial state 2–3, 17–8,
33, 35, 37–8, 40, 44, 98, 112,
120, 144, 159, 177; see also
postcolonial India, post-
independence India
Post-independence India 98, 133;
see also postcolonial India,
postcolonial state
Poststructuralism 9, 21, 54, 104,
107
Poulantzas, Nicos 44–5, 49–51
Poverty 2, 73, 132, 135, 141, 154,
193, 199, 211, 214, 231, 260, 266
Poverty alleviation 228
Prakash, Gyan 6, 8–10, 15, 26, 57
Prashad, Vijay 26
Praxis
Precarious labour 56, 62, 69, 73–4
Precarity 55, 62–3, 65, 244
Predatory growth 197
Pre-political 99, 149
Primitive accumulation 24–5,
74, 179, 181–2, 189–90, 192,
197–8, 226–32, 236, 238–9, 241,
247–50, 253
PRISM 161–2
Prison Notebooks 12, 259
Private sector employment 89
Privilege 22, 24, 76–8, 96, 98–9,
154, 192, 249

Thiruvananthapuram 131
Thomas, M. M. 134
Thomas, Peter 48–51, 59–60, 251
Thompson, E. P. 46, 53, 199, 258–9
Tilly, Charles 45
Tombeur, James 134–5
Trafficking 107, 119, 246
Transfer of technical knowledge 81
Transition to capitalism, transition
    to modernity 24, 26, 182, 227
Translational agent 236
Transnational mobility 77, 98
Travancore 133
Tribal *see* adivasis
Tribal areas 226, 230, 234–5, 237,
    240, 253; *see also* adivasis
Tributary modes of production 36
Trinamul Congress (TMC) 206–7,
    210, 219, 222
Turn to affect 156
Typicality 115, 267

Universalism 81, 98, 231, 247–8,
    250
Universality 167, 263
Unlawful Activities Prevention
    Act 233
Unrepresentable 23, 104
Unwilling farmers 202, 204–7,
    214–5, 224
Uplift 129
Upper caste 3, 24, 63–4, 68, 77–80,
    89–94, 97, 99, 153
    Upper caste flight 77
    Upper-caste hegemony 22
Upper-order discourses of the state
    (Sudipta Kaviraj) 37, 39
Urban growth 243
Urban middle classes 74, 228–9
Urban poor 228, 245, 253

Uttar Pradesh 41–2, 241, 246

Vanaik, Achin 3, 26
Vanvasi Kalyan Ashrams 235
Varma, Rashmi 12, 23, 103, 120,
    149, 261
Vatican II *see* Second Vatican
    Ecumenical Council
Vertreten (Spivak) 106, 108
Vikas 64–5, 70
Village India 178, 181–2, 186–8
Village struggle committee
    (Sangam) 190, 198
Vision 2023 (Tamil Nadu) 180

Wage workers 227
Waghmore, Suryakant 2
Walker, Kathy Le Mons 2, 197
War of manoeuvre 77
Welfare 25, 41–2, 62–3, 65, 74, 85,
    182, 197, 200, 226, 228, 230,
    245
    Welfare programmes, welfare
        projects 25, 153, 177, 229,
    235
West Bengal 5, 25, 112, 202–4, 206,
    223
Williams, Raymond 19, 158, 163,
    188
Wolf, Eric 24, 187, 197, 199
Women 3, 9–10, 13–14, 41–2, 53,
    62, 66–7, 70, 117, 121–2, 128,
    135, 137, 139, 142–4, 147,
    153–5, 159–60, 162–4, 221, 237,
    246, 253, 260, 264, 268
Working class 6, 11, 65, 154, 217
World Bank 120
World capitalism 177

Zone of non-capital 227

Editors and Contributors

David Arnold is Emeritus Professor, Department of History, University of Warwick, UK.

Kenneth Bo Nielsen is Postdoctoral Fellow, Department of Sociology, University of Bergen, Norway.

Manali Desai is Lecturer, Department of Sociology, University of Cambridge.

Alf Gunvald Nilsen is Associate Professor, Department of Sociology, University of Bergen, Norway, and Visiting Professor, Centre for Indian Studies in Africa, University of the Witwatersrand, South Africa.

Srila Roy is Senior Lecturer, Department of Sociology, University of the Witwatersrand, South Africa.

Subir Sinha is Senior Lecturer, Department of Development Studies, The School of Oriental and African Studies (SOAS), UK.

Luisa Steur is Assistant Professor, Department of Anthropology, University of Copenhagen, Denmark.

Ajantha Subramanian is Professor, Department of Anthropology, Harvard University, US.

Aparna Sundar is Associate Professor, Azim Premji University, Bangalore, India.

Rashmi Varma is Associate Professor, Department of English and Comparative Literary Studies, University of Warwick, UK.